D1357842

jQuery UI 1.8
The User Interface Library for jQuery

Build highly interactive web applications with
ready-to-use widgets from the jQuery User
Interface Library

Dan Wellman

[PACKT] open source ✿
PUBLISHING   community experience distilled

BIRMINGHAM - MUMBAI

jQuery UI 1.8
The User Interface Library for jQuery

First published: August 2011

Production Reference: 1120811

Livery Place
35 Livery Street
Birmingham B3 2PB, UK.

ISBN 978-1-849516-52-5

www.packtpub.com

Cover Image by Karl Swedberg (karl@englishrules.com)

Credits

Author
Dan Wellman

Reviewers
Vijay Joshi

Jake Kronika

Acquisition Editor
Sarah Cullington

Development Editor
Hithesh Uchil

Technical Editors
Lubna Shaikh

Merwine Machado

Project Coordinator
Michelle Quadros

Proofreader
Aaron Nash

Indexers
Tejal Daruwale

Hemangini Bari

Graphics
Nilesh Mohite

Production Coordinators
Aparna Bhagat

Nilesh Mohite

Cover Work
Aparna Bhagat

Nilesh Mohite

About the Author

Dan Wellman is an author and web developer based on the South Coast of the UK. By day he works alongside some of the most talented people he has had the pleasure of calling colleagues, for a small, yet accomplished digital agency called Design Haus. By night he writes books and tutorials on a range of front-end topics. He is hopelessly addicted to jQuery. His life is enriched by his four wonderful children, a beautiful wife, and a close circle of family and friends. This is his sixth book.

Thanks to everyone who was involved in the book, the editorial team at Packt, the reviewers, and the hugely talented team responsible for jQuery UI. Props to my friends Steev Bishop, Andrew Herman, Dan Goodall, Aaron Matheson, James Zabiela, Jon Adams, Eamon O'Donoghue, and Dan Isles.

About the Reviewers

Vijay Joshi is a programmer with over six years of experience on various platforms. He discovered his passion for open source four years back when he started playing with PHP on a hobby project after completing his Masters in Computer Applications.

Vijay is now a freelance web developer, independent consultant for a few selected companies, and a blogger at `http://vijayjoshi.org`. He specializes in developing custom web applications, mashups, creating apps using PHP frameworks, and enhancing existing web apps using PHP and front-end libraries like jQuery, jQUI, and so on.

Vijay is also the author of PHP jQuery Cookbook and a technical reviewer of PHP AJAX Cookbook both of which have been published by Packt.

Outside of work, he enjoys reading, trekking, and sometimes gets obsessed with fitness.

Jake Kronika is a web designer and developer with over fifteen years of experience, and brings to this book a strong background in front-end development with JavaScript and jQuery, as well as significant training in server-side languages and frameworks.

Having earned a Bachelors of Science degree in Computer Science from Illinois Wesleyan University in 2005, with a minor in Business Administration, he went on to become Senior User Interface (UI) Specialist for Imaginary Landscape, LLC, a small web development firm in the Ravenswood neighborhood on the north side of Chicago. In this role, the foundations of his strengths in Cascading Style Sheets (CSS) and JavaScript (JS) were honed and finely tuned.

From there, Jake went on to work for the Sun-Times News Group, owner of the Chicago Sun-Times and numerous suburban newspapers in Chicagoland. It was in this role that he was initially exposed and rapidly gained expert skills with the jQuery framework for JS.

Following intermediate positions as Technology Consultant with Objective Arts, Inc, and as UI Prototyper for JP Morgan Chase, Jake moved across the contiguous United States to Seattle, WA, where he assumed his current role of Senior UI Software Engineer with the Cobalt Group, a marketing division of ADP's Dealer Services. Since 1999, he has also operated Gridline Design & Development (so named in 2009), a sole proprietorship for web design, development, and administration.

Jake has also reviewed Django JavaScript Integration: AJAX and jQuery, a Packt Publishing text authored by Jonathan Howard and published in January of 2011.

www.PacktPub.com

Support files, eBooks, discount offers and more

You might want to visit www.PacktPub.com for support files and downloads related to your book.

Did you know that Packt offers eBook versions of every book published, with PDF and ePub files available? You can upgrade to the eBook version at www.PacktPub.com and as a print book customer, you are entitled to a discount on the eBook copy. Get in touch with us at service@packtpub.com for more details.

At www.PacktPub.com, you can also read a collection of free technical articles, sign up for a range of free newsletters and receive exclusive discounts and offers on Packt books and eBooks.

http://PacktLib.PacktPub.com

Do you need instant solutions to your IT questions? PacktLib is Packt's online digital book library. Here, you can access, read and search across Packt's entire library of books.

Why Subscribe?

- Fully searchable across every book published by Packt
- Copy and paste, print and bookmark content
- On demand and accessible via web browser

Free Access for Packt account holders

If you have an account with Packt at www.PacktPub.com, you can use this to access PacktLib today and view nine entirely free books. Simply use your login credentials for immediate access.

For my wonderful mother Sue

Table of Contents

Preface

Modern web application user interface design requires rapid development and proven results. jQuery UI, a trusted suite of official plugins for the jQuery JavaScript library, gives you a solid platform on which you can build rich and engaging interfaces with maximum compatibility, stability, and a minimum of time and effort.

jQuery UI has a series of ready-made, great-looking user interface widgets and a comprehensive set of core interaction helpers designed to be implemented in a consistent and developer-friendly way. With all this, the amount of code that you need to write personally to take a project from conception to completion is drastically reduced.

Specially revised for version 1.8+ of jQuery UI, this book has been written to maximize your experience with the library by breaking down each component and walking you through examples that progressively build upon your knowledge, taking you from beginner to advanced usage in a series of easy-to-follow steps.

In this book, you'll learn how each component can be initialized in a basic default implementation and then see how easy it is to customize its appearance and configure its behavior to tailor it to the requirements of your application. You'll look at the configuration options and the methods exposed by each component's API to see how these can be used to bring out the best of the library.

Events play a key role in any modern web application if it is to meet the expected minimum requirements of interactivity and responsiveness, and each chapter will show you the custom events fired by the component covered and how these events can be intercepted and acted upon.

What this book covers

Chapter 1, Introducing jQuery UI, lets you find out exactly what the library is, where it can be downloaded from, and how the files within it are structured. We also look at ThemeRoller, which browsers support the library, how it is licensed, and how the API has been simplified to give the components a consistent and easy-to-use programming model.

Chapter 2, The CSS Framework and Other Utilities, looks in detail at the extensive CSS framework, which provides a rich environment for integrated theming through Themeroller, or allows developers to easily supply their own custom themes or skins. We also cover the new position utility, as well as a whole section dedicated to writing your own jQuery UI plugins using the widget factory.

Chapter 3, Using the Tabs Component, looks at the first widget, which is the tabs component, a simple but effective means of presenting structured content in an engaging and interactive widget.

Chapter 4, The Accordion Widget, looks at the accordion widget, another component dedicated to the effective display of content. Highly engaging and interactive, the accordion makes a valuable addition to any web page and its API is exposed in full to show exactly how it can be used.

Chapter 5, The Dialog, focuses on the dialog widget. The dialog behaves in the same way as a standard browser alert, but it does so in a much less intrusive and more visitor-friendly manner. We look at how it can be configured and controlled to provide maximum benefit and appeal.

Chapter 6, The Slider Widget, provides a less commonly used, but no less valuable user interface tool for collecting input from your visitors. We look closely at its API throughout this chapter to see the variety of ways in which it can be implemented.

Chapter 7, The Datepicker Widget, looks at the date picker. This component packs a huge amount of functionality into an attractive and highly usable tool, allowing your visitors to effortlessly select dates. We look at the wide range of configurations that its API makes possible as well as seeing how easy common tasks such as skinning and localization are made.

Chapter 8, The Progressbar Widget, looks at the progressbar widget, examining its compact API and seeing a number of ways in which it can be put to good use in our web applications.

Chapter 9, The Button and Autocomplete Widgets, looks at the brand new button, and recently revivied autocomplete. Longtime users of the library will remember the autocomplete from a previous version of the library. The widget is now back, fully updated to fit in with the latest version of the library and in this chapter we get to see how it can be used to great effect.

Chapter 10, Drag and Drop, begins to look at the low-level interaction helpers, tackling first the related drag-and-droppable components. We look at how they can be implemented individually and how they can be used together to enhance your user interfaces.

Chapter 11, The Resizable Component, looks at the resizing component and how it is used with the dialog widget seen earlier in the book. We see how it can be applied to any element on the page to allow it be resized in a smooth and attractive way.

Chapter 12, The Selectables Component, looks at the selectable component, which allows us to add behavior to elements on the page and allows them be selected individually or as a group. We see that this is one component that really brings the desktop and the browser together as application platforms.

Chapter 13, The Sortables Component, looks at the final interaction helper in this chapter–the sortable component. This is an especially effective component that allows you to create lists on a page that can be reordered by dragging items to a new position on the list. This is another component that can really help you to add a high level of professionalism and interactivity to your site with a minimum of effort.

Chapter 14, UI Effects, the last chapter of the book, is dedicated solely to the special effects that are included with the library. We look at an array of different effects that allow you to show, hide, move, and jiggle elements in a variety of attractive and appealing animations.

What you need for this book

All you need to work through most of the examples in this book is a simple text or code editor and a browser. One or two of the more advanced examples rely on PHP, but for convenience, I've put these examples up on my site for you to use if need be. You can find them at http://danwellman.co.uk/examples/jqueryui/.

Who this book is for

This book is for front-end developers who need to quickly learn how to use jQuery UI, or designers who wish to see how jQuery UI functions, behaves, and looks. To get the most out of this book you should have a good working knowledge of HTML, CSS, and JavaScript, and should ideally be comfortable using jQuery.

Conventions

In this book, you will find a number of styles of text that distinguish between different kinds of information. Here are some examples of these styles, and an explanation of their meaning.

Code words in text are shown as follows: "When prompted for a location to unpack the archive to, choose the `jqueryui` folder that we just created."

A block of code is set as follows:

```
<link rel="stylesheet"
  href="development-bundle/themes/base/jquery.ui.tabs.css">
<link rel="stylesheet"
  href="development-bundle/themes/base/jquery.ui.theme.css">
```

When we wish to draw your attention to a particular part of a code block, the relevant lines or items are set in bold:

```
$(".ui-positioned-element").position({
  of: ".ui-positioning-element",
  my: "right bottom",
  at: "right bottom"
});
```

New terms and important words are shown in bold. Words that you see on the screen, in menus or dialog boxes for example, appear in the text like this: "When we view the page and select the **Images** tab, after a short delay we should see six new images".

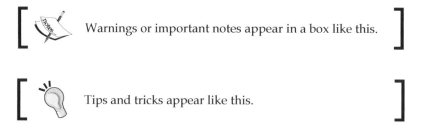

> Warnings or important notes appear in a box like this.

> Tips and tricks appear like this.

Reader feedback

Feedback from our readers is always welcome. Let us know what you think about this book—what you liked or may have disliked. Reader feedback is important for us to develop titles that you really get the most out of.

To send us general feedback, simply send an e-mail to feedback@packtpub.com, and mention the book title via the subject of your message.

If there is a book that you need and would like to see us publish, please send us a note in the **SUGGEST A TITLE** form on www.packtpub.com or e-mail suggest@packtpub.com.

If there is a topic that you have expertise in and you are interested in either writing or contributing to a book, see our author guide on www.packtpub.com/authors.

Customer support

Now that you are the proud owner of a Packt book, we have a number of things to help you to get the most from your purchase.

Downloading the example code

You can download the example code files for all Packt books you have purchased from your account at http://www.PacktPub.com. If you purchased this book elsewhere, you can visit http://www.PacktPub.com/support and register to have the files e-mailed directly to you.

Errata

Although we have taken every care to ensure the accuracy of our content, mistakes do happen. If you find a mistake in one of our books—maybe a mistake in the text or the code—we would be grateful if you would report this to us. By doing so, you can save other readers from frustration and help us improve subsequent versions of this book. If you find any errata, please report them by visiting http://www.packtpub.com/support, selecting your book, clicking on the **errata submission form** link, and entering the details of your errata. Once your errata are verified, your submission will be accepted and the errata will be uploaded on our website, or added to any list of existing errata, under the Errata section of that title. Any existing errata can be viewed by selecting your title from http://www.packtpub.com/support.

Piracy

Piracy of copyright material on the Internet is an ongoing problem across all media. At Packt, we take the protection of our copyright and licenses very seriously. If you come across any illegal copies of our works, in any form, on the Internet, please provide us with the location address or website name immediately so that we can pursue a remedy.

Please contact us at copyright@packtpub.com with a link to the suspected pirated material.

We appreciate your help in protecting our authors, and our ability to bring you valuable content.

Questions

You can contact us at questions@packtpub.com if you are having a problem with any aspect of the book, and we will do our best to address it.

1
Introducing jQuery UI

Welcome to jQuery UI 1.8: The User Interface Library for jQuery. This resource aims to take you from your first steps to an advanced usage of the JavaScript library of UI widgets and interaction helpers that are built on top of the hugely popular and easy-to-use jQuery.

jQuery UI extends the underlying jQuery library to provide a suite of rich and interactive widgets along with code-saving interaction helpers, built to enhance the user interfaces of your websites and web applications. It's the official UI library for jQuery and although it is not the only library built on top of jQuery, in my opinion it is without a doubt the best.

This chapter will cover the following topics:

- How to obtain a copy of the library
- How to set up a development environment
- The structure of the library
- ThemeRoller
- Browser support
- How the library is licensed
- The format of the API

jQuery has quickly become one of the most popular JavaScript libraries in use today. jQuery UI will definitely become the extension library of choice, thanks to its ever-growing range of common UI widgets, high levels of configurability, and its exceptional ease of implementation.

jQuery UI runs on top of jQuery so the syntax used to initialize, configure, and manipulate the different components is in the same comfortable, easy-to-use style as jQuery. We automatically get all of the great jQuery functionality at our disposal as well. The library is also supported by a range of incredibly useful tools, such as the CSS framework that provides a range of helper CSS classes, and the excellent ThemeRoller application that allows us to visually create our own custom themes for the widgets, or choose from a growing library of pre-existing themes.

Over the course of this book, we'll look at each of the existing components that make up the library. We will also be looking at their configuration options and try out their methods in order to fully understand how they work and what they are capable of. By the end of the book, you'll be an expert in its configuration and use.

We already have a basic working knowledge of the components when we add a new widget or interaction helper, because of the consistency in how we implement the different components that make up the library. Therefore, we only need to learn any widget-specific functionality to master the particular component we wish to use.

Downloading the library

To obtain a copy of the library, we should visit the download builder at `http://jqueryui.com/download`. This tool gives us a range of different options for building a download package that is tailored for our particular implementational requirements. The following screenshot shows the download builder:

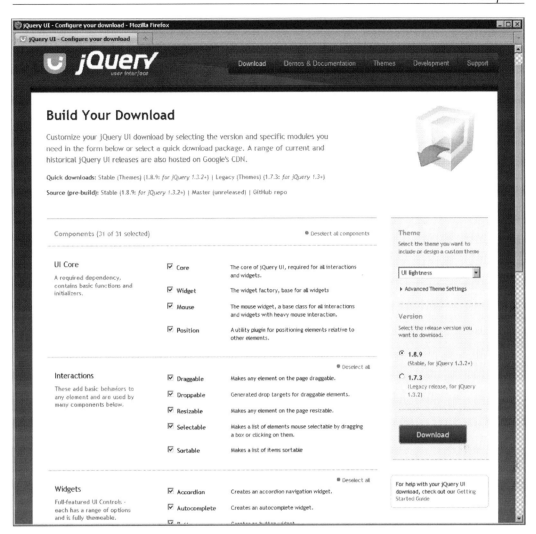

We can either download the complete current release of the library (version 1.8.9 at the time of writing), or a complete package of a legacy version. We can also select just the components that we want and download a custom package.

This book is specifically tailored towards version 1.8, which is above of jQuery UI and requires jQuery 1.3.2 or higher. To support older versions of jQuery, the legacy version 1.7.3 is also available from the download builder.

The page is laid out in a really friendly and easy-to-use way. It lists all of the different components in their respective groupings (core, interaction helpers, and widgets) and allows us to choose from one of 24 different predesigned themes (or no theme at all). The page also provides information about the package (including both its compressed and uncompressed size).

We'll look at the different files found within the library in just a moment, but for now we should download the complete library. It will contain everything we need, including the JavaScript and CSS files, as well as any images from the current theme that different components rely on. It even contains the latest version of jQuery itself, so we don't need to worry about downloading this separately.

For now, just use the **Stable** link at the top of the page. This will give us the default theme, which is called **smoothness**. We'll look at downloading and using other themes in the next chapter.

Hosted Files

We don't even need to download the library in order to implement it in a production web application. Both jQuery and jQuery UI are hosted on Google and Microsoft's **Content Delivery Networks (CDN)**, so we can include `<script>` elements that link to these files instead of using local versions. Only the complete library (not individual components) is available, although there are a range of different releases.

 On a live site that receives a lot of international traffic, using a CDN will help ensure that the library files are downloaded to a visitor's computer from a server that is geographically close to them. This helps in making the response quicker for them and saving our own bandwidth. This is not recommended for local development however.

Google's CDN can be found at: `http://code.google.com/apis/libraries/`.

Microsoft's CDN can be found at: `http://www.asp.net/ajaxlibrary/cdn.ashx`.

Setting up a development environment

We'll need a location to unpack the jQuery UI library in order to easily access the different parts of it within our own files. We should first create a project folder, into which all of our example files, as well as all of the library and other associated resources, can be saved.

Create a new directory in your C: drive, or in your home directory, and call it jqueryui. This will be the root folder of our project and will be the location where we store all of the example files that we'll make over the course of the book.

 The structure of the accompanying code download for this book will mirror the local environment we are creating.

To unpack the library, open it up in a compression program, such as the open source 7-zip, and choose the extract or unzip command. When prompted for a location to unpack the archive to, choose the jqueryui folder that we just created.

 7-zip can be found at: http://www.7-zip.org/

The code examples that we'll be looking at use other resources, mostly images, but occasionally some PHP files too. The accompanying code download available on Packt's website contains all of the images that we'll be using. You should download this now if you can. Visit: http://www.packtpub.com/support/book/user-interface-library-for-jquery. You'll need to create a new folder within the jqueryui project folder and call it img, then unpack all of the images within the img folder in the archive, to this new folder.

The code download also contains all the examples files as well as the library itself. These files are provided in the hope that they will be used for reference purposes only. I'd urge you to follow the examples in the book as you go along, manually creating each file as it is shown, instead of just referring to the files in the code download. The best way to learn code is to code.

This is all that we need to do, no additional platforms or applications need to be installed and nothing needs to be configured or set up. As long as you have a browser and some kind of code or text editor, everything is in place to begin developing with the library.

The structure of the library

Let's take a moment to look at the structure of the library once it has been unpacked, so that we know where to look for specific utilities and files. This will give us a feel for its composition and structure. Open up the `jqueryui` folder where we unpacked the library. The contents of this folder should be as follows:

- A `css` directory
- A `development-bundle` directory
- A `js` directory
- An `index` file

The `css` folder is used to store the complete CSS framework that comes with the library. Within this folder will be a directory that has the name of the theme we chose when building the download package. Inside this is a single file that contains all of the CSS, and a folder that holds all the images used by the theme. We can also store the CSS files that we will be creating in this `css` directory.

The `js` folder contains minified versions of jQuery and the complete jQuery UI library, with all components rolled into one file. In a live project, it is the `js` and `css` folders that we'd want to drop into our site.

The index is an HTML file that gives a brief introduction to the library and displays all of the widgets along with some of the CSS classes. If this is the first time you've ever used the library, you can take a look at this file to see some of the things that we'll be working with throughout the course of this book.

The `development-bundle` directory contains a series of resources to help us develop with the library. It consists of the following subdirectories:

- A `demos` folder
- A `docs` folder
- An `external` folder
- A `themes` folder
- A `ui` folder

Also present in the directory are the license files, documents showing the version of the library and its main contributors, and an uncompressed version of jQuery.

The `demos` folder contains a series of basic examples, showing all of the different components in action. The `docs` folder contains API documents for each of the different components.

The `external` folder contains a set of tools that may be of use to developers. They are as follows:

- The `bgiframe` plugin
- The `cookie` plugin
- The unit testing suite `qunit` (consisting of a JavaScript and a CSS file)
- The `simulate` plugin
- The `metadata` plugin used to parse metadata from elements

The `bgiframe` plugin is used to fix the issue in IE6 where `<select>` elements appear above other content, regardless of `z-index`. The `cookie` plugin makes it easy to use browser cookies. `qunit` is jQuery's unit testing suite and can be used to run unit tests on widgets and plugins that we may create. For more information on QUnit, visit `http://docs.jquery.com/QUnit`.

The `themes` folder contains the default theme, or the theme that was selected during in the download builder. Other themes that we download at a later point or themes we create ourselves, can also be stored here.

The `ui` folder contains the individual and uncompressed source files of each of the different components of the library.

ThemeRoller

ThemeRoller is a custom tool written with jQuery and PHP. It allows us to visually produce our own custom jQuery UI theme and package it up in a convenient and downloadable archive, which we can drop into our project with no further coding (other than using the style sheet in an HTML `<link>` element of course).

ThemeRoller was created by **Filament Group, Inc.** and makes use of a number of jQuery plugins released into the open source community. It can be found at `http://ui.jquery.com/themeroller`. It is due to be updated shortly to coincide with the 1.9 release of jQuery UI.

ThemeRoller is certainly the most comprehensive tool available for creating your own jQuery UI themes. We can very quickly and easily create an entire theme comprised of all of the styles needed for targeting the different widgets that make up the library, including the images we'll need.

If you looked at the `index.html` file a little earlier, then the ThemeRoller landing page will instantly be familiar, as it shows all of the UI widgets on the page, skinned with the default **smoothness** theme.

The page features an interactive menu on the left that is used to work with the application. Each item within the menu expands to give you access to the available style settings for each part of the widget, such as the content and the clickable areas: the header and content areas of the widget, and other associated things such as warnings and error messages.

Here we can create our custom theme with ease and see the changes instantly, as they are applied to the different visible parts of each widget on the page:

When you're not feeling particularly inspired while creating a theme, there is also a gallery of pre-configured themes that you can instantly use to generate a fully configured theme. Aside from convenience, the best thing about these pre-selected themes is that when you select one, it is loaded into the left menu. Therefore, you can easily make little tweaks as required.

This is an excellent way to create a visually appealing custom theme that matches the style of your existing site, and is the recommended method of creating custom skins.

Installing and using the new theme is as easy as selecting or creating it. The **Download theme** button in the above screenshot takes us back to the download builder, which has the CSS and images for the new theme, integrated into the download package.

If it's just the new theme we want, we can deselect the actual components and just download the theme. Once downloaded, the css folder within the downloaded archive will contain a folder that has the name of the theme. We can simply drag this folder into our own local css folder, and then link to the style sheet from our pages.

We won't be looking at this tool in much detail throughout the book. We'll be focusing instead on the style rules that we need to manually override in our own custom style sheets to generate the desired look of the examples manually.

Component categories

There are three types of components found within the jQuery UI library:

1. **Low-level interaction helpers**: designed to work primarily with mouse events.
2. **Widgets**: produce visible objects on the page.
3. **Core components**: components that other parts of the library rely on.

The core components consist of:

*   Core
*   Widget
*   Mouse
*   Position

The core file sets up the construct that all components use to function, and adds some core functionality which is shared by all of the library components, such as keyboard mappings, parent-scrolling, and a z-index manager. This file isn't designed to be used standalone, and exposes no functionality that can be used outside of another component.

The interaction helpers are comprised of the following components:

*   Draggable
*   Droppable
*   Resizable
*   Selectable
*   Sortable

The higher-level widgets (at the time of writing) include:

- Accordion
- Autocomplete
- Button
- Datepicker
- Dialog
- Progressbar
- Slider
- Tabs

The widget factory literally creates the basis for all of the visible widgets exposed by the library. It implements the shared API common to all widgets, such as the create and destroy methods, and provides the event callback logic. It also allows us to create custom jQuery UI widgets which inherit the shared API.

Apart from these components and interaction-helpers, there are also a series of UI effects that produce different animations or transitions on targeted elements on the page. These are excellent for adding flair and style to our pages. We'll be looking at these effects in the final chapter of the book.

The great thing about jQuery UI's simplified API is that once you have learned to use all of the existing components (as this book will show you), you'll be able to pick up any new components very quickly. As this book is being written, there are already a number of new components nearing release, with many more in the pipeline, and all of these components will automatically be ThemeRoller-ready.

Browser support

Like jQuery itself, jQuery UI supports all of the major browsers in use today, including the following:

- IE6, IE7, IE8, and IE9
- Firefox 2, Firefox 3, and Firefox 4, and Firefox 5
- Opera 9, Opera 10, and Opera 11
- Safari 3, Safari 4, and Safari 5
- Chrome 1 to Chrome 9

The widgets are built from semantically correct HTML elements generated, as needed by the components. Therefore, we won't see excessive or unnecessary elements being created or used.

Book examples

The library is as flexible as standard JavaScript. By this, I mean that there is often more than one way of doing the same thing, or achieving the same end. For example, the callback events used in the configuration objects for different components, can usually take either references to functions or inline anonymous functions, and use them with equal ease-and-efficiency.

In practice, it is advisable to keep your code as minimal as possible (which jQuery can really help with anyway). But to make the examples more readable and understandable, we'll be separating as much of the code as possible into discrete modules. Therefore, callback functions and configuration objects will be defined separately from the code that calls or uses them.

To reduce the number of files that we have to create and work with, all of the JavaScript will go into the host HTML page on which it runs, as opposed to in separate files. Please keep in mind that this is not advisable for production websites. When scripts reside within external `js` files, the browser is able to cache them for vastly improved loading speeds. When scripts are in the `<body>` element of a page, the browser cannot store them in the cache.

I'd also just like to make it clear that the main aim throughout the course of this book is to learn how to use the different components that make up jQuery UI. If an example seems a little convoluted, it may simply be that this is the easiest way to expose the functionality of a particular method or property, as opposed to a situation that we would find ourselves coding for in regular implementations.

I'd like to add here that the jQuery UI library is currently undergoing a rapid period of expansion and development. It is also constantly growing and evolving, with bug fixes and feature enhancements continually being added. It would be impossible to keep entirely up-to-date with this aggressive expansion and cover components that are literally about to be released.

Library licensing

Like jQuery, the jQuery UI library is dual licensed under the MIT and GPL open source licenses. These are both very unrestrictive licenses that allow the creators of the library to take credit for its production and retain intellectual rights over it, without preventing us as developers from using the library in any way that we like on any type of site.

The MIT license explicitly states that users of the software (jQuery UI in this case) are free to use, copy, merge, modify, publish, distribute, sublicense, and sell. This lets us do pretty much whatever we want with the library. The only requirement imposed by this license is that we must keep the original copyright and warranty statements intact.

This is an important point to make. You can take the library and do whatever you like with it. Build applications on top of the library and then sell those applications, or give them away for free. Put the library in embedded systems like cell phone OS and sell those. But whatever you do, leave the original text file with John Resig's name present in it. You may also duplicate it word-for-word in the help files or documentation of your application.

The MIT license is very lenient, but because it is not copyrighted itself, we are free to change it. We could therefore demand that users of our software give attribution to us instead of the jQuery team, or pass off the code as our own.

The GPL license is copyrighted, and offers an additional layer of protection for the library's creators and the users of our software. jQuery is provided for free and is open source. The GPL license ensures that it will always remain that way, regardless of the environment it may end up in, and that the original creators of the library are given the credit they deserve. Again, the original GPL license file must be available in some form, within your application or site.

The licenses are not there to restrict us in any way, and are not the same as the kind of license that comes with software you might purchase and install on your own computer. In most cases, how the library is licensed will not be a consideration when using it. Plugin authors, however, will want to ensure that their plugins are released under a similar license.

API introduction

Once you've worked with one of the components from the library, you'll instantly feel at home when working with any of the other components, since the methods of each component are called in exactly the same way.

The API for each component consists of a series of different methods. While these are all technically methods, it may be useful to categorize them based on their particular function.

Method type	Description
The `plugin` method	This method is used to initialize the component and is simply the name of the component, followed by parentheses. I will refer to this throughout the book as the `plugin` method or `widget` method.
Shared API methods	The `destroy` method can be used with any of the components, to completely disable the widget being used and in most cases, returns the underlying HTML to its original state.
	The `option` method is used by all components to get or set any configuration option after initialization.
	The `enable` and `disable` methods are used by most library components to enable or disable the component.
	The `widget` method, exposed by all widgets, returns a reference to the current widget.
Specialized methods	Each component has one or more methods unique to that particular component that perform specialized functions.

Methods are consistently called throughout each of the different components by passing the method that we'd like to call, as a simple string to the component's `plugin` method, with any arguments that the method accepts passed as strings after the method name.

For example, to call the `destroy` method of the accordion component, we would simply do the following:

```
$("#someElement").accordion("destroy");
```

See how easy that was? Every single method exposed by all of the different components, is called in this same simple way.

Some methods, like standard JavaScript functions, accept arguments that trigger different behavior in the component. If we wanted to call the `disable` method on a particular tab in the tabs widget for example, we would do the following:

```
$("#someElement").tabs("disable", 1);
```

The `disable` method, when used in conjunction with the tabs widget, accepts an integer, which refers to the index of the individual tab within the widget. Similarly, to enable the tab again we would use the `enable` method:

```
$("#someElement").tabs("enable", 1);
```

Again, we supply an argument to modify how the method is used. Sometimes the arguments that are passed to the method vary between components. The accordion widget, for example, does not enable or disable individual accordion panels, only the whole widget, so no additional arguments following the method name are required.

The `option` method is slightly more complex than the other common methods, but it's also more powerful and is just as easy-to-use. The method is used to either get or set any configurable option, after the component has been initialized.

To use the option method in `getter` mode to retrieve the current value of an option, we could use the following code:

```
$("#someElement").accordion("option", "navigation");
```

This code would return the current value of the `navigation` option of the accordion widget. So to trigger `getter` mode, we just supply the option name that we'd like to retrieve.

In order to use the `option` method in `setter` mode instead, we can supply the option name and the new value as arguments:

```
$("#someElement").accordion("option", "navigation", true);
```

This code would set the value of the `navigation` option to `true`. Note that, an object literal can also be passed to the `option` method in order to set several different options at once, for example:

```
$("#someElement").accordion("option", {
  navigation: true,
  autoHeight: false
});
```

As you can see, although the `option` method gives us the power to both get and set configuration options, it still retains the same easy-to-use format of the other methods.

Using jQuery UI feels just like using jQuery and having built up confidence coding with jQuery, moving on to jQuery UI is the next logical step to take.

Events and callbacks

The API for each component also contains a rich event model that allows us to easily react to different interactions. Each component exposes its own set of unique custom events, yet the way in which these events are used is the same, regardless of which event is used.

We have two ways of working with events in jQuery UI. Each component allows us to add callback functions that are executed when the specified event is fired, as values for configuration options. For example, to use the `select` event of the tabs widget, which is fired every time a tab is selected, we could use the following code:

```
var config = {
  select: function() {
  }
};
```

The name of the event is used as the `option` name and an anonymous function is used as the `option` value. We'll look at all of the individual events that are used with each component in later chapters.

The other way of working with events is to use jQuery's `bind()` method. To use events in this way, we simply specify the name of the component followed by the name of the event:

```
$("#someElement").bind("tabsselect", function() {
});
```

Usually, but not always, callback functions used with the `bind()` method are executed after the event has been fired, while callbacks specified using configuration options are executed directly before the event is fired.

The callback functions are called in the context of the DOMElement that triggered the event. For example, in a tabs widget with several tabs, the `select` event will be triggered by the actual tab that is selected, not the tabs widget as a whole. This is extremely useful to us, because it allows us to associate the event with a particular tab.

Some of the custom events fired by jQuery UI components are cancellable and if stopped, can be used to prevent certain actions from taking place. The best example of this (which we'll look at later in the book) is preventing a dialog widget from closing, by returning `false` in the callback function of the `beforeclose` event:

```
beforeclose: function() {
  if (readyToClose === false) {
    return false
  }
```

If the arbitrary condition in this example was not met, `false` would be returned by the callback function and the dialog would remain open. This is an excellent and powerful feature that can give us fine-grained control over each widget's behavior.

Callback arguments

Any anonymous functions that we supply as callback functions to the different events, automatically pass two arguments, the original event object, and an object containing useful information about the widget. The information contained with the second object varies between components. We'll look at it in greater detail in later chapters.

To use these two objects we just specify them as arguments to the function:

```
select: function(e, ui) {
  e.target
  ui.index
}
```

Every single component will automatically supply these objects to any callback functions we define.

Summary

jQuery UI removes the difficulty of building engaging and effective user interfaces. It provides a range of components that can quickly and easily be used out of the box with little configuration. They each expose a comprehensive set of properties and methods for integration with your pages or applications, if a more complex configuration is required.

Each component is designed to be efficient, lightweight, and semantically correct, along with making use of the latest object-oriented features of JavaScript. When combined with jQuery, it provides an awesome addition to any web developer's toolkit.

So far, we've seen how the library can be obtained, how your system can be set up to utilize it, and how the library is structured. We've also looked at how the different widgets can be themed or customized, how the API simply and consistently exposes the library's functionality, and the different categories of component.

We've covered some important topics during the course of this chapter, but now we can get on with using the components of jQuery UI and get down to some proper coding.

2
The CSS Framework and Other Utilities

Version 1.7 of jQuery UI was an exciting release because it introduced the comprehensive new CSS framework. All widgets are effectively and consistently themed by the framework. There are many helper classes that we can use in our own code, even if we aren't using any of the library components.

In this chapter we'll be covering the following subjects:

- The files that make up the framework
- How to use the classes exposed by the framework
- How to switch themes quickly and easily
- Overriding the theme
- Using the position utility

The files that make up the framework

There are two locations within the library's structure where the CSS files that make the framework reside. They are the following:

- **The css folder**: This folder holds the complete CSS framework, including the theme that was selected when the download package was built. All the necessary CSS has been placed in a single, lean, and mean style sheet to minimize HTTP requests in production environments. The CSS file is stored in a directory, named after the theme selected on the download builder.

  This version of the framework will contain styles for all the components that were selected in the download builder, so its size will vary depending on how much of the library is being used. The full version of each theme weighs in at 26.7 KB and is not compressed.

- **The** themes **folder**: Another version of the framework exists within the development-bundle\themes folder. Two themes are provided in this folder—the base theme and whichever theme that was selected when the library was downloaded. The base theme is a grey, neutral theme which is visually identical to smoothness theme.

Within each of these theme folders are all the individual files that make up the framework. Each of the different components of the framework is split into its own respective files.

Component	Use
jquery.ui.all.css	All the required files for a theme can be linked by using this file in development. It consists of @import directives that pull in the ui.base.css and the ui.theme.css files.
jquery.ui.base.css	This file is used by ui.all.css. It also contains @ import directives that pull in the ui.core.css file, as well as in each of the widget CSS files. However, it contains none of the theme styles that control each widget's appearance.
jquery.ui.core.css	This file provides core framework styles such as the clear-fix helper and a generic overlay.
jquery.ui.accordion.css jquery.ui.datepicker.css jquery.ui.dialog.css jquery.ui.progressbar. css jquery.ui.resizable.css jquery.ui.slider.css jquery.ui.tabs.css	These files are the individual source files that control the layout and basic appearance of each widget.
jquery.ui.theme.css	This file contains the complete visual theme and targets of all the visual elements that make up each widget in the library.

Let's take a look at each of these files in more detail.

jquery.ui.all.css

The `jquery.ui.all.css` file makes use of CSS imports, using the `@import` rule to read in two files—the `jquery.ui.base.css` file and the `jquery.ui.theme.css` file. This is all that is present in the file and all that is needed to implement the complete framework and the selected theme.

From the two directives found in this file, we can see the separation between the part of the framework that makes the widgets function and the theme that gives them their visual appearance.

jquery.ui.base.css

The `jquery.ui.base.css` file also consists of only `@import` rules, and imports the `jquery.ui.core.css` file along with each of the individual widget CSS files. At this point, I should mention that the resizable component has its own framework file, along with each of the widgets.

jquery.ui.core.css

The `jquery.ui.core.css` file provides generic styles for the framework that are used by all components. It contains the following classes:

Class	Use
`.ui-helper-hidden`	Hides elements with `display:none`.
`.ui-helper-hidden-accessible`	Hides elements by clipping them, so that the element remains fully accessible. The element is not hidden or positioned off-screen at all.
`.ui-helper-reset`	This is the reset mechanism for jQuery UI (it doesn't use a separate reset style sheet), which neutralizes the margins, padding, and other common default styles applied to common elements by browsers. For an introduction to see the importance of resetting default browser styling, visit: `http://sixrevisions.com/css/css-tips/css-tip-1-resetting-your-styles-with-css-reset/`.

Class	Use

`.ui-helper-clearfix:after`
 	
`.ui-helper-clearfix`
 	
`* html .ui-helper-clearfix`
	These classes provide a cross-browser solution for automatically clearing floats. Whenever an element is floated, the `.ui-helper-clearfix` class is added to the floated element's container. The `.ui-helper-clearfix:after` styles are added after the parent container (it uses the content style to insert new content) to automatically clear the float.

`.ui-helper-clearfix`	The `.ui-helper-clearfix` styles are applied to the container itself, and the `*` hack is used to target older versions of Internet Explorer.
`.ui-helper-zfix`	The `.ui-helper-zfix` class provides rules that are applied to `<iframe>` elements, in order to fix `z-index` issues when overlays are used.
`.ui-state-disabled`	This class sets the `cursor` to `default` for disabled elements and uses the `!important` directive to ensure that it is not overridden.
`.ui-icon`	This rule is the library's method of replacing the text content of an element with a background image. The responsibility of setting the background images for the different icons found in the library is delegated to the `jquery.ui.theme.css` file.
`.ui-widget-overlay`	This class sets the basic style properties of the overlay that is applied to the page when dialogs and other modal pop ups are shown. As images are used by the overlay, some styles for this class are also found in the `theme` file.

The core file lays the foundation for the rest of the framework. We can also give these class names to our own elements, to clear floats or hide elements whenever we use the library, and especially when building new jQuery UI plugins for consistent theming with ThemeRoller.

The individual component framework files

Each widget in the library, as well as the resizable interaction helper, has a framework file that controls the CSS, which makes the widget function correctly. For example, the tab headings in the tabs widget must be floated left, in order to display them as tabs. These framework files set this rule. These styles will need to be preserved when we are overriding the framework in a custom theme.

These files are brief, with each component using the smallest number of rules possible for it to function correctly. Generally the files are quite compact (usually not more than 20 style rules long). The `dialog` and `datepicker` source files are the exception, with each requiring a large number of rules to function correctly as a pop up.

jquery.ui.theme.css

This file will be customized to the theme that was selected or created with ThemeRoller and it sets all of the visual properties (colors, images, and so on) for the different elements that make up each widget.

Within the `jquery.ui.reset.css` file, there are many comments that contain descriptive labels, enclosed within curly braces. These are called **placeholders** and the CSS styles that precede them are updated by ThemeRoller automatically when the theme is generated.

This is the file that will be generated for the complete theme and it contains styles for all the visible parts of each widget, when creating or selecting a theme using ThemeRoller. When overriding the framework to create a custom theme, it is mostly rules in this file that will be overridden.

Each widget is constructed from a set of common elements. For example, the outer container of each widget has the class named `ui-widget`, while any content within the widget will be held in a container with the class named `ui-widget-content`. It is this consistent layout and classing convention that makes the framework so effective.

This is the biggest style sheet used by the framework and contains too many classes to list here in its entirety (but feel free to open it up at this point and take a look through it). The following table lists the different categories of classes:

Category	Use
Containers	Sets style properties for widget, heading, and content containers.
Interaction states	These classes set the default, hover, and active states for any clickable elements.
Interaction cues	This category applies visual cues to elements including highlight, error, disabled, primary, and secondary styles.
States and images	These classes set the images used for icons displayed in the content and heading containers, as well as any clickable elements including default, hover, active, highlight, focus, and error states.
Image positioning	All of the icon images used by the theme are stored in a single file (known as a **sprite** file), and are displayed individually by manipulating the `background-position` properties of the sprite file. This category sets the background positions for all individual icons.
Corner radius	CSS3 is used to give rounded corners to supporting browsers (just Firefox 3+, Safari 3+, Chrome 1+, Opera 10+, and IE9+).
Overlays	The image used for the generic overlay defined in the core CSS file is set here, as it is a class that implements a semi-transparent overlay over specified elements.

The jQuery UI documentation features an extensive overview of the theming API at: `http://docs.jquery.com/UI/Theming/API`.

Linking to the required framework files

For rapid theming of all jQuery UI widgets in a development environment, we can link to all of the individual files using `jquery.ui.all.css`:

```
<link rel="stylesheet"
  href="development-bundle/themes/smoothness/jquery.ui.all.css">
```

To use each file individually when testing a component such as the tabs widget for example, we would use the following `<link>` elements:

```
<link rel="stylesheet"
  href="development-bundle/themes/base/jquery.ui.core.css">
<link rel="stylesheet"
  href="development-bundle/themes/base/jquery.ui.tabs.css">
<link rel="stylesheet"
  href="development-bundle/themes/base/jquery.ui.theme.css">
```

The CSS resources, when linked to separately, should be added to the HTML page in the following order—`core.css`, the widget's CSS file, and the `theme.css` file.

In a production environment of course, we'd use the super-efficient combined file to minimize the number of HTTP requests for CSS files. We need to link to the combined `jquery-ui-x.x.x.css` style sheet found in the `css/themename/` directory:

```
<link rel="stylesheet"
  href="css/smoothness/jquery-ui-x.x.x.custom.css">
```

For easier coding and convenience, we'll be linking to the `jquery-ui-1.8.9.custom.css` file in all our examples. If you have unpacked the library as shown in *Chapter 1, Introducing jQuery UI*, and the `.html` files that are stored in the top-level directory alongside the `css`, `development-bundle`, and `js` directories, the previous path to the CSS file will be correct. If you are using a different folder structure, please ensure the path to this CSS file is correct.

Using the framework classes

Along with using the framework while we're implementing official jQuery UI widgets, we can also use it when we're deploying our own custom plugins.

Containers

Containers are recommended because it means that widgets or plugins that we write, will be ThemeRoller-ready and easier for end-developers to theme and customize. Let's look at how easy it is to use the framework with our own elements.

In your text editor, create a new file and add the following code:

```
<!DOCTYPE html>
<html>
  <head>
    <meta charset="utf-8">
    <title>CSS Framework - Containers
    </title>
    <link rel="stylesheet"
      href="development-bundle/themes/base/jquery.ui.all.css">
  </head>
  <body>
    <div class="ui-widget">
      <div class="ui-widget-header ui-corner-top">
        <h2>This is a .ui-widget-header container</h2>
      </div>
```

```
      <div class="ui-widget-content ui-corner-bottom">
        <p>This is a .ui-widget-content container</p>
      </div>
    </div>
  </body>
</html>
```

Save this page as `containers.html` within the `jqueryui` project folder that we created in *Chapter 1, Introducing jQuery UI*, when we unpacked the library. We're linking to the `jquery.ui.all.css` file from the `base` development theme in the library. If we were building a more complex widget, we'd probably want to link to the `jquery.ui.core.css` file as well.

Working with this file when creating widgets or plugins is essential, because it lets us verify that the class names we give our containers will pick up appropriate styling, and reassures us that they will be ThemeRoller-ready. Any style that we need to apply ourselves would go into a separate style sheet, like each widget from the library has its own custom style sheet.

We use only a couple of elements in this example. Our outer container is given the class name `ui-widget`. If we were making a custom widget, we'd also want to put a custom class name on this element. For example, if we were making a content scroller, we might add the class `ui-widget-scroller`.

Within the outer container, we have two other containers—one is the `ui-widget-heading` container and the other is the `ui-widget-content` container. We also give these elements variants of the corner-rounding classes—`ui-corner-top` and `ui-corner-bottom` respectively.

Inside the header and content containers, we just have a couple of appropriate elements that we might want to put in, such as `<h2>` in the header and `<p>` in the content element. These elements will inherit some rules from their respective containers, but are not styled directly by the theme file.

When we view this basic page in a browser, we should see that our two container elements pick up the styles from the `theme` file as shown in the following screenshot:

Interactions

Let's look at some more of the framework classes in action. Create the following new page:

```html
<!DOCTYPE html>
<html>
  <head>
    <meta charset="utf-8">
    <title>CSS Framework - Interaction states
    </title>
    <link rel="stylesheet"
      href="development-bundle/themes/base/jquery.ui.all.css">
  </head>
  <body>
    <div class="ui-widget">
      <div
        class="ui-state-default ui-state-active ui-corner-all">
        <a href="#">I am clickable and selected</a>
      </div>
      <div class="ui-state-default ui-corner-all">
        <a href="#">I am clickable but not selected
        </a>
      </div>
    </div>
  </body>
</html>
```

Save this file as `interactions.html` in the `jqueryui` project folder. We've defined two clickable elements in these examples, which are comprised of a container `<div>` and an `<a>` element. Both containers are given the class names `ui-state-default` and `ui-corner-all`, but the first is also given the selected state `ui-state-active`. This will give our clickable elements the following appearance:

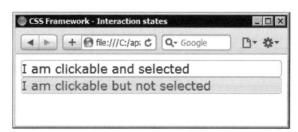

The CSS framework doesn't provide styles on the `:hover` CSS pseudo-class, instead it applies a set of styles using a class name, which is added using JavaScript. To see this in action before the closing `</body>` tag, add the following code:

```
<script src="development-bundle/jquery-1.4.4.js">
</script>
<script>
  (function($) {
    $(".ui-widget a").hover(function() {
      $(this).parent().addClass("ui-state-hover");
    }, function() {
      $(this).parent().removeClass("ui-state-hover");
    });
  })(jQuery);
</script>
```

Save this variation of the previous example file as `interactionsHovers.html`.

 The version number of jQuery will change as the library continues to evolve.

Our simple script adds the `ui-state-hover` class name to a clickable element when the mouse pointer moves on to it, and then removes it when the mouse pointer moves off. When we run the page in a browser and hover over the second clickable element, we should see the `ui-state-hover` styles:

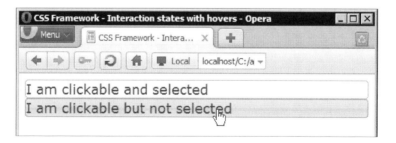

Icons

The framework provides a series of images that we can use as icons. Change the contents of the ui-widget container in `interactionsHovers.html` so that it appears as follows:

```
<div class="ui-widget">
  <div class="ui-state-default ui-state-active ui-corner-all">
```

```
      <div class="ui-icon ui-icon-circle-plus">
      </div>
      <a href="#">I am clickable and selected</a>
    </div>
    <div class="ui-state-default ui-corner-all">
      <div class="ui-icon ui-icon-circle-plus">
      </div>
        <a href="#">I am clickable but not selected
        </a>
    </div>
  </div>
</div>
```

Save this as `icons.html` in the `jqueryui` directory. In this example, our nested `<div>` elements, which have the classes `ui-icon` and `ui-icon-circle-plus`, are given the correct icon from a sprite file:

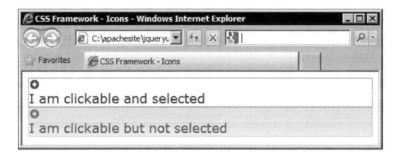

As you can see, the `ui-state-active` icon differs slightly from the `ui-state-default` icon (as well as the `ui-state-hover` icon). We haven't positioned the icons at all in this example, because this would necessitate the creation of a new style sheet. The point of this example is to see how the icons can be automatically added using the class names from the framework.

Interaction cues

Another set of classes we can use is the interaction cues. We will look at another example using these. In a new page in your text-editor, add the following code:

```
<!DOCTYPE html>
<html>
  <head>
    <meta charset="utf-8">
    <title>CSS Framework - Interaction cues</title>
    <link rel="stylesheet"
      href="development-bundle/themes/base/jquery.ui.all.css">
```

```
        <link rel="stylesheet" href="css/jquery.ui.form.css">
    </head>
    <body>
      <div class="ui-widget ui-form">
        <div class="ui-widget-header ui-corner-all">
          <h2>Login Form</h2>
        </div>
        <div class="ui-widget-content ui-corner-all">
          <form action="#" class="ui-helper-clearfix">
            <label>Username</label>
            <div class="ui-state-error ui-corner-all">
              <input type="text">
              <div class="ui-icon ui-icon-alert"></div>
              <p class="ui-helper-reset ui-state-error-text">
                Required field
              </p>
            </div>
          </form>
        </div>
      </div>
    </body>
</html>
```

Save this file as cues.html in the jqueryui folder. This time we link to a custom file jquery.ui.form.css that we'll create in a moment.

On the page, we have the outer widget container, with the class names ui-form and ui-widget. The ui-form class will be used to pick up our custom styles from the jquery.ui.form.css style sheet. Within the widget, we have ui-widget-header and ui-widget-content containers.

Within the content section, we've got a <form> with a single row of elements, a <label> element followed by a <div> element that has the ui-state-error and ui-corner-all class names hardcoded to it.

Within this <div> element,we have a standard <input>, a <div> with the ui-icon, and ui-icon-alert classes added along with a <p> element with the ui-state-error-text class name added to it. Because the <form> will have child elements that are floated due to styles we will add in jquery.ui.form.css, we can make use of the ui-helper-clearfix class to clear the floats, which we add as a class name.

We should now create the custom jquery.ui.form.css style sheet. In a new page in your text editor, add the following code:

```
.ui-form { width:470px; margin:0 auto; }
.ui-form .ui-widget-header h2 { margin:10px 0 10px 20px; }
```

```
.ui-form .ui-widget-content { padding:20px; }
.ui-form label, .ui-form input, .ui-form .ui-state-error,
.ui-form .ui-icon, .ui-form .ui-state-error p { float:left; }
.ui-form label, .ui-state-error p {
  font-size:12px; padding:10px 10px 0 0;
}
.ui-form .ui-state-error { padding:4px; }
.ui-form .ui-state-error p {
  font-weight:bold; padding-top:5px;
}
.ui-form .ui-state-error .ui-icon { margin:5px 3px 0 4px; }
```

Within our `jqueryui` project folder, there is a folder called `css` that is used to store the single-file production version of the framework. All of the CSS files we create throughout the book will also be saved in here for convenience. Save this file as `jquery.ui.form.css` in the css folder.

Imagine we have more forms of elements and a submit button. By adding the `ui-state-error` class to the `<div>` element, we can use the error classes for form validation, which upon an unsuccessful submission would show the icon and text. The following screenshot shows how the page should look:

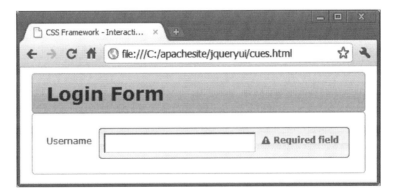

Switching themes quickly and easily

After developing a new widget using the base theme, we may decide that we want to switch to a fancier theme or one that fits in better with our site when we deploy it. People might want to use a different theme than the one we chose when downloading the library, if we wrote and released a new plugin.

Thankfully, the CSS framework makes switching themes a painless task. Looking at the previous example, all we need to do to change the skin of the widget is choose a new theme using ThemeRoller, and then download the new theme (we can download just the new theme by deselecting all of the components in the download builder).

Within the downloaded archive, there would be a directory with the name of the chosen theme, such as **dot-luv**. We drag the theme folder out of the archive into the `development-bundle\themes` folder and link the new theme file from our page, giving our form a completely new look as shown in the following screenshot:

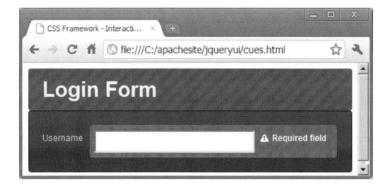

The theme I used to obtain the this screenshot is dot-luv. We'll be using the **smoothness** theme, or themes of our own creation for the remainder of the book.

Overriding the theme

Using the ThemeRoller gallery and customization tools, we can generate an extraordinary number of unique themes. But there may be times when we need a deeper level of customization than we are able to reach using ThemeRoller; in this situation we have two options.

We can either create a complete theme file from scratch by ourselves, or we can create an additional style sheet that overrides only those rules in the `jquery.ui.theme.css` file that we need. The latter is probably the easiest method and results in having to write less code.

We'll now take a look at this aspect of theming. Switch back to the base theme in the
`<head>` of `cues.html`, if you changed it for the previous example. Save the page as
`cuesOverridden.html` and then create the following new style sheet:

```
.ui-corner-all {
  -moz-border-radius:0; -webkit-border-radius:0;
  border-radius:0;
}
.ui-widget-header {
  font-family:Georgia; background:#534741;
  border:1px solid #362f2d; color:#c7b299;
}
.ui-form .ui-widget-header h2 {
  margin:0; border:1px solid #998675; padding:10px;
  font-style:italic; font-weight:normal;
}
.ui-form .ui-widget-content {
  background:#c7b299; border:1px solid #362f2d; border-top:0;
  padding:0;
}
.ui-widget-content form {
  padding:20px; border:1px solid #f3eadf;
}
.ui-widget-content .ui-state-error {
  border:1px solid #e7cc17; background:#fbf5cd;
}
.ui-widget-content .ui-state-error-text {
  color:#e7cc17; padding-left:10px;
}
.ui-state-error .ui-icon { display:none; }
```

Save this as `overrides.css` in the `css` folder. In this style sheet we're mostly
overriding rules from the `jquery.ui.theme.css` file. These are simple styles
and we're just changing colors, backgrounds, and borders. Link to this style
sheet by adding the following line of code below the other style sheets in
`cuesOverridden.html`:

```
<link rel="stylesheet" href="css/overrides.css">
```

Our humble form should now appear as in the following screenshot:

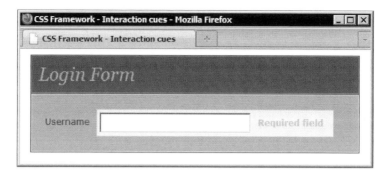

As long as we match or exceed the specificity of the selectors used in the `jquery.ui.theme.css` file, and as long as our style sheet appears after the theme file, our rules will take precedence. A long discussion on CSS selector weight is beyond the scope of this book. However, a brief explanation of specificity may be beneficial as it is the key to overriding the selected theme.

CSS specificity refers to how specific a CSS selector is — the more specific it is, the more weight it will have, and will subsequently override other rules that are applied to the element being targeted by other selectors. For example, consider the following selectors:

```
#myContainer .bodyText
.bodyText
```

The first selector is more specific than the second selector, because it not only uses the class name of the element being targeted, but also the id of its parent container. It will therefore override the second selector, regardless of whether the second selector appears after it.

In this example, we have full control over the elements that we're skinning. But when working with any widgets from the library or with plugins authored by third-parties, a lot of markup could be generated automatically, which we have no control over (without hacking the actual library files themselves).

Therefore, we may need to rely on overriding styles in this way. All we need to do to find which styles to override, is open up the `jquery.ui.theme.css` file in a text editor and take a look at the selectors used there. Failing to do that, we can use Firebug's CSS viewer to see the rules that we need to override:

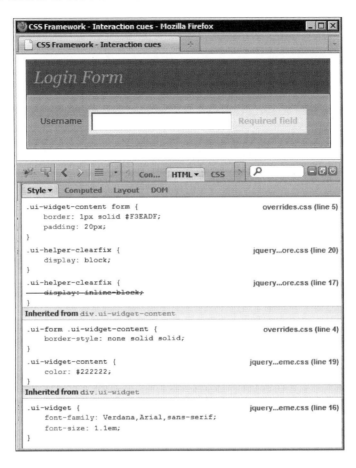

DOM Explorers

All modern browsers have DOM explorers and CSS inspectors like Firebug that can be used to see the order in which CSS rules are being applied. Using the browser's CSS inspector is usually the most convenient way of checking CSS order.

The position utility

The position utility is a powerful stand-alone utility that is used to position any element relative to the window, the document, a specific element, or the mouse pointer. It is unique among library components, in that it doesn't require `jquery.ui.core.js` or `jquery.effects.core.js` as dependencies.

It exposes no unique or custom methods (other than the `position()` method) and fires no events, but it does come with a series of configuration options that allow us to use it. These options are listed in the following table:

Option	Format	Used to...
at	string	Specify the edges of the element that is being positioned against. Formatted as, for example, `left bottom`.
collision	string	Move the positioned element to an alternative position when the positioned element overflows its container.
my	string	Specify the edges of the element being positioned that are expected to be aligned to the element being positioned against, for example `right top`.
of	selector, jQuery, object, event object	Specify the element to position against the positioned element. When a selector or jQuery object is provided, the first matched element is used. When an event object is provided, the `pageX` and `pageY` properties are used
offset	string	Move the positioned element to the specified number of pixels. Formatted as, for example, `10, 20` with the value for the horizontal axis appearing first, then the vertical.
using	function	Accepts a function, which actually positions the positioned element. This function receives an object containing the `top` and `left` values of the new position.

Using the position utility

Using the position utility is easy. Let's look at a few examples; create the following page in your text editor:

```
<!DOCTYPE html>
<html>
  <head>
    <meta charset="utf-8">
    <title>Position Utility - position
    </title>
    <link rel="stylesheet" href="css/position.css">
  </head>
  <body>
    <div class="ui-positioning-element">
      I am being positioned against
    </div>
    <div class="ui-positioned-element">
      I am being positioned
    </div>
    <script src="development-bundle/jquery-1.4.4.js">
    </script>
    <script
      src="development-bundle/ui/jquery.ui.position.js">
    </script>
    <script>
      (function($) {
        $(".ui-positioned-element").position({
          of: ".ui-positioning-element"
        });
      })(jQuery);
    </script>
  </body>
</html>
```

Save this as `position.html`. We also use a very basic style sheet in this example consisting of the following styles:

```
.ui-positioning-element {
  width:200px; height:200px; border:1px solid #000;
}
.ui-positioned-element {
  width:100px; height:100px; border:1px solid #ff0000;
}
```

Save this file in the `css` folder as `position.css`. The element that we are positioning against, as well as element that we are positioning itself, can be set to either `relative`, `absolute`, or `static` positioning, without affecting how the positioned element behaves. If the element we are positioning against is moved using its `top`, `left`, `bottom`, or `right` style properties, the element we are positioning will take account of this and still work correctly.

On the page we just have two `<div>` elements: one is what we will be positioning against, and the other is the actual element we will be positioning. jQuery itself is a requirement so we link to that at the bottom of the `<body>` element, and also we link to the position utility's source file. As I mentioned earlier, we don't need to link to the `jquery.ui.core.js` file when using position by itself.

The minimum configuration we can use, as we have in this example, is to set the `of` option, which we use to specify the element we are positioning against. When we set just this one option, the element we are positioning is placed exactly in the center of the element we are positioning against, as shown in the following screenshot:

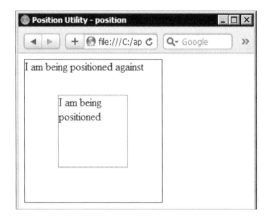

This alone is incredibly useful as the element is not only centered horizontally, but vertically too.

By using the `my` and `at` properties as well, we can place any edge of the positioned element against any edge of the element we are positioning against. Change the code within the outer function so that it appears as follows (new/altered code is shown in bold):

```
$(".ui-positioned-element").position({
    of: ".ui-positioning-element",
    my: "right bottom",
    at: "right bottom"
});
```

The following screenshot shows the output of this code:

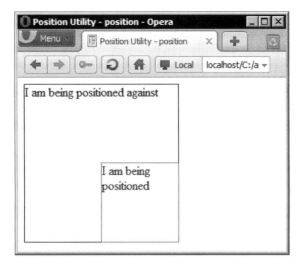

The `my` option refers to the element that is being positioned. The first part of the string, which is supplied as the value of this option, is the horizontal axis, and can be set to `left`, `center`, or `right`. The second part is the vertical axis, and can be set to `top`, `center`, or `bottom`.

The `at` option refers to the horizontal and vertical edges of the element being positioned against. It also accepts a string in the same format as the `my` configuration option.

> At the time of writing, there appears to be an issue in Webkit browsers that causes the positioning to be reversed. This is due to the default value of `flip` being applied even when no collision occurs. We can work around this issue by setting the `collision` option to `none` (see the *Collision avoidance*, section below).

Collision avoidance

The position utility has a built-in collision detection system to prevent the element that is being positioned from overflowing the viewport. There are two different options that we can use to set what happens when a collision is detected. The default is `flip`, which causes the element to flip and align the opposite edges, of those configured.

For example, if we position a `<div>` element's right edge to align to the left edge of another element, it will be flipped to have its right edge aligned to the positioning element's right edge instead, if it overflows the viewport. Change the configuration in `position.html` to the following:

```
$(".ui-positioned-element").position({
    of: ".ui-positioning-element",
    my: "right",
    at: "left"
});
```

This would result in the following positioning:

The other mode of collision avoidance is `fit`, which will honor the configured positioning as much as possible, but adjust the offset, so that the positioned element stays within the viewport. Configure the collision option as follows:

```
$(".ui-positioned-element").position({
    collision: "fit",
    of: ".ui-positioning-element",
    my: "right",
    at: "left",
});
```

Save this file as `positionFit.html`. This time, the element is positioned as close as possible to its intended position:

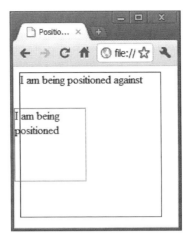

 We can also set the value of the `collision` option to `none` to disable collision detection entirely, and allow the positioned element to overflow the viewport.

Positioning with a function

We can set the `using` option to a function, and position the positioned element manually. Change the configuration so that it appears as follows:

```
$(".ui-positioned-element").position({
  of: ".ui-positioning-element",
  my: "right bottom",
  at: "right bottom",
  using: function(pos) {
    $(this).css({
      backgroundColor: "#fc7676",
      top: pos.top,
      left: pos.left
    });
  }
});
```

Save this change as `positionFunction.html`. We supply an anonymous function as the value of the `using` option. This function is passed as a single argument that is an object containing the properties `top` and `left`, which correspond to the values that the element we are positioning, should be given.

As you can see from this code, we still need to position the element manually, but the function allows us to do any pre-processing of the element that may be required. Within the function, the `this` object is set to the element being positioned.

The widget factory

Version 1.8 of jQuery UI split the functionality that allows widgets to be easily created into a separate and standalone utility file. This is the `jquery.ui.widget.js` file and we can use it to create our very own jQuery UI plugins with ease. Like jQuery itself, which provides the `fn.extend()` method for easily creating plugins, jQuery UI also provides mechanisms to make plugin creation easier, and to ensure that the common API functionality is retained in new plugins.

In this section, we'll create a very simple jQuery UI plugin so that we can see the conventions that should be adhered to and the different features we have at our disposal. The widget we'll create will be a simple JavaScript calculator. The following screenshot shows how the calculator will appear once we are finished:

Creating the widget

We'll start by creating the script file for our plugin; in a new file in your text editor add the following code:

```
(function($) {
  $.widget("ui.calculator", {
    options: {
      autoShow: true,
      currentSum: []
    },
    _create: function() {
    },
    destroy: function() {
    },
    disable: function() {
    },
    enable: function() {
    },
  });
})(jQuery);
```

Save this file as `jquery.ui.calculator.js` in the `js` folder. jQuery UI plugins should always be named using this convention. This is just the shell of our plugin; we still have to add a good deal of code, but let's look at what we have so far.

jQuery UI plugins should always be encapsulated in a self-executing anonymous function, which aliases the `$` character to ensure that jQuery's `noConflict()` method works as intended.

Next we use the `$.widget()` method to define our plugin. This method accepts two arguments; the first is the name of our widget, which should always be added to the `ui` namespace, and the second is the `options` prototype, which contains the properties and methods that make the plugin function.

Plugins should normally have configurable options that the end developer can use to customise a particular implementation of the plugin. These are defined using the key `options` in the second argument to the `widget()` method. The value of this property should be an object literal containing the actual options. The widget factory will handle interacting with the `options` object; all we need to do is define it.

In this basic example, we have just two configurable options: `autoShow`, which determines (or will determine once we have added the code for it) whether the widget is displayed when the page loads, and `currentSum`, which starts out as an empty array.

The next property of the `options` prototype has the key `_create`. This is used to add an initialisation function for our widget, so that we can build any mark-up required by the plugin, attach event handlers, or do any other processing that may be required. The function supplied as the value of `_create` can only be executed internally by jQuery UI; it is generally not accessible from outside of the plugin. As nothing in JavaScript is ever truly private, in the sense that other languages can have public and private methods, this is not entirely true. But to invoke this code from outside of our plugin, would require extremely advanced code and is not something that could be done accidentally.

Any additional functions that we want our plugin to use internally, which should not be exposed as methods for implementing developers to use, should be prefixed with an underscore. Any functions we wish to be exposed as useable methods, should not have an underscore. This makes it incredibly easy to write robust code that only exposes the functionality that is required to use the plugin.

After the `_create` function, we have also added `destroy`, `disable`, and `enable` methods (these will be available for use by developers implementing the plugin). In order to maintain consistency with the common API exposed by the rest of the library, we should always define these methods.

The _create function

The code we looked at in the previous section forms the shell of the plugin; we'll now move on to add some more internal functions, and fill out those already defined, starting with the `_create` function. Add the following code to the `_create` function:

```
_create: function() {
  var div = $("<div />"),
  list = $("<ul></ul>", {
    "class": "ui-helper-reset ui-helper-clearfix"
  }),
  li = $("<li />", {
    "class": "ui-corner-all ui-state-default"
  }),
  a = $("<a />", {
    href: "#",
    "class": "ui-calculator-button"
  }),
  container = div.clone()
    .addClass("ui-calculator-container ui-corner-all ui-widget-
    content ui-helper-clearfix"),
```

```
      display = div.clone()
        .addClass("ui-corner-all ui-widget-content ui-calculator-
        display").text("0").appendTo(container),
      numberpad = div.clone()
        .addClass("ui-calculator-numberpad").appendTo(container),
      functionpad = div.clone()
        .addClass("ui-calculator-functionpad").appendTo(container),
      numberlist = list.clone().appendTo(numberpad),
      functionlist = list.clone().appendTo(functionpad),
      buttons = ["","clear",7,8,9,4,5,6,1,2,3,0,"."],
      functions = ["/", "*", "-", "+", "="];
      for (var x = 0; x < buttons.length; x++) {
        var listitem = li.clone().appendTo(numberlist),
        linky = a.clone().text(buttons[x]).appendTo(listitem);
        if(x === 0) {
          $("<span />", {
            "class": "ui-calculator-icon ui-icon ui-icon-arrowthick-1-w",
            text: "Backspace"
          }).appendTo(linky);
        } else if (x === 1 || buttons[x] === 0) {
          linky.addClass("ui-calculator-button-wide");
        }
      }
      for (var y = 0; y < functions.length; y++) {
        var listitem2 = li.clone().addClass("ui-state-default")
          .appendTo(functionlist),
        linky2 = a.clone().text(functions[y]).appendTo(listitem2);
      }
      this.element
        .addClass("ui-calculator ui-widget ui-helper-reset");
      (this.options.autoShow) ?
      container.appendTo(this.element) :
      container.appendTo(this.element).hide();
      this.element.this("li").bind({
        mouseenter: this._addHoverState,
        mouseleave: this._removeHoverState,
        click: this._buttonClick
      });
    },
```

We start out by defining a series of variables. The first four variables are a series of elements that we create and then use to build the mark-up required by the widget including a <div>, a <ul>, an <li>, and an <a>. We add any general attributes that will be required each time we make use of one of these base elements, such as class names, or in the case of the anchor, an href.

The next six variables are the actual elements that are used to build the widget, which are created by cloning our base elements and augmenting them with additional class names that are required for theming purposes.

Once created, these elements are appended to each other to form the required DOM structure, although they aren't yet added to the page. We also define two arrays here, where each contains the different labels that will be used for the calculator buttons.

Next, we use a `for` loop to build the buttons contained in the `buttonpad` container. The buttons are built from `<a>` elements, wrapped in `<li>` elements. Some of these buttons will not be number buttons, such as the `backspace` and `clear` buttons. The `backspace` button has an extra `<span>` element added to it, which will be used to show an icon (a back-arrow). This is the first item in the buttons array.

The `clear` and `0` buttons are wider than the rest of the buttons. We know that the `clear` label is the second item in the buttons array, so we can detect this using the array index `1`. The `0` button is checked by looking at the actual array value, to see if it is `0`.

When either of these conditions are met, we add the class `ui-calculator-button-wide` (normal buttons have the class name `ui-calculator-button` added to them) to the newly created `<a>` element.

 The custom class names used by our plugin are in the same format as other class names used by jQuery UI for consistency.

We then use another `for` loop to create the function buttons (division, multiplication, and so on), and append them to the second container within the calculator. This time, none of the buttons have additional elements or special class names added to them, so we don't need a conditional `if` statement.

Within the functions we define, the `this` object is scoped to our plugin. jQuery UI adds two special properties to the `this` object for us: the first is called `element` and points to the actual element that the plugin method is called on, the second is called `options` and refers to the `options` configuration object that we defined at the start of the plugin.

We use `this.element` to add some class names to the element when the `plugin` method is called on. We then check the `autoShow` option within our `options` object; if the option is set to its default value of `true`, we simply append our widget to the page. If it is set to `false`, we still append it, but hide it straight away.

The last thing we do in our `_create` function is attach some event handlers to the `<li>` elements within the widget. We haven't added the event-handling functions yet, but when we do, these will be added to the widget, so we can access them via the `this` object. As the event handling functions should not be directly accessible to implementing developers, we prefix them with an underscore.

The common API methods

Next, we can add the code that will make the common API methods, `destroy`, `disable`, and `enable`, function correctly:

```
destroy: function() {
  $.Widget.prototype.destroy.call(this, arguments);
  this.element
    .removeClass("ui-calculator ui-widget ui-helper-reset");
  this.element.find("li").unbind();
  this.element.children(":first").remove();
},
disable: function() {
  $.Widget.prototype.disable.call(this, arguments);
  this.element.find("li").unbind();
},
enable: function() {
  $.Widget.prototype.enable.call(this, arguments);
  this.element.find("li").bind({
    mouseenter: this._addHoverState,
    mouseleave: this._removeHoverState,
    click: this._buttonClick
  });
},
```

All of these functions follow a common format, with jQuery UI doing most of the heavy lifting for us. The widget factory already defines these methods for us; all we need to do is call the original method defined by the widget factory using the JavaScript `call()` function. The original method can be accessed through the widget prototype using the name of the method we wish to call, appended to `$.Widget.prototype`. We then provide any additional code, specific to our plugin.

In our `destroy` function, we remove the class names we added to the element our `plugin()` method is called on, unbind the event handlers we attached, and then remove the DOM structure we created. This is done to tidy-up after our plugin, which other plugins do, and to prevent memory leaks in the case of older versions of IE.

In our `disable` function, we again call the widget factory's original `disable` function, and then simply unbind the handlers we attached to stop the over-states and clicks working on the buttons, while the widget is disabled.

In our `enable` function, we again call the widget factory's original `enable()` method and then re-attach our event handlers.

Adding custom methods

As we've provided the `autoShow` option, so that the widget can be appended to the page but not shown immediately, we should provide a method that can be used to show the widget when required. Add the following function directly after the `enable()` method:

```
show: function() {
  var el = this.element.children(":first");
  if (el.is(":hidden")) {
    el.show();
  }
  this._trigger("show", null, this.element);
},
```

Our method is stored with the key `show`, so developers can use this in the same way as the standard API methods we have already defined, for example, `$("#el").calculator("show")`. All we need to do in this function is find the first child of the outer element that the widget is appended to, and show it if it is currently hidden.

Once we have shown the calculator, we then trigger a custom event. This makes it useful for developers using our widget to hook into key interaction points. The `_trigger()` method accepts three arguments: the first is for the event we are triggering, the second is for the original browser event object (which we don't need to use in this implementation because it is a custom event and hence, there is no browser event for it), and the third is a reference to the element stored in `this.element`, which is the element that the main widget method is called on. Even in custom methods, the `this` object is still scoped to our widget instance. Note that this can be any hash of key/value pairs we wish to pass to the handler function that a developer defines for our custom event.

In the `_create()` function, (as well as the `enable` function), we bind to several events, namely `mouseenter`, `mouseleave`, and `click`. We now need to add the handler function that will react to these events being detected by our plugin. After the `show()` method, add the following code:

```
_addHoverState: function() {
  $(this).addClass("ui-state-hover");
```

```
  },
  _removeHoverState: function() {
    $(this).removeClass("ui-state-hover");
  },
  _buttonClick: function() {
    var buttonText = $(this).text(),
    display = $(".ui-calculator-display"),
    newArray = $.ui.calculator.prototype.options.currentSum;
    if (buttonText == "Backspace") {
      if (display.text() !== "0" && display.text().length > 1) {
        newArray.pop();
        $.ui.calculator.prototype.options.currentSum = newArray;
        display.text(function(i, orig) {
          return orig.substring(0, orig.length - 1);
        });
      }
    } else if (buttonText == "clear") {
      $.ui.calculator.prototype.options.currentSum = [];
      display.text("0");
    } else if (buttonText == "=") {
      result = eval
        ($.ui.calculator.prototype.options.currentSum.join(""));
      display.text(result);
      $.ui.calculator.prototype.options.currentSum = [result];
    } else if (buttonText == "/" || buttonText == "*" || buttonText
      == "-" || buttonText == "+") {
      $.ui.calculator.prototype.options.currentSum.push(buttonText);
      display.text(buttonText);
    } else {
      $.ui.calculator.prototype.options.currentSum.push(buttonText);
      if (display.text() == "0" || display.text() == "/" ||
        display.text() == "*" || display.text() ==  "-" ||
        display.text() == "+") {
        display.text("");
    }
      display.text(function(i, orig) {
        return orig + buttonText;
      });
    }
  }
}
```

The functions called when the `mouseenter` and `mouseleave` events are detected are really straight-forward; we just add and remove the appropriate state class names so that the over state is applied and removed respectively.

The `click` handler is a little more complex, but all we are really doing is checking which button was clicked and reacting to the different types of button in different ways.

The first thing we do in the `click` handler is cache some variables, including the text of the button that was clicked, the display element of the widget, and a copy of the `currentSum` configuration option. Because the `this` object is no longer scoped to our widget instance, we can't access the options using `this.options`, but we can still access them through the prototype of our widget using `$.ui.calculator.prototype.options`.

We then have an `if` statement that checks for each type of button, including the `backspace` button, the `clear` button, the `=` button, any other function button (`/`, `+`, and so on), or any number button.

If the `backspace` button was clicked, we check that the `display` doesn't consist of just `0`, and that the length of the text being displayed is longer than a single character. If these conditions are met, we remove the last item from the `currentSum` that we obtained from our widget's prototype, update the `currentSum` with the new shortened array, and then remove the last character from the text being displayed.

If the `clear` button was clicked, we just empty the `currentSum` option by setting its value to an empty array, and then reset the display back to `0`.

If the `=` button was clicked, we evaluate the expression stored in the `currentSum` array, show the result in the `display` element, and then update the `currentSum`, so that it just contains the result.

If any of the function buttons are clicked, we simply add the text of the button to the `currentSum` array and then set the text of the `display` element to the text of the button that was clicked.

Finally, if any number button is clicked, we first check what is currently being displayed on the calculator, and if it is either `0` or one of the functions, we empty the `display` element. We then update the `display` with the new number. This is so that if a number has already been pressed, then the `display` is updated to include the original number as well as the new number, but if a function key has been pressed, the number is added as a new number to avoid displaying things like `+1`, and so on.

The widget style sheet

We need to add some basic styling specific to our widget. A lot of styling will come from the jQuery UI class names we added, but we will still need to define the layout. In a new file in your text editor add the following code:

```css
.ui-calculator { width:9.65em; }
.ui-calculator-container { padding:.2em .2em 0; }
.ui-calculator-display {
  width:12.3em; padding:.3em; margin-bottom:.3em;
  font-size:0.7em; overflow:auto;
}
.ui-calculator-numberpad {
  width:7em; float:left;
}
.ui-calculator-functionpad { width:2em; float:left; }
.ui-calculator li {
  float:left; margin:0 .2em .2em 0;
}
.ui-calculator-button {
  display:block; width:2em; height:1.2em;
  padding:.3em 0 .5em; text-align:center; border:0;
}
.ui-calculator-button-wide { width:4.3em; }
.ui-calculator-icon { margin:.2em auto; }
```

Save this in the `css` folder as `jquery.ui.calculator.css`.

Using the widget

Our widget is now pretty much complete. There's still a lot of functionality we could add, and probably a number of bugs to fix, but this simple demonstration was more to see how to make a jQuery UI plugin, not how to make a JavaScript calculator.

To use the plugin, a developer could use the following code:

```html
<!DOCTYPE html>
<html>
  <head>
  <meta charset="utf-8">
  <title>Widget Factory - calculator
  </title>
  <link rel="stylesheet"
    href="css/smoothness/jquery-ui-1.8.9.custom.css">
  <link rel="stylesheet"
```

```
      href="css/jquery.ui.claculator.css">
  </head>
  <body>
    <div id="calc">
    </div>
    <script src="development-bundle/jquery-1.4.4.js">
    </script>
    <script src="development-bundle/ui/jquery.ui.core.js">
    </script>
    <script
      src="development-bundle/ui/jquery.ui.widget.js">
    </script>
    <script src="js/jquery.ui.calculator.js">
    </script>
    <script>
      (function($) {
        $("#calc").calculator();
      })(jQuery);
    </script>
  </body>
</html>
```

This page can be saved in the main project folder as `calculator.html`. The basic calculator can be added using just the widget method:

```
$("#calc").calculator();
```

```
To configure the autoShow option, we could use:
$("#calc").calculator({
  autoShow: false
});
```

```
To add a handler for the custom show event we defined, we could do
this:
$("#calc").calculator({
  autoShow: false,
  show: function(e, ui) {
    alert(e + ", " + $(ui).attr("id");
  }
});
```

To actually show the calculator, we could use our custom `show()` method:

```
$("#calc").calculator("show");
```

This could then display an alert, for example, showing the name of the event, and the id of the element that the widget method was called on:

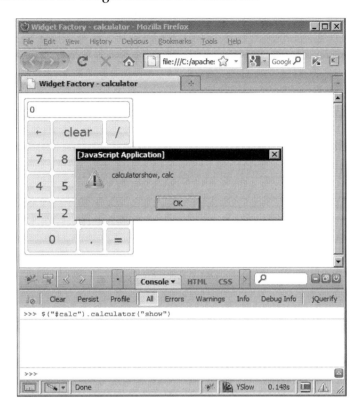

Summary

In this chapter, we've seen how the CSS framework consistently styles each of the library components. We've looked at the files that make it and how they work together to provide the complete look-and-feel of the widgets. We also saw how tightly integrated the ThemeRoller application is with the framework.

We saw how easy it is to install or change a theme using ThemeRoller. We also looked at how we can override the theme file if we require a radical customization of a widget that we cannot obtain with ThemeRoller alone.

The chapter also covered building our own widgets or plugins in a way that is compatible with and can make use of the framework, as well as to ensure that our creations are ThemeRoller ready. We can also make use of the helper classes provided by the framework, such as the `ui-helper-clearfix` class, to quickly implement common CSS solutions.

We also looked at some of the other utilities included with the library including the `position` utility, which allows us to align any edge of one element with any edge of another element, giving us a powerful and flexible way of positioning elements that we create or manipulate.

We ended the chapter with an extensive look at the widget factory and how it allows us to quickly and easily create our very own jQuery UI plugins. We saw how easy it was to make our widget conform to the common API exposed by official jQuery plugins, how we can add custom methods for implementing developers to use, how to add protected functions that are only accessible from within our plugin, and how to add custom events that implementing developers can easily hook into.

In the next chapter, we'll move on to start looking at the widgets provided by the library, starting with the `tabs` widget.

3
Using the Tabs Widget

Now that we've been formally introduced to the jQuery UI library, the CSS framework, and some of the utilities, we can move on to begin looking at the individual components included in the library. Over the next six chapters, we'll be looking at the widgets. These are a set of visually engaging, highly configurable user interface widgets.

The UI tabs widget is used to toggle visibility across a set of different elements, with each element containing content that can be accessed by clicking on its tab heading. Each **panel** of content has its own tab. The tab headings are usually displayed across the top of the widget, although it is trivial to reposition them so that they appear along the bottom of the widget instead.

The tabs are structured so that they line up next to each other horizontally, whereas the content sections are all set to `display: none` except for the active panel. Clicking a tab will highlight the tab and show its associated content panel, while ensuring all of the other content panels are hidden. Only one content panel can be open at a time. The tabs can be configured so that no content panels are open.

In this chapter, we will look at the following topics:

- The default implementation of the widget
- How the CSS framework targets tab widgets
- How to apply custom styles to a set of tabs
- Configuring tabs using their options
- Built-in transition effects for content panel changes
- Controlling tabs using their methods
- Custom events defined by tabs
- AJAX tabs

The following screenshot shows the different elements that a set of jQuery UI tabs consists of:

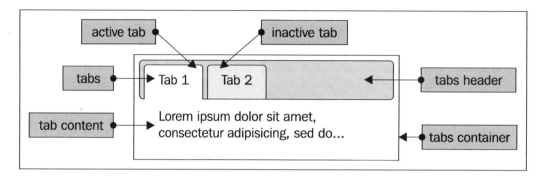

A basic tab implementation

The structure of the underlying HTML elements on which tabs are based is fairly rigid, and widgets require a certain number of elements for them to work.

The tabs must be created from a list element (ordered or unordered) and each list item must contain an <a> element. Each link will need to have a corresponding element with a specified id that is associated with the href attribute of the link. We'll clarify the exact structure of these elements after the first example.

In a new file in your text editor, create the following page:

```
<!DOCTYPE html>
<html>
  <head>
    <meta charset="utf-8">
    <title>Tabs</title>
    <link rel="stylesheet"
      href="css/smoothness/jquery-ui-1.8.9.custom.css">
  </head>
  <body>
    <div id="myTabs">
      <ul>
        <li><a href="#a">Tab 1</a></li>
        <li><a href="#b">Tab 2</a></li>
      </ul>
      <div id="a">This is the content panel linked to the first tab,
        it is shown by default.
      </div>
      <div id="b">This content is linked to the second tab and will
        be shown when its tab is clicked.
```

```
          </div>
        </div>
        <script src="development-bundle/jquery-x.x.x,js">
        </script>
        <script src="development-bundle/ui/jquery.ui.core.js">
        </script>
        <script
          src="development-bundle/ui/jquery.ui.widget.js">
        </script>
        <script src="development-bundle/ui/jquery.ui.tabs.js">
        </script>
        <script>
          (function($){
            $("#myTabs").tabs();
          })(jQuery);
        </script>
      </body>
    </html>
```

Save the code as `tabs1.html` in your `jqueryui` working folder. Let's review what was used. The following script and CSS resources are needed for the default tab widget configuration:

```
jquery.ui.all.css
jquery-x.x.x.js
jquery.ui.core.js
jquery.ui.widget.js
jquery.ui.tabs.js
```

A tab widget is usually constructed from several standard HTML elements arranged in a specific manner:

- An outer container element, which the tabs method is called on
- A list element (`<ul>` or `<ol>`)
- An `<a>` element within an `<li>` element for each tab
- An element for the content panel of each tab

 These elements can be either hardcoded into the page, added dynamically, or can be a mixture of both, depending upon the requirements.

The list and anchor elements within the outer container make the clickable tab headings, which are used to show the content section that is associated with the tab. The `href` attribute of the link should be set to a fragment identifier, prefixed with #. It should match the `id` attribute of the element that forms the content section with which it is associated.

The content sections of each tab are created using `<div>` elements. The `id` attribute is required and will be targeted by its corresponding `<a>` element. We've used `<div>` elements in this example as the content panels for each tab, but other elements can also be used as long as the relevant configuration is provided and the resulting HTML is valid. The `panelTemplate` and `tabTemplate` configuration options can be used to change the elements used to build the widget (see the *Configuration* section, later in the chapter for more information).

We link to several `<script>` resources from the library at the bottom of the `<body>` before its closing tag. Loading scripts last, after style sheets and page elements, is a proven technique for improving the apparent loading time of a page, and should therefore be used whenever possible.

After linking first to jQuery, we link to the `jquery.ui.core.js` file that is required by all components (except the effects, which have their own core file), and the `jquery.ui.widget.js` file. We then link to the component's source file, which in this case is `jquery.ui.tabs.js`.

After the three required script files from the library, we can turn to our custom `<script>` element in which we add the code that creates the tabs. We use an anonymous function which is executed immediately (thanks to the extra set of parentheses following the function) and aliases the $ character.

Aliasing the $ character in this way is considered a current best-practice, and although not strictly necessary unless writing our own custom jQuery UI plugins, it does make our code more portable by ensuring that other JavaScript libraries, which may use the $ character, do not break it.

Within this anonymous function we simply call the `tabs()` widget method on the jQuery object, representing our tabs container element (the `<ul>` with an `id` of `myTabs`). When we run this file in a browser, we should see the tabs as they appeared in the first screenshot of this chapter (without the annotations of course).

Tab CSS framework classes

Using Firebug for Firefox (or another generic DOM explorer), we can see that a variety of class names are added to the different underlying HTML elements that the tabs widget is created from.

Let's review these classnames briefly and see how they contribute to the overall appearance of the widget. To the outer container `<div>`, the following classnames are added:

Classname	Purpose
ui-tabs	Allows tab-specific structural CSS to be applied.
ui-widget	Sets generic font styles that are inherited by nested elements.
ui-widget-content	Provides theme-specific styles.
ui-corner-all	Applies rounded corners to the container.

The first element within the container is the `<ul>` element. This element receives the following classnames:

Classname	Purpose
ui-tabs-nav	Allows tab-specific structural CSS to be applied.
ui-helper-reset	Neutralizes browser-specific styles applied to `<ul>` elements.
ui-helper-clearfix	Applies the clear-fix as this element has children that are floated.
ui-widget-header	Provides theme-specific styles.
ui-corner-all	Applies rounded corners.

The individual `<li>` elements that form a part of the tab headings are given the following classnames:

Classname	Purpose
ui-state-default	Applies the standard, non-active, non-selected, non-hovered state to the tab headings.
ui-corner-top	Applies rounded corners to the top edges of the elements.
ui-tabs-selected	This is only applied to the active tab. On page-load of the default implementation, this will be the first tab. Selecting another tab will remove this class from the currently selected tab and apply it to the newly selected tab.
ui-state-active	Applies theme-specific styles to the currently selected tab. This class name will be added to the tab that is currently selected, just like the previous classname. The reason there are two class names is that ui-tabs-selected provides the functional CSS, while ui-state-active provides the visual, decorative styles.

The `<a>` elements within each `<li>` are not given any classnames, but they still have both structural and theme-specific styles applied to them by the framework.

Finally, the panel elements that hold each tab's content are given the following classnames:

Classname	Purpose
ui-tabs-panel	Applies structural CSS to the content panels.
ui-widget-content	Applies theme-specific styles.
ui-corner-bottom	Applies rounded corners to the bottom edges of the content panels.

All of these classes are added to the underlying HTML elements automatically by the library. We don't need to manually add them when coding the page or adding the base markup.

Applying a custom theme to the tabs

In the next example, we can see how to change the tabs' basic appearance. We can override any rules used purely for display purposes with our own style rules for quick and easy customization, without changing the rules related to the tab functionality or structure.

In a new file in your text editor, create the following very small style sheet:

```
#myTabs {
  width:400px; padding:5px; border:1px solid #636363;
  background:#c2c2c2 none;
}
.ui-widget-header {
  border:0; background:#c2c2c2 none; font-family:Georgia;
}
#myTabs .ui-widget-content {
  border:1px solid #aaa; background:#fff none; font-size:80%;
}
.ui-state-default, .ui-widget-content .ui-state-default {
  border:1px solid #636363; background:#a2a2a2 none;
}
.ui-state-active, .ui-widget-content .ui-state-active {
  border:1px solid #aaa; background:#fff none;
}
```

This is all we need. Save the file as `tabsTheme.css` in your `css` folder. If you compare the classnames with the tables on the previous pages, you'll see that we're overriding the theme-specific styles. Because we're overriding the theme file, we need to meet or exceed the specificity of the selectors in `theme.css`. This is why we target multiple selectors sometimes.

In this example, we override some of the rules in `jquery.ui.tabs.css`. We need to use the `ID` selector of our container element along with the selector from `jquery.ui.theme.css` (`.ui-widget-content`), in order to beat the double class selector `.ui-tabs .ui-tabs-panel`.

Add the following reference to this new style sheet in the `<head>` of `tabs1.html` and resave the file as `tabs2.html`:

```
<link rel="stylesheet" href="css/tabsTheme.css">
```

 Make sure the custom style sheet we just created appears after the `jquery.ui.tabs.css` file, because the rules that we are trying to override will be not overridden by our custom theme file if the style sheets are not linked in the correct order.

If we view the new page in a browser, it should appear as in the following screenshot:

Our new theme isn't dramatically different from the default smoothness (as shown in the first screenshot), but we can see how easy it is, and how little code it requires to change the appearance of the widget to suit its environment.

Configurable options

Each of the different components in the library has a series of options that control which features of the widget are enabled by default. An object literal, or an object reference, can be passed in to the `tabs()` widget method to configure these options.

The available options to configure non-default behaviors are shown in the following table:

Option	Default value	Used to...
ajaxOptions	null	Specify additional AJAX options. We can use any of the options exposed by jQuery's `$.ajax()` method such as `data`, `type`, `url`, and so on.
cache	false	Control whether the remote data is loaded only once when the page initializes, or is reloaded every time the corresponding tab is clicked.
collapsible	false	Allow an active tab to be unselected if it is clicked, so that all of the content panels are hidden and only the tab headings are visible.
cookie	null	Show the active tab using cookie data on page load. The cookie plugin is required for this option to be used.
disabled	false	Disable the widget on page load. We can also pass an array of tab indices (zero-based) in order to disable specific tabs.
event	"click"	Specify the event that triggers the display of content panels.
fx	null	Specify an animation effect when changing tabs. Supply an object literal or an array of animation effects.
idPrefix	"ui-tabs-"	Generate a unique `ID` and fragment identifier when a remote tab heading's `<a>` element has no `title` attribute.
panelTemplate	"<div></div>"	Specifying the elements used for the content section of a tab panel.
selected	0	Show a tab panel other than the first one on page load (overrides the cookie property).

Option	Default value	Used to...
spinner	"Loading&#8230"	Specify the loading spinner for remote tabs.
tabTemplate	`<li><a href="#{href}"><span>#{label}</span></a></li>`	Specify the elements used when creating new tabs. The #{href} and #{label} strings are replaced by the widget internally when the new tab is created.

Selecting a tab

Let's look at how these configurable properties can be used. For example, let's configure the widget so that the second tab is displayed when the page loads. Remove the `<link>` for `tabsTheme.css` in the `<head>` of `tabs2.html` and change the final `<script>` element so that it appears as follows:

```
<script>
  (function($){
    var tabOpts = {
      selected: 1
    };
    $("#myTabs").tabs(tabOpts);
  })(jQuery);
</script>
```

Save this as `tabs3.html`. The different tabs and their associated content panels are represented by a numerical index starting at zero. Specifying a different tab to open by default is as easy as supplying its index number as the value for the `selected` property. When the page loads now, the second tab should be selected by default.

Along with changing which tab is selected, we can also specify that no tabs should be initially selected by supplying `null` as the value for this property. This will cause the widget to appear as follows on page load:

Disabling a tab

You may want a particular tab to be disabled until a certain condition is met. This is easily achieved by manipulating the `disabled` property of the tabs. Change the `tabOpts` configuration object in `tabs3.html` to this:

```
var tabOpts = {
  disabled: [1]
};
```

Save this as `tabs4.html` in your `jqueryui` folder. In this example, we remove the `selected` property and add the index of the second tab to the `disabled` array. We could add the indices of other tabs to this array as well, separated by a comma, to disable multiple tabs by default.

When the page is loaded in a browser, the second tab has the classname `ui-widget-disabled` applied to it, and will pick up the disabled styles from `ui.theme.css`. It will not respond to mouse interactions in any way, as shown in the following screenshot:

Transition effects

We can easily add attractive transition effects using the `fx` property. These are displayed when tabs are opened or closed. This option is configured using another object literal (or an array) inside our configuration object, which enables one or more effects. We can enable fading effects, for example, using the following configuration object:

```
var tabOpts = {
  fx: {
    opacity: "toggle",
    duration: "slow"
  }
};
```

Save this file as `tabs5.html` in your `jqueryui` folder. The `fx` object that we created has two properties. The first property is the animation to use when changing tabs. To use fading animations we specify `opacity`, as this is what is adjusted. Toggling the `opacity` simply reverses its current setting. If it is currently visible, it is made invisible and vice-versa.

The second property, `duration`, specifies the speed at which the animation occurs. The values for this property are `slow` or `fast`, which correspond to `200` and `600` milliseconds respectively. Any other string will result in the default duration of `400` milliseconds. We can also supply an integer representing the number of milliseconds the animation should run for.

When we run the file we can see that the tab content slowly fades-out as a tab closes and fades-in when a new tab opens. Both animations occur during a single tab interaction. To only show the animation once, when a tab closes, for example, we would need to nest the `fx` object within an array. Change the configuration object in `tabs5.html` so that it appears as follows:

```
var tabOpts = {
  fx: [{
    opacity: "toggle",
    duration: "slow"
  },
  null]
};
```

The closing effect of the currently open content panel is contained within an object in the first item of the array, and the opening animation of the new tab is the second. By specifying `null` as the second item in the array, we disable the opening animations when a new tab is selected.

We can also specify different animations and speeds for opening and closing animations, by adding another object as the second array item instead of `null`. Save this as `tabs6.html` and view the results in a browser.

Collapsible tabs

By default when the currently active tab is clicked, nothing happens. But we can change this so that the currently open content panel closes when its tab heading is selected. Change the configuration object in `tabs6.html` so that it appears as follows:

```
var tabOpts = {
  collapsible: true
};
```

Save this version as `tabs7.html`. This option allows all of the content panels to be closed, much like when we supplied null to the `selected` property earlier on. Clicking a deactivated tab will select the tab and show its associated content panel. Clicking the same tab again will close it, shrinking the widget down so that only tab headings are visible.

Tab events

The tab widget defines a series of useful options that allow you to add callback functions to perform different actions, when certain events exposed by the widget are detected. The following table lists the configuration options that are able to accept executable functions on an event:

Event	Fired when...
add	A new tab is added.
disable	A tab is disabled.
enable	A tab is enabled.
load	A tab's remote data has loaded.
remove	A tab is removed.
select	A tab is selected.
show	A tab is shown.

Each component of the library has callback options (such as those in the previous table), which are tuned to look for key moments in any visitor interactions. Any functions we use within these callbacks are usually executed before the change happens. Therefore, you can return `false` from your callback and prevent the action from occurring.

In our next example, we will look at how easy it is to react to a particular tab being selected, using the standard non-bind technique. Change the final `<script>` element in `tabs7.html` so that it appears as follows:

```
<script>
  (function($){
    var handleSelect = function(e, tab) {
      $("<p></p>", {
        text: "Tab at index " + tab.index + " selected",
        "class": "status-message ui-corner-all"
      }).appendTo(".ui-tabs-nav", "#myTabs").fadeOut(5000, function()
      {
        $(this).remove();
      });
```

```
    },
    tabOpts = {
      select: handleSelect
    }
    $("#myTabs").tabs(tabOpts);
  })(jQuery);
</script>
```

Save this file as `tabs8.html`. We also need a little CSS to complete this example. In the `<head>` of the page we just created, add the following `<link>` element:

```
<link rel="stylesheet" href="css/tabSelect.css">
```

Then in a new page in your text editor, add the following code:

```
.status-message {
  padding:11px 8px 10px; margin:0; border:1px solid #aaa;
  position:absolute; right:10px; top:9px; font-size:11px;
  background-color:#fff;
}
```

Save this file as `tabSelect.css` in the `css` folder. We made use of the `select` callback in this example, although the principle is the same for any of the other custom events fired by tabs. The name of our callback function is provided as the value of the `select` property in our configuration object.

Two arguments will be passed automatically by the widget to the callback function we define, when it is executed. These are the original event object and custom object containing useful properties from the tab, which was selected.

To find out which of the tabs was clicked, we can look at the `index` property of the second object (remember these are zero-based indices). This is added, along with a little explanatory text, to a paragraph element that we create on the fly and append to the widget header:

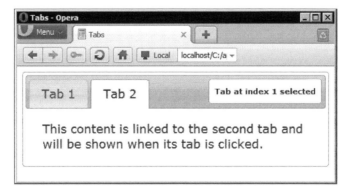

Whenever a tab is selected, the paragraph before it fades away. Note that the event is fired before the change occurs.

Binding to events

Using the event callbacks exposed by each component is the standard way of handling interactions. However, in addition to the callbacks listed in the previous table, we can also hook into another set of events fired by each component at different times.

We can use the standard jQuery `bind()` method to bind an event handler to a custom event, fired by the tabs widget in the same way that we could bind to a standard DOM event, such as a click.

The following table lists the tab widget's custom binding events and their triggers:

Event	Fired when...
tabsselect	A tab is selected.
tabsload	A remote tab has loaded.
tabsshow	A tab is shown.
tabsadd	A tab has been added to the interface.
tabsremove	A tab has been removed from the interface.
tabsdisable	A tab has been disabled.
tabsenable	A tab has been enabled.

The first three events are fired in succession, in the order of events in which they appear in the table. If no tabs are remote, then `tabsselect` and `tabsshow` are fired in that order. These events are sometimes fired before and sometimes after the action has occurred, depending on which event is used.

Let's see this type of event usage in action; change the final `<script>` element in `tabs8.html` to the following:

```
<script>
  (function($) {
    $("#myTabs").tabs();
    $("#myTabs").bind("tabsselect", function(e, tab) {
      alert("The tab at index " + tab.index + " was selected");
    });
  })(jQuery);
</script>
```

Save this change as `tabs9.html`. Binding to the `tabsselect` in this way produces the same result as the previous example, using the `select` callback function. Like last time, the alert should appear before the new tab is activated.

All the events exposed by all the widgets can be used with the `bind()` method, by simply prefixing the name of the widget to the name of the event.

Using tab methods

The tabs widget contains many different methods, which means it has a rich set of behaviors. It also supports the implementation of advanced functionality that allows us to work with it programmatically. Let's take a look at the methods, which are listed in the following table:

Method	Used to...
abort	Stop any animations or AJAX requests that are currently in progress.
add	Add a new tab programmatically, specifying the URL of the tab's content, a label, and optionally its index number as arguments.
destroy	Completely remove the tabs widget.
disable	Disable a specific tab by passing a zero-based index number to the method, or pass nothing to the method to disable the entire set of tabs.
enable	Enable a disable tab by passing a zero-based index number to the method, or enable the entire widget by passing nothing to the method.
length	Return the number of tabs in the widget.
load	Reload an AJAX tab's content, specifying the index number of the tab.
option	Get or set any property after the widget has been initialized.
remove	Remove a tab programmatically, specifying the index of the tab to remove. If no index is supplied, the first tab is removed. Tabs can also be removed using their `href` value.
rotate	Automatically changes the active tab after a specified number of milliseconds have passed, either once or repeatedly.
select	Select a tab programmatically, which has the same effect as when a visitor clicks a tab, based on index number.
url	Change the URL of content given to an AJAX tab. The method expects the index number of the tab and the new URL. See also `load` (earlier in this table).
widget	Return the element that the `tabs()` widget method is called on.

Enabling and disabling tabs

We can make use of the enable or disable methods to programmatically enable or disable specific tabs. This will effectively switch on any tabs that were initially disabled or disable those that are currently active.

Let's use the enable method to switch on a tab, which we disabled by default in an earlier example. Add the following new <button> elements directly after the existing markup for the tabs widget in tabs4.html:

```
<button type="button" id="enable">Enable</button>
<button type="button" id="disable">Disable</button>
```

Next, change the final <script> element so that it appears as follows:

```
<script>
  (function($){
    $("#myTabs").tabs({
      disabled: [1]
    });
    $("#enable").click(function() {
      $("#myTabs").tabs("enable", 1);
    });
    $("#disable").click(function() {
      $("#myTabs").tabs("disable", 1);
    });
  })(jQuery);
</script>
```

Save the changed file as tabs10.html. On the page, we've added two new <button> elements—one will be used to enable the disabled tab and the other is used to disable it again.

In the JavaScript, we use the click event of the **Enable** button to call the tabs() widget method. To do this, we pass the string enable, to the tabs() method as the first argument. Additionally, we pass the index number of the tab we want to enable as a second argument. All methods in jQuery UI are called in this way. We specify the name of the method we wish to call as the first argument to the widget method.

The disable method is used in the same way. Note that a tab cannot be disabled while it is active. Don't forget that we can use both of these methods without additional arguments, in order to enable or disable the entire widget.

Adding and removing tabs

Along with enabling and disabling tabs programmatically, we can also remove them or add completely new tabs on the fly. In `tabs10.html`, remove the existing `<button>` elements and add the following:

```
<label>Enter a tab to remove:</label>
<input for="indexNum" id="indexNum">
<button type="button" id="remove">Remove!</button><br>
<button type="button" id="add">Add a new tab!</button>
```

Then change the final `<script>` element to this:

```
<script>
  (function($){
    $("#myTabs").tabs();
    $("#remove").click(function() {
      $("#myTabs").tabs("remove", parseInt($("#indexNum").val(),
        10));
    });
    $("#add").click(function() {
      $("#myTabs").tabs("add", "remoteTab.txt", "A New Tab!");
    });
  })(jQuery);
```

Save this as `tabs11.html`. On the page we've added a new instructional `<label>`, an `<input>`, and a `<button>` that are used to specify a tab to remove. We've also added a second `<button>`, which is used to add a new tab.

In the `<script>`, the first of our new functions handle removing a tab, using the `remove` method. This method requires one additional argument—the index number of the tab to be removed. We get the value entered into the textbox and pass it to the method as the argument. The data returned by jQuery's `val()` method is in string format, so we wrap the call in the JavaScript `parseInt` function to convert it.

 If no index is passed to the `remove` method, the first tab will be removed.

The `add` method that adds a new tab to the widget, can be made to work in several different ways. In this example, we've specified that the content found in the file `remoteTab.txt` should be added as the content of the new tab. In addition to passing the string `add`, and specifying a reference to the file containing the new content, we also specify a label for the new tab in string format as the third argument.

Optionally, we can also specify the index number of where the new tab should be inserted as a fourth argument. If the index is not supplied, the new tab will be added as the last tab.

After adding and perhaps removing some tabs, the page should appear something like this:

 There is a bug in the current version of the tabs widget that causes an extra content panel to be added to the tabs widget, when using the add method (see ticket #5069 at http://bugs.jqueryui.com/ticket/). It is this bug that causes the extra space to appear when the new tab is initially added in the previous example.

Simulating clicks

There may be times when you want to programmatically select a particular tab and show its content. This could happen as the result of some other interaction by the visitor.

We can use the select() method to do this, which is completely analogous with the action of clicking a tab. Alter the final <script> block in tabs11.html, so that it appears as follows:

```
<script>
  (function($){
    $("#myTabs").tabs();
    $("#remove").click(function() {
      $("#myTabs")
        .tabs("remove", parseInt($("#indexNum").val(), 10));
    });
    $("#add").click(function() {
      $("#myTabs").tabs("add", "#newTab", "A New Tab!")
        .tabs("select", $("#myTabs").tabs("length") - 1);
    });
  });
</script>
```

Save this as `tabs12.html` in your `jqueryui` folder. Now when the new tab is added, it is automatically selected. The `select()` method requires just one additional argument, which is the index number of the tab to select.

As any tab that we add will, by default (although this can be changed), be the last tab in the interface, and as the tab indices are zero based, all we have to do is use the `length` method to return the number of tabs, and then subtract 1 from this figure to get the index. The result is passed to the `select` method.

Interestingly, selecting the newly-added tab straight away fixes, or at least hides, the extra space issue from the last example.

Creating a tab carousel

One method that creates quite an exciting result is the `rotate` method. This method will make all of the tabs (and their associated content panels) display one after the other automatically.

It's a great visual effect and is useful for ensuring that all, or a lot, of the individual tab's content panels get seen by the visitor. For an example of this kind of effect in action, see the homepage of `http://www.cnet.com`. There is a tabs widget (not a jQuery UI one) that shows blogs, podcasts, and videos.

Like the other methods we've seen, the `rotate` method is easy-to-use. Change the final `<script>` element in `tabs9.html` to this:

```
<script>
  (function($){
    $("#myTabs").tabs().tabs("rotate", 1000, true);
  })(jQuery);
</script>
```

Save this file as `tabs13.html`. We've reverted back to a simplified page with no additional elements other than the underlying structure of the widget. Although we can't call the `rotate` method directly using the initial `tabs()` method, we can chain it to the end like we would with methods from the standard jQuery library.

Chaining UI methods

Chaining widget methods is possible because like the methods found in the underlying jQuery library, they almost always return the jQuery ($) object. Note that this is not possible when using getter methods that return data, such as the `length` method.

The `rotate` method is used with two additional parameters. The first parameter is an integer that specifies the number of milliseconds each that tab should display before the next tab is shown. The second parameter is a Boolean that indicates whether the cycle through the tabs should occur once or continuously.

The tab widget also contains a `destroy` method. This is a method common to all the widgets found in jQuery UI. Let's see how it works. In `tabs13.html`, after the widget add a new `<button>` as follows:

```
<button type="button" id="destroy">Destroy the tabs</button>
```

Next, change the final `<script>` element to this:

```
<script>
  (function($){
    $("#myTabs").tabs();
    $("#destroy").click(function() {
      $("#myTabs").tabs("destroy");
    });
  })(jQuery);
</script>
```

Save this file as `tabs14.html`. The `destroy` method that we invoke with a click on the button, completely removes the tab widget, returning the underlying HTML to its original state. After the button has been clicked, you should see a standard HTML list element and the text from each tab, just like in the following screenshot:

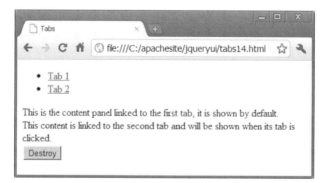

 Only the original tabs hard-coded in the page will remain if the tabs are destroyed, not those added with the add method.

Getting and setting options

Like the `destroy` method, the `option` method is exposed by all the different components found in the library. This method is used to work with the configurable options and functions in both getter and setter modes. Let's look at a basic example; add the following `<button>` after the tabs widget in `tabs9.html`:

```
<button type="button" id="show">Show Selected!</button>
```

Then change the final `<script>` element so that it is as follows:

```
<script>
  (function($){
    $("#myTabs").tabs();
    $("#show").click(function() {
      $("<p></p>", {
        text: "Tab at index " + $("#myTabs")
          .tabs("option", "selected") + " is active"
      }).appendTo(".ui-tabs-nav").fadeOut(5000);
    });
  })(jQuery);
</script>
```

Save this file as `tabs15.html`. The `<button>` on the page has been changed, so that it shows the currently active tab. All we do is add the index of the selected tab to a status bar message, as we did in the earlier example. We get the `selected` option by passing the string `selected` as the second argument. Any value of any option can be accessed in this way.

To trigger setter mode instead, we can supply a third argument containing the new value of the option that we'd like to set. Therefore, to change the value of the `selected` option, in order to change the tab being displayed, we could use the following HTML:

```
<label for="newIndex">Enter a tab index to activate</label>
<input id="newIndex" type="text">
<button type="button2" id="set">Change Selected</button>
```

And the following click-handler:

```
<script>
  (function($){
    $("#set").click(function() {
      $("#myTabs")
        .tabs("option", "selected", parseInt($("#newIndex").val()));
    });
  })(jQuery);
```

Save this as `tabs16.html`. The new page contains a `<label>`, an `<input>`, as well as a `<button>` that is used to harvest the index number that the `selected` option should be set to. When the button is clicked, our code will retrieve the value of the `<input>` and use it to change the `selected` index. By supplying the new value we put the method in setter mode.

When we run this page in our browser, we should see that we can switch to the second tab by entering its index number (1) and clicking the **Change Selected** button.

AJAX tabs

We saw how we can use the `add` method to add an AJAX tab to the widget dynamically, but we can also add remote content to tabs using the underlying HTML. In this example, we want the tab that will display the remote content to be available all the time, not just after clicking the button. Add the following new `<a>` element to the underlying HTML for the widget in `tabs16.html`:

```
<li><a href="remoteTab.txt">AJAX Tab</a></li>
```

We should also remove the `<button>` from the last example.

The final `<script>` element can be used to just call the `tabs` method; no additional configuration is required:

```
$("#myTabs").tabs();
```

Save this as `tabs17.html`. All we're doing is specifying the path to the remote file (the same one we used in the earlier example) using the `href` attribute of an `<a>` element in the underlying markup, from which the tabs are created.

Unlike static tabs, we don't need a corresponding `<div>` element with an `id` that matches the `href` of the link. The additional elements required for the tab content will be generated automatically by the widget.

If you use a DOM explorer, you can see that the file path that we added to link to the remote tab has been removed. Instead, a new fragment identifier has been generated and set as the `href`. The new fragment is also added as the `id` of the new tab (minus the # symbol of course) so that the tab heading still shows the tab.

Along with loading data from external files, it can also be loaded from URLs. This is great when retrieving content from a database using query strings or a web service. Methods related to AJAX tabs include the `load` and `url` methods. The `load` method is used to load and reload the contents of an AJAX tab, which could come in handy for refreshing content that changes very frequently.

> There is no inherent cross-domain support built into the AJAX functionality of tabs widget. Therefore, unless additional PHP or some other server-scripting language is employed as a proxy, you may wish to make use of JSON structured data and jQuery's JSONP functionality. Files and URLs should be under the same domain as the page running the widget.

Changing the URL of a remote tab's content

The `url` method is used to change the URL that the AJAX tab retrieves its content from. Let's look at a brief example of these two methods in action. There are also a number of properties related to AJAX functionality.

Add the following new `<select>` element after the tabs widget in `tabs17.html`:

```
<select id="fileChooser">
  <option value="remoteTab1">tabContent.html</option>
  <option value="remoteTab2">tabContent2.html</option>
</select>
```

Then change the final `<script>` element to the following:

```
<script>
  $(function(){
    $("#myTabs").tabs();
    $("#fileChooser").change(function() {
      $("#myTabs").tabs("url", 2, $(this).val());
    });
  });
</script>
```

Save the new file as `tabs18.html`. We've added a simple `<select>` element to the page that lets you choose the content to display in the AJAX tab. In the JavaScript, we set a change handler for the `<select>` and specified an anonymous function to be executed each time the event is detected.

This function simply calls the `url` method, passing in the index of the tab whose URL we want to update and the new URL as arguments.

We'll also need a second local content file. Change the text in the `remoteTab.txt` file and resave it as `remoteTab2.txt`.

Run the new file in a browser and use the dropdown `<select>` to choose the second remote file, then switch to the remote tab. The contents of the second text file should be displayed.

Reloading a remote tab

One thing you may have noticed in the previous example is that if the remote tab was already selected when its URL was changed, the content was not updated until you switched to a different tab and then back to the remote tab. To fix this, we can make use of the `load` method, which reloads a remote tab's content. Update the change event-handler in `tabs18.html` to the following:

```
$("#fileChooser").change(function() {
  $("#myTabs").tabs("url", 2, $(this).val()).tabs("load", 2);
});
```

The `load` method accepts a single argument, which is the index number of the tab whose content we want to reload. We should find now that we can change the URL of the remote tab with the `<select>` element, even while the remote tab is selected and the content will be automatically updated.

The slight flicker in the tab heading is the string value of the `spinner` option that by default is set to `Loading`. We don't really get a chance to see it in full here, as the tab content is changed too quickly as its running locally.

Displaying data obtained via JSONP

Let's pull-in some external content for our final tabs example. If we use the tabs widget, in conjunction with the standard jQuery library `getJSON` method, we can bypass the cross-domain exclusion policy and pull-in a feed from another domain, to display in a tab. In `tabs19.html`, change the tabs widget so that it appears as follows:

```
<div id="myTabs">
  <ul>
    <li><a href="#a"><span>Nebula Information</span></a></li>
    <li><a href="#flickr"><span>Images</span></a></li>
  </ul>
```

```html
<div id="a">
  <p>A nebulae is an interstellar cloud of dust, hydrogen gas, and
     plasma. It is the first stage of a star's cycle. In these re
     gions the formations of gas, dust, and other materials clump
     together to form larger masses, which attract further matter,
     and eventually will become big enough to form stars. The re
     maining materials are then believed to form planets and other
     planetary system objects. Many nebulae form from the gravita
     tional collapse of diffused gas in the interstellar medium or
     ISM. As the material collapses under its own weight, massive
     stars may form in the center, and their ultraviolet radiation
     ionizes the surrounding gas, making it visible at optical wave
     lengths.
  </p>
</div>
<div id="flickr"></div>
</div>
```

Next, change the final `<script>` to the following:

```html
<script>
  (function($){
    var img = $("<img/>", {
      height: 100,
      width: 100
    }),
    tabOpts = {
      select: function(event, ui) {
        if (ui.tab.toString().indexOf("flickr") != -1 ) {
          $("#flickr").empty();
          $.getJSON("http://api.flickr.com/services/feeds/
photos_public.gne?tags = nebula&format = json&jsoncallback = ?",
function(data) {
            $.each(data.items, function(i,item){
              img.clone()
              .attr("src", item.media.m).appendTo("#flickr");
              if (i == 5) {
                return false;
              }
            });
          });
        }
      }
    };
    $("#myTabs").tabs(tabOpts);
  })(jQuery);
</script>
```

Save the file as `tabs20.html` in your `jqueryui` folder. We first create a new `<img>` element and store it in a variable. We also create a configuration object and add the `select` event option to it. Every time a tab is selected, the function we set as the value of this option will check to see if it was the tab with an `id` of `flickr` that was selected. If it was, the jQuery `getJSON` method is used to retrieve an image feed from `http://www.flickr.com`.

Once the data is returned, first empty the contents of the **Flickr** tab to prevent a build-up of images, then use jQuery's `each()` utility method to iterate over each object within the returned JSON, and create a clone of our stored image.

Each new copy of the image has its `src` attribute set using the information from the current feed object, and is then added to the empty **Flickr** tab. Once iteration over six of the objects in the feed has occurred, we exit jQuery's `each` method. It's that simple.

When we view the page and select the **Images** tab, after a short delay we should see six new images, as seen in the following screenshot:

Summary

The tabs widget is an excellent way of saving space on your page by organizing related (or even completely unrelated) sections of content that can be shown or hidden, with simple click-input from your visitors. It also lends an air of interactivity to your site that can help improve the overall functionality and appeal of the page on which it is used.

Let's review what was covered in this chapter. We first looked at how, with just a little underlying HTML and a single line of jQuery-flavored JavaScript, we can implement the default tabs widget.

We then saw how easy it is to add our own basic styling for the tabs widget so that its appearance, but not its behavior, is altered. We already know that in addition to this, we can use a predesigned theme or create a completely new theme using ThemeRoller.

We then moved on, to look at the set of configurable options exposed by the tabs' API. With these, we can enable or disable different options that the widget supports, such as whether tabs are selected by clicks or another event, whether certain tabs are disabled when the widget is rendered, and so on.

We took some time to look at how we can use a range of predefined callback options that allow us to execute arbitrary code, when different events are detected. We also saw that the jQuery bind() method can listen for the same events if necessary.

Following the configurable options, we covered the range of methods that we can use to programmatically make the tabs perform different actions, such as simulating a click on a tab, enabling or disabling a tab, and adding or removing tabs.

We briefly looked at some of the more advanced functionality supported by the tabs widget such as AJAX tabs and the tab carousel. Both these techniques are easy to use and can add value to any implementation.

In the next chapter, we'll move on to look at the **accordion** widget, which like the tabs widget, is used to group content into related sections that are shown one at a time.

4
The Accordion Widget

The accordion widget is another UI widget that allows you to group content into separate panels that can be opened or closed by visitor interaction. Therefore, most of its content is initially hidden from view, much like the tabs widget that we looked at in the previous chapter.

Each container has a heading element associated with it that is used to open the container and display the content. When you click on a heading, its content will slide into view (with an animation) below it. The currently visible content is hidden, while the new content is shown whenever we click on an accordion heading.

In this chapter, we are going to cover the following topics:

- The structure of an accordion widget
- The default implementation of an accordion
- Adding custom styling
- Using the configurable options to set different behaviors
- Working with methods for controlling the accordion
- The built-in types of animation
- Custom accordion events

The accordion widget is a robust and highly configurable widget that allows you to save space on your web pages, by displaying only a single panel of content at any time. The following screenshot shows an example of an accordion widget:

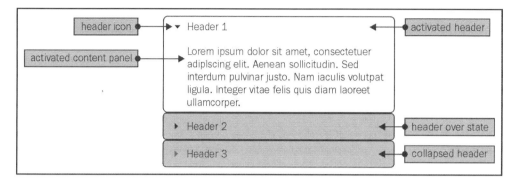

It's easy for our visitors to use and easy for us to implement. It has a range of configurable options that can be used to customize its appearance and behavior, and exposes a series of methods that allow you to control it programmatically. It also comes with a rich set of interaction events that we can use to hook into key interactions between our visitors and the widget.

The height of the accordion's container element will be set automatically, so that there is room to show the tallest content panel in addition to the headers. Also, by default, the size of the widget will remain fixed, so that it won't push other elements on the page around it out of the way, when content panels open or close.

Accordion's structure

Let's take a moment to familiarize ourselves with the underlying markup that an accordion is made of. Within the outer container is a series of links. These links are the headings within the accordion and each heading will have a corresponding content panel that opens when the header is clicked.

It's worth remembering that only one content panel can be open at a time when using the accordion widget. In a blank page in your text editor, create the following page:

```
<!DOCTYPE html>
<html>
  <head>
    <meta charset="utf-8">
```

```
  <link rel="stylesheet"
    href="css/smoothness/jquery-ui-1.8.9.custom.css">
  <title>Accordion
  </title>
</head>
<body>
  <div id="myAccordion">
    <h2>
      <a href="#">Header 1
      </a>
    </h2>
    <div>Lorem ipsum dolor sit amet, consectetuer adipiscing
      elit. Aenean sollicitudin. Sed interdum pulvinar justo.
      Nam iaculis volutpat ligula. Integer vitae felis quis
      diam laoreet ullamcorper.
    </div>
    <h2>
      <a href="#">Header 2
      </a>
    </h2>
    <div>Etiam tincidunt est vitae est. Ut posuere, mauris at
      sodales rutrum, turpis tellus fermentum metus, ut
      bibendum velit enim eu lectus. Suspendisse potenti.
    </div>
    <h2>
      <a href="#">Header 3
      </a>
    </h2>
    <div>Donec at dolor ac metus pharetra aliquam.
      Suspendisse purus. Fusce tempor ultrices libero. Sed
      quis nunc.        Pellentesque tincidunt viverra felis.
      Integer elit mauris, egestas ultricies, gravida vitae,
      feugiat a, tellus.
    </div>
  </div>
  <script
    src="development-bundle/jquery-1.3.2.js">
  </script>
  <script
    src="development-bundle/ui/ui.core.js">
  </script>
  <script
    src="development-bundle/ui/ui.accordion.js">
  </script>
  <script>
```

```
      $(function() {
        $("#myAccordion").accordion();
      });
    </script>
  </body>
</html>
```

Save the file as `accordion1.html` in the `jqueryui` folder, and try it out in a browser. The widget should appear as it did in the screenshot at the start of the chapter, fully skinned and ready for action.

The following list shows the required dependencies of the widget:

- `jquery.ui.all.css`
- `jquery-x.x.x.js`
- `jquery.ui.core.js`
- `jquery.ui.accordion.js`

Each widget also has its own source file, and may depend on other components as well. For example, we could include some effect files to use non-standard animations on the opening accordion panels.

The order in which these files appear is important. The jQuery library must always appear first, followed by the `jquery.ui.core.js` file. After these files, any other files that the widget depends upon, should appear before the widget's own script file. The library components will not function as expected if files are not loaded in the correct order.

The underlying markup required for the accordion is flexible, and the widget can be constructed from a variety of different structures. In this example, the accordion headings are formed from links wrapped in `<h2>` elements, and the content panels are simple `<div>` elements.

For the accordion to function correctly, each content panel should appear directly after its corresponding header. All of the elements for the widget are enclosed within a container `<div>` that is targeted with the `accordion()` widget method.

After the required script dependencies from the library, we use a custom `<script>` block to transform the underlying markup into the accordion.

To initialize the widget, we use a simple `id` selector `$("#myAccordion")`, to specify the element that contains the markup for the widget, and then chain the `accordion()` widget method after the selector to create the accordion.

In this example, we used an empty fragment (#) as the value of the href attribute in our tab heading elements, such as:

```
<h2><a href="#">Header 1</a></h2>
```

You should note that any URL supplied for accordion headers will not be followed, when the header is clicked in the default implementation.

Similar to the tabs widget that we looked at in the previous chapter, the underlying markup that is transformed into the accordion has a series of classnames added to it, when the widget is initialized.

A number of different elements that make up the widget are given role and aria- attributes. **ARIA** stands for **Accessible Rich Internet Applications** and is a W3C recommendation for ensuring that rich-internet applications remain accessible to assisted technologies.

The accordion panels that are initially hidden from view are given the attribute aria-expanded="false" to ensure that screen readers don't discard or cannot access content that is hidden using display:none. This makes the accordion widget highly accessible.

Styling the accordion

ThemeRoller is the recommended tool for choosing or creating the theme of the accordion widget, but there may be times when we want to considerably change the look and style of the widget beyond what is possible with ThemeRoller. In that case, we can just style our own accordion.

In a new page in your text editor add the following code:

```
#myAccordion {
  width:400px; border:1px solid #636363; padding-bottom:1px;
}
.ui-accordion-header {
  border:1px solid #fff;
  font-family:Georgia; background:#e2e2e2 none;
}
.ui-widget-content { font-size:70%; border:none; }
.ui-corner-bottom {
  -moz-border-radius:4px 4px 0 0;
  -webkit-border-radius:4px 4px 0 0;
  border-radius:4px 4px 0 0;
}
```

```css
.ui-corner-all {
  -moz-border-radius:0; -webkit-border-radius:0;
  border-radius:0;
}
.ui-accordion .ui-accordion-header { margin:0 0 -1px; }
#myAccordion .ui-state-active, #myAccordion .ui-widget-content .ui-
state-active { background:#fff; }
.ui-state-hover, .ui-widget-content .ui-state-hover {
  background:#d2d2d2;
}
```

Save this file as `accordionTheme.css` in the `css` folder, and link to it after the jQuery UI style sheet in the `<head>` of `accordion1.html`:

```html
<link rel="stylesheet" href="css/accordionTheme.css">
```

Save the new file as `accordion2.html` in the `jqueryui` folder and view it in a browser. It should appear something like this:

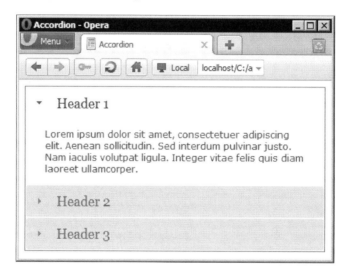

As you can see from this screenshot, we've disabled the built-in rounded corners that are added by the theme file and have set alternative fonts, background colors, and border colors.

We haven't changed the widget much, but we haven't used many style rules. It would be easy to continue overriding rules in this way to build a much more complex custom theme.

Configuring an accordion

The accordion has a range of configurable options that allow us to change the default behavior of the widget. The following table lists the available options, their default values, and gives a brief description of their usage:

Option	Default value	Used to...
active	`first child` (the first panel is open)	Set the active heading on page load.
animated	`"slide"`	Animate the opening of content panels.
autoHeight	`true`	Automatically set height according to the biggest drawer.
clearStyle	`false`	Clear the height and overflow styles after a panel opens.
collapsible	`false`	Allow all of the content panels to be closed at the same time.
disabled	`false`	Disable the widget.
event	`"click"`	Specify the event on headers that trigger drawers to open.
fillSpace	`false`	Allow the accordion to fill the height of its container instead of sizing itself according to the content within it.
header	`"> li >:first-child,> :not(li):even"`	Specify the selector for header elements. Although it looks complex, this is a standard jQuery selector that simply targets the first-child within every odd `<li>` element.
icons	`'header': 'ui-icon-triangle-1-e', 'headerSelected': 'ui-icon-triangle-1-s'`	Set the icons for the header elements and the selected state.
navigation	`false`	Enable `navigation` mode for accordion.
navigationFilter	`location.href`	Change the function used to obtain the ID of the content panel that should be open when the widget is initialized.

Changing the trigger event

Most of the options are self-explanatory, and the values they accept are usually Booleans, strings, or element selectors. Let's put some of them to use, so that we can explore their functionality. Change the final `<script>` element in `accordion2.html` so that it appears as follows:

```
<script>
  (function($) {
    var accOpts = {
      event:"mouseover"
        }
        $("#myAccordion").accordion(accOpts);
  })(jQuery);
</script>
```

Save these changes as `accordion3.html`. First, we create a new object literal called `accOpts` that contains the key `event` and the value `mouseover`, which is the event we wish to use to trigger the opening of an accordion panel. We pass this object to the `accordion()` method as an argument and it overrides the default option of the widget, which is `click`.

The `mouseover` event is commonly used as an alternative trigger event. Other events can also be used, for example, we can set `keydown` as the event, but in order for this to work, the accordion panel that we wish to open, must already be focused.

You should note that you can also set options using an inline object within the widget method, without creating a separate object. Using the following code would be equally as effective, and would often be the preferred way of coding:

```
<script>
  (function($) {
    $("#myAccordion").accordion({
      event:"mouseover"
    });
  })(jQuery);
</script>
```

Changing the default active header

By default, the first header of the accordion will be selected when the widget is rendered, with its content panel open. We can change which header is selected on page load using the `active` option. Change the configuration object in `accordion3.html`, so that it appears as follows:

```
var accOpts = {
   active: 2
};
```

Save this version as `accordion4.html`. We set the `active` option to the integer 2 to open the last content panel by default, and like the tab headers that we saw in the previous chapter, accordion's headers use a zero-based index. Along with an integer, this option also accepts a jQuery selector or raw DOM element.

We can also use the Boolean value of `false` to configure the accordion, so that none of the content panels are open by default. Change the configuration object once again to the following:

```
var accOpts = {
   active: false
};
```

Save this as `accordion5.html`. Now when the page loads, all of the content panels are hidden from view:

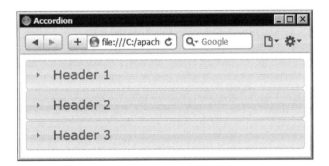

The widget will only remain closed until one of the headers is selected, and then one panel will remain open at all times. This behavior can be changed by employing the `collapsible` option in the configuration object:

```
var accOpts = {
   active: false,
   collapsible: true
};
```

Save this as `accordion6.html`. Now, not only is the accordion closed when the page loads, but also clicking an active header will close its associated content panel as well. As expected, when a closed header is clicked, it will show its content panel in the usual way. For usability, it is best to avoid configuring both this and the `mouseover` event option together in the same implementation, as the open panels would close even when the user inadvertently moused off-and-back over them.

Filling the height of its container

If the `fillSpace` option is set, it will override `autoHeight`, and force the accordion to take the full height of its container. In our examples so far, the container of the accordion has been the body of the page, and the height of the body will only be the height of its largest element. We'll need to use a new container element with a fixed height to see this option in action.

In the `<head>` of `accordion6.html`, add the following `<style>` element:

```
<style>
  #container { height:600px; width:400px; }
</style>
```

Then wrap all of the underlying markup for the accordion in a new container element as follows:

```
<div id="container">
  <div id="myAccordion">
    <h2><a href="#">Header 1</a></h2>
    <div>Lorem ipsum dolor sit amet, consectetuer adipiscing elit.
      Aenean sollicitudin. Sed interdum pulvinar justo. Nam iaculis
      volutpat ligula. Integer vitae felis quis diam laoreet ullam
      corper.
    </div>
    <h2><a href="#">Header 2</a></h2>
    <div>Etiam tincidunt est vitae est. Ut posuere, mauris at sodales
      rutrum, turpis tellus fermentum metus, ut bibendum velit enim
      eu lectus. Suspendisse potenti.
    </div>
    <h2><a href="#">Header 3</a></h2>
    <div>Donec at dolor ac metus pharetra aliquam. Suspendisse
      purus. Fusce tempor ultrices libero. Sed quis nunc.
      Pellentesque tincidunt viverra felis. Integer elit mauris,
      egestas ultricies, gravida vitae, feugiat a, tellus.
    </div>
  </div>
</div>
```

Finally, change the configuration object to use the `fillSpace` option:

```
var accOpts = {
  fillSpace: true
};
```

Save the changes as `accordion7.html`. The new container is given a fixed height and width using the CSS specified in the `<head>` of the page.

 This is not the best way to add style to our pages. But when we only have a single selector and two rules, it seems excessive to create a new style sheet.

The `fillSpace` option forces the accordion to take the entire height of its container, and restricting the width of the container naturally reduces the width of the widget too. This page should appear as follows:

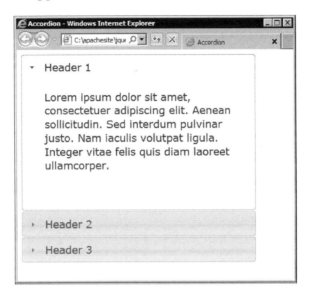

Accordion animation

The accordion widget comes with the built-in `slide` animation that is enabled by default, and has been present in all of our examples so far. Disabling this animation is as easy as supplying `false` as the value of the `animated` option. Remove the `<style>` tag from the `<head>` of the page in `accordion7.html`, and remove the additional container `<div>`, then change the configuration object so that it appears as follows:

```
var accOpts = {
   animated: false
};
```

Save this as `accordion8.html`. This will cause each content panel to open immediately instead of sliding-open nicely whenever a header is clicked.

An alternate animation has also been built into the widget—the `bounceslide` animation. However, to use this alternate animation, we need to add a link to the `jquery.effects.core.js` file.

Directly after the link to `ui.accordion.js` at the bottom of the `<body>`, add the following line of code:

```
<script
  src="development-bundle/ui/jquery.effects.core.js">
</script>
```

Now, change the configuration object in our custom `<script>` element so that it appears like this:

```
var accOpts = {
  animated: "bounceslide"
};
```

Save these changes as `accordion9.html`. Although the accordion panels close in exactly the same way as they did in previous examples, when they open they bounce a few times at the end of the animation. It's a great effect, and as we saw in this example, it's easy to use.

In addition to the two preconfigured animations, we can also use any of the different easing effects defined within the `jquery.effects.core.js` file, including the following:

- `easeInQuad`
- `easeInCubic`
- `easeInQuart`
- `easeInQuint`
- `easeInSine`
- `easeInExpo`
- `easeInCirc`
- `easeInElastic`
- `easeInBack`
- `easeInBounce`

Each of these easing methods is complimented by `easeOut` and `easeInOut` counterparts. For the complete list, see the `jquery.effects.core.js` file, or refer to the *easing table* in *Chapter 14, UI Effects*.

 See the jQuery UI demo site for some great examples of the accordion effects: `http://jqueryui.com/demos/accordion/`

The easing effects don't change the underlying animation, which will still be based on the slide animation. But they do change how the animation progresses. For example, we can make the content panels bounce both on opening and closing animations, by using the `easeOutBounce` easing effect in our configuration object:

```
var accOpts = {
    animated: "easeOutBounce"
};
```

Save this file as `accordion10.html` and view it in a browser. Most of the easing effects have opposites, for example, instead of making the content panels bounce at the end of the animation, we can make them bounce at the start of the animation using the `easeInBounce` easing effect.

Another option that has an effect on animations is the `clearStyle` property, which resets `height` and `overflow` styles after each animation. Remember that animations are enabled by default, but this option isn't. Change the configuration object in `accordion10.html` to the following:

```
var accOpts = {
    clearStyle: true,
    animated: "easeOutBounce"
};
```

Save this as `accordion11.html`. Now when the page is run, the accordion will not keep to a fixed size; it will grow or shrink depending on how much content is in each panel. It doesn't make much of a difference in this example, but the property really comes into its own when using dynamic content, when we may not always know how much content will be within each panel when the panel content changes frequently.

Accordion events

The accordion exposes three custom events, which are listed in the following table:

Event	Triggered when...
change	The active header has changed.
changestart	The active header is about to change.
create	The widget has been created.

The change event is triggered every time the active header (and its associated content panel) is changed. It fires at the end of the content panel's opening animation, or if animations are disabled, immediately (but still after the active panel has been changed).

The changestart event is fired as soon as the new header is selected, that is before the opening animation (or before the active panel has changed, if animations are disabled). The create event is fired as soon as the widget has been initialized.

Using the change event

Let's see how we can use these events in our accordion implementations. In accordion11.html, change the configuration object so that it appears as follows:

```
var accOpts = {
  change: function(e, ui) {
    $(".notify").remove();
    $("<div />", {
      "class": "notify",
      text: ([
        ui.newHeader.find("a").text(),
        "was activated,",
        ui.oldHeader.find("a").text(),
        "was closed"].join(" ")
      )
    }).insertAfter("#myAccordion").fadeOut(2000, function(){
      $(this).remove();
    });
  });
  $("#myAccordion").accordion(accOpts);
});
```

Save this as accordion12.html. In this example, we use the change configuration option, to specify an anonymous callback function that is executed every time the active panel is changed. This function will automatically receive two objects as arguments. The first object is the event object, which contains the original browser event object.

The second argument is an object, which contains useful information about the widget, such as the header element that was activated (ui.newHeader) and the header that was deactivated (ui.oldHeader). The second object is a jQuery object, so we can call jQuery methods directly on it.

In this example, we navigate down to the `<a>` element within the header and display its text content in an information box, which is appended to the page and then removed after a short interval with a fading animation.

For reference, the `ui` object also provides information on the content panels in the form of `ui.newContent` and `ui.oldContent` properties.

Once a header has been activated, and its content panel shown, the notification will be generated:

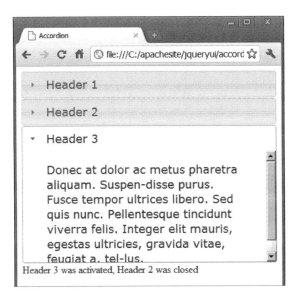

The changestart event

The `changestart` event can be used in exactly the same way, and any callback function we specify using this event also receives the `e` and `ui` objects to use. Change the configuration object from the last example to as follows:

```
var accOpts = {
  changestart: function(e, ui) {
  $("<div />", {
    "class": "notify",
    text: ([ui.newHeader.find("a").text(),
    "was activated,", ui.oldHeader.find("a").text(),
    "was closed"].join(" "))
  }).insertAfter("#myAccordion").fadeOut(2000, function(){
    $(this).remove();
  });
};
```

Save this as `accordion13.html`. All that's changed, is the property that we're targeting with our configuration object. When we run the page, we should find that everything is exactly as it was before, except that our notification is produced before the content panel animation instead of after it.

There are also events such as `accordionchange` and `accordionchangestart` for use with the standard `jQuery bind()` method, so that we can specify a callback function to execute outside of the accordion configuration.

Accordion navigation

Along with a standard content accordion, the widget can also be put to good use as a navigation menu through the simple addition of some proper `href` attributes and the `navigation` option. We'll need to create two new pages to fully appreciate the effect of this option. In `accordion13.html`, change the underlying markup for the accordion to the following:

```
<div id="container" class="ui-helper-clearfix">
  <div id="navCol">
    <h2><a href="#me" title="About Me">About Me</a></h2>
    <div>
      <a href="accordionMe.html#me" title="Bio">My Bio</a>
      <a href="accordionMe.html#me" title="Contact Me">Contact Me</a>
      <a href="accordionMe.html#me" title="Resume">My Resume</a>
    </div>
    <h2><a href="#js" title="JavaScript"></a></h2>
    <div>
      <a href="accordionJS.html#js" title="Tutorials">Tutorials</a>
      <a href="accordionJS.html#js" title="AJAX">AJAX</a>
      <a href="accordionJS.html#js" title="JavaScript
        Apps">JavaScript Apps</a>
    </div>
  </div>
  <div id="contentCol">
    <h1>Page 1</h1>
  </div>
</div>
```

Then change the configuration object, so that it appears as follows:

```
var accOpts = {
  navigation: true
};
```

Save this file as `accordion14.html`, then save it again as `accordionMe.html` and `accordionJS.html`, to give us the two extra example pages we need for this example. In the `<body>` of the page, we've added a new outer container to hold all the page content and have added two inner containers within this—one for the accordion widget that will appear as a navigation menu, and the other for content. In this example, the two pages just have `<h1>` elements denoting which page is open.

The underlying markup that the accordion is built from has also changed. We've added classnames and `href` attributes to the links within the accordion headers that include fragment identifiers. Adding the `href` is critical to the functioning of the navigation accordion.

In the final `<script>` element, we set the `navigation` option to `true`. The `navigation` option changes how the widget appears when the page is initially loaded.

Instead of activating the first header when the accordion is initialized, it instead looks at the `location.href` property of the window. If the contents of the `location.href` property match the `href` attribute of one of the accordion headers, that header will be activated.

When we run `accordion14.html` in a browser, and select one of the links in the second content panel, the page will navigate to `accordionJS.html` and the second header will automatically be activated. The `navigation` property gives us a great way of maintaining state between pages for the widget.

We also need some additional styles in order to make sure that the accordion and the page appear correctly. In a new page in your text editor, create the following file:

```
#navCol { width:250px; float:left; }
#contentCol { float:left; }
#contentCol h1 { text-indent:20px; font-family:Georgia; }
#navCol .ui-accordion-header {
  display:block; padding-left:40px;
}
.ui-accordion-content a {
  font-size:70%; text-decoration:none; display:block;
}
.ui-accordion-content a:hover { text-decoration:underline; }
```

Save this in the `css` folder as `accordionTheme2.css`. We don't need many styles for this example; we just need to arrange the containers and set some basic aesthetics for the accordion and the links within it.

The following screenshot shows how the page will appear when navigating from `accordion14.html` to `accordionJS.html`:

When going back to the first page from the second page, the first header should once again be activated.

Accordion methods

The accordion includes a selection of methods that allow you to control and manipulate the behavior of the widget programmatically. Some of the methods are common to each component of the library, such as the `destroy` method that is used by every widget. The following table lists the unique methods for the accordion widget:

Method	Use
activate	Programmatically activates a header. This is analogous to the header being selected by the visitor.
resize	Resizes the accordion when the `fillSpace` option is set to `true` and when the contents on an accordion has changed.

 In addition to the accordion-specific `activate` and `resize` methods, the `destroy`, `enable`, `disable`, `option`, and `widget` methods are also available.

Header activation

The `activate` method can be used to programmatically show or hide different drawers. We can easily test this method using a textbox and a new button. In `accordion15.html`, add the following new markup directly after the accordion:

```
<label for="activateChoice">Enter a header index to activate</label>
<input id="activateChoice">
<button type="button" id="activate">Activate</button>
```

Now change the final <script> element so that it appears as follows:

```
<script>
  (function($) {
    $("#myAccordion").accordion();
    $("#activate").click(function() {
      $("#myAccordion").accordion("activate",
      parseInt($("#activateChoice").val(), 10));
    });
  })(jQuery);
</script>
```

Save the new file as `accordion15.html`. The `activate` method takes an additional argument. It expects to receive the index (zero-based) number of the header element to activate. In this example, we obtain the header to activate, by returning the value of the text input. We convert it to an integer using the `parseInt()` function of JavaScript because the `val()` jQuery method returns a string.

If an index number that doesn't exist is specified, nothing will happen. The first header will be activated if no index is specified. If a value other than an integer is specified, nothing will happen; the script will fail silently, without errors, and the accordion will continue to function as normal.

Resizing an accordion panel

Change the underlying markup for the accordion widget in `accordion11.html`, so that the third header points to a remote text file and the third panel is empty. The heading element should also be given an `id` attribute:

```
<div id="myAccordion">
  <h2><a href="#">Header 1</a></h2>
  <div>Lorem ipsum dolor sit amet, consectetuer adipiscing elit.
    Aenean sollicitudin. Sed interdum pulvinar justo. Nam iaculis
    volutpat ligula. Integer vitae felis quis diam laoreet
    ullamcorper.
```

```
    </div>
    <h2><a href="#">Header 2</a></h2>
    <div>Etiam tincidunt est vitae est. Ut posuere, mauris at sodales
        rutrum, turpis tellus fermentum metus, ut bibendum velit enim eu
        lectus. Suspendisse poten-ti.
    </div>
    <h2 id="remote"><a href="remoteAccordion.txt">Remote</a></h2>
    <div></div>
</div>
```

Then change the final `<script>` element, so that it appears as follows:

```
(function($) {
    var accOpts = {
        changestart: function(e, ui) {
            if (ui.newHeader.attr("id") === "remote") {
                $.get(ui.newHeader.find("a").attr("href"),
                function(data) {
                    ui.newHeader.next().text(data);
                });
            }
        },
        change: function(e, ui) {
            ui.newHeader.closest("#myAccordion").accordion("resize");
        }
    };
    $("#myAccordion").accordion(accOpts);
})(jQuery);
```

Save this file as `accordion16.html`. In our configuration object, we use the `changestart` event to check whether the `id` of the element matches the `id` we gave to our remote accordion heading.

If it does, we get the contents of the text file specified in the `<a>` element's `href` attribute, using jQuery's `get()` method. If the request returns successfully, we add the contents of the text file to the empty panel after the header. This all happens before the panel opens.

We then use the `change` event to call the `resize` method on the accordion, after the panel has opened.

When we run the page in a browser, the contents of the remote text file should be sufficient to cause a scroll bar to appear within the content panel. Calling the `resize` method allows the widget to read just itself, so that it can contain all of the newly added content without displaying the scroll bar.

The widget will automatically display the configured spinner when loading remote content.

Accordion interoperability

Does the accordion widget play nicely with other widgets in the library? Let's take a look and see whether the accordion can be combined with the widget from the previous chapter, the tabs widget.

Change the underlying markup for the accordion, so that the third content panel now contains the markup for a set of tabs, and the third heading no longer points to the remote text file:

```
<div id="myAccordion">
  <h2><a href="#">Header 1</a></h2>
  <div>Lorem ipsum dolor sit amet, consectetuer adipiscing elit.
    Aenean sollicitudin. Sed interdum pulvinar justo. Nam iaculis
    volutpat ligula. Integer vitae felis quis diam laoreet
    ullamcorper.
  </div>
  <h2><a href="#">Header 2</a></h2>
  <div>Etiam tincidunt est vitae est. Ut posuere, mauris at sodales
    rutrum, turpis tellus fermentum metus, ut bibendum velit enim eu
    lectus. Suspendisse potenti.
  </div>
  <h2><a href="#">Header 3</a></h2>
  <div>
    <div id="myTabs">
      <ul>
        <li><a href="#0"><span>Tab 1</span></a></li>
        <li><a href="#1"><span>Tab 2</span></a></li>
      </ul>
      <div id="0">This is the content panel linked to the first
       ab, it is shown by default.</div>
      <div id="1">This content is linked to the second tab and
        will be shown when its tab is clicked.</div>
    </div>
  </div>
</div>
```

We should also link to the source file for the tabs widget, after the accordion's source file. Next, change the final `<script>` element so that it appears as follows:

```
<script>
  (function($) {
    $("#myAccordion").accordion();
    $("#myTabs").tabs();
  })(jQuery);
</script>
```

Save this file as `accordion17.html`. All we've done with this file is add a simple tab structure to one of the accordion's content panels. In the `<script>` at the end of the page, we just call the accordion and tab's widget methods. No additional or special configuration is required.

The page should appear as follows, when the third accordion heading is activated:

The widgets are compatible the other way round; that is we can have an accordion within one of the tab's content panels without any adverse effects as well.

Summary

We first looked at what the accordion does and how it is targeted by the CSS framework. We then moved on, to look at the configurable options that can be used with accordion. We saw that we can use these options to change the behavior of the widget, such as specifying an alternative heading to be open by default, whether the widget should expand to fill the height of its container, or the event that triggers the opening of a content drawer.

Along with configurable options, we saw that the accordion exposes several custom events. Using them, we can specify callback functions during configuration, or bind to them after configuration to execute additional functionality, in reaction to different things happening to the widget.

Next, we looked at the accordion's default animation and how we can add simple transition effects to the opening of content panels in the form of easing effects. We saw that to make use of non-standard animations or easing effects, the `jquery.effects.core.js` file needs to be included.

In addition to looking at these options, we also saw that there are a range of methods which can be called on the accordion to make it do things programmatically. Like the tabs widget that we looked at in the previous chapter, the accordion is a flexible and robust widget that provides essential functionality in an aesthetically pleasing format. In the next chapter, we get to play with the dialog widget, which allows us to create a flexible, highly configurable overlay that floats above the page and displays any content we specify.

5
The Dialog

Traditionally, the way to display a brief message or ask a visitor a question would've been to use one of JavaScript's native dialog boxes (such as `alert` or `confirm`), or to open a new web page with a predefined size, styled to look like a dialog box.

Unfortunately, as I'm sure you're aware, neither of these methods is particularly flexible to us as developers, or particularly engaging for our visitors. For each problem they solve, several new problems are usually introduced.

The dialog widget lets us display a message, supplemental content (such as images or text), or even interactive content (such as forms). It's also easy to add buttons, such as simple **ok** and **cancel buttons** to the dialog, and define callback functions for them in order to react to their being clicked; the dialog can also be modal or non-modal.

In this chapter, we will cover the following topics:

- Creating a basic dialog
- Working with dialog options
- Modality
- Enabling the built-in animations
- Adding buttons to the dialog
- Working with dialog callbacks
- Controlling the dialog programmatically

The following screenshot shows a dialog widget and the different elements that it is made of:

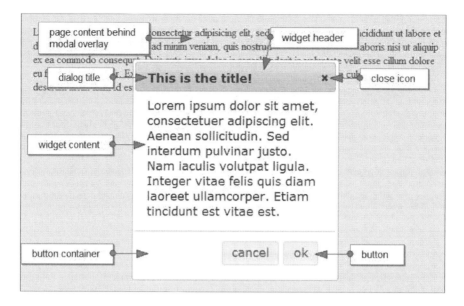

Creating a basic dialog

A dialog has a lot of default behavior built-in, but few methods are needed to control it programmatically, making this an easy-to-use widget that is also highly configurable and powerful.

Generating the widget is simple and requires a minimal underlying markup structure. The following page contains the minimum markup that's required to implement the dialog widget:

```
<!DOCTYPE html>
<html>
  <head>
    <meta charset="utf-8">
    <link rel="stylesheet"
      href="css/smoothness/jquery-ui-1.8.9.custom.css">
    <title>Dialog
    </title>
  </head>
  <body>
    <div id="myDialog" title="This is the title!">
      Lorem ipsum dolor sit amet, consectetuer adipiscing elit.
```

```
      Aenean sollicitudin. Sed interdum pulvinar justo. Nam iaculis
      volutpat ligula. Integer vitae felis quis diam laoreet
      ullamcorper. Etiam tincidunt est vitae est.
    </div>
    <script
      src="development-bundle/jquery-1.4.4.js">
    </script>
    <script
      src="development-bundle/ui/jquery.ui.core.js">
    </script>
    <script
      src="development-bundle/ui/jquery.ui.widget.js">
    </script>
    <script
      src="development-bundle/ui/jquery.ui.position.js">
    </script>
    <script
      src="development-bundle/ui/jquery.ui.dialog.js">
    </script>
    <script>
      (function($){
        $("#myDialog").dialog();

      })(jQuery);
    </script>
  </body>
</html>
```

Save this file as `dialog1.html` in the `jqueryui` project folder. To use the dialog, the following dependencies are required:

- `jquery-ui-x.x.x.custom.css`
- `jquery-x.x.x.js`
- `jquery.ui.core.js`
- `jquery.ui.widget.js`
- `jquery.ui.position.js`
- `jquery.ui.dialog.js`

Optionally, we can also include the following files to make the dialog draggable and resizable:

- `jquery.ui.mouse.js`
- `jquery.ui.draggable.js`
- `jquery.ui.resizable.js`

The dialog widget is initialized in the same way as the other widgets that we have already looked at—by calling the widget's plugin method. When you run this page in your browser, you should see the default dialog widget, as shown in the screenshot at the start of this chapter.

As with the previous widgets we've covered, a variety of classnames from the CSS framework are added to different elements within the widget to give them the appropriate styling for their respective elements, and any additional elements that are required are created on the fly.

The dialog in the first example is fixed both in size and position, and will be positioned in the top-left of the viewport. We can make the widget draggable, resizable, or both easily. All we need to do is include the draggable and resizable component's source files, as well as the mouse utility, with the other `<script>` resources at the end of the `<body>`.

It's not important that the draggable and resizable files are included in the page before the dialog's source file, they can come before or after, and the widget will still inherit these behaviors. Any styling that is required, such as the resize indicator that appears in the bottom-left of the dialog, will be picked up automatically from the master CSS file.

Add the following three `<script>` elements directly before the closing `</body>` tag in `dialog1.html`:

```
<script src="development-bundle/ui/jquery.ui.mouse.js">
</script>
<script
  src="development-bundle/ui/jquery.ui.draggable.js">
</script>
<script
  src="development-bundle/ui/jquery.ui.resizable.js">
</script>
```

Save this as `dialog2.html` and view it in a browser. The dialog should now be draggable and can be moved to any part of the viewport, but will not cause it to scroll if the widget is moved to an edge.

The dialog should also be resizable—by clicking and holding the resize indicator in the bottom-right and dragging, the widget can be made bigger or smaller. If the dialog is made bigger than the viewport, then it will cause the window to scroll.

Dialog options

An options object can be used in a dialog's widget method to configure various dialog options. Let's look at the available options:

Option	Default value	Used to...
autoOpen	true	Shows the dialog as soon as the dialog() method is called, when set to true.
buttons	{}	Supplies an object containing buttons to be used with the dialog. Each key becomes the text on the <button> element, and each value is a callback function, which is executed when the button is clicked.
closeOnEscape	true	If set to true, the dialog will close when the *Esc* key is pressed.
closeText	close	Sets the text on the close button.
dialogClass	""	Sets additional classnames on the dialog for theming purposes.
disabled	false	Disables the widget.
draggable	true	Makes the dialog draggable (use jquery.ui.draggable.js).
height	auto	Sets the starting height of the dialog.
hide	null	Sets an effect to be used when the dialog is closed.
maxHeight	false	Sets a maximum height for the dialog.
maxWidth	false	Sets a maximum width for the dialog.
minHeight	150	Sets a minimum height for the dialog.
minWidth	150	Sets a minimum width for the dialog.
modal	false	Enables modality while the dialog is open.
position	center	Sets the starting position of the dialog in the viewport. Can accept a string, or an array of strings, or an array containing exact coordinates of the dialog offset from the top and left of the viewport (use jquery.ui.position.js).
resizable	true	Makes the dialog resizable (also requires jquery.ui.resizable.js).
show	null	Sets an effect to be used when the dialog is opened.
stack	true	Causes the focused dialog to move to the front, when several dialogs are open.

Option	Default value	Used to...
title	""	Alternative to specifying the title attribute on the widget's underlying container element.
width	300	Sets the starting width of the dialog.
zIndex	1000	Sets the starting CSS z-index of the widget. When using multiple dialogs and the stack option is set to true, the z-index will change as each dialog is moved to the front of the stack.

As you can see, we have a wide range of configurable options to work with when implementing the dialog. Many of these options are Boolean, or numerical, or string-based, making them easy to set and work with.

Showing the dialog

In our examples so far, the dialog has been displayed as soon as the page has loaded. The autoOpen option is set to true by default, so the dialog will be displayed as soon as it has been initialized.

We can change this, so that the dialog is opened when something else occurs, like a button being clicked, by setting the autoOpen option to false. Change the final <script> element at the bottom of dialog2.html to the following:

```
<script>
  $(function(){
    var dialogOpts = {
      autoOpen: false
    };
    $("#myDialog").dialog(dialogOpts);
  })
</script>
```

Save this as dialog3.html. The widget is still created; the underlying markup is removed from the page, transformed into the widget, and then re-appended to the end of the <body>. It will remain hidden until the open method is called on it. We'll come back to this option when we look at the open method, a little later on.

The title of the dialog

The options table shows a title option. Although the title of the dialog (the actual text in the header of the widget) can be set using the title attribute of the underlying HTML container element, using the title configuration option gives us more control over how the title is displayed on the widget.

By default, the title text of the dialog will not be selectable and will also not be displayed in the operating system's default tool tip style. When using the `title` attribute on the underlying element, the text will appear within a `<span>` element, which is inside a `<div>` with the class name `ui-dialog-titlebar`. These elements will appear in the header of the widget.

If we want to inject additional elements into the DOM structure of the dialog (for additional styling perhaps or different behavior), we could do it using the `title` option. Change the configuration object in `dialog3.html` to the following:

```
var dialogOpts = {
   title: '<a href="#">A link title!</a>'
};
```

Save this file as `dialog4.html`. The change in the widget should be apparent immediately; the `span` element in the widget header will now contain our new `link` element. The following screenshot shows our new title:

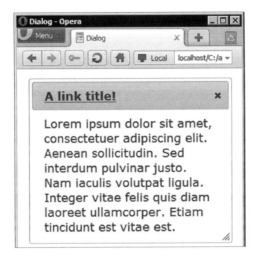

 As a cautionary note, I should advise that the system will display the default OS tooltip, and if a `title` attribute is specified on any new elements we add to the widget in this way.

Modality

One of the dialog's greatest assets is modality. This feature creates an overlay that covers the underlying page below the dialog while it is open. The overlay is removed as soon as the dialog is closed. None of the underlying page content can be interacted with in any way while the dialog is open.

The benefit of this feature is that it ensures the dialog is closed before the underlying page becomes interactive again, and gives a clear visual indicator to the visitor that the dialog must be interacted with before they can proceed.

Change the configuration object in `dialog4.html` to the following:

```
var dialogOpts = {
  modal: true
};
```

This file can be saved as `dialog5.html`. Only a single property is required when adding modality and that is the `modal` option. When you view the page in a browser, you'll see the modal effect immediately.

The repeated background image that is used to create the overlay is styled completely by the CSS framework and is therefore fully themeable through ThemeRoller. We can also use our own image if we need to. The class name `ui-widget-overlay` is added to the overlay, so this is the selector to override if customization is required.

The following screenshot shows the modal effect (I've added some fake content to the page, so that the effect of the modal can be fully appreciated):

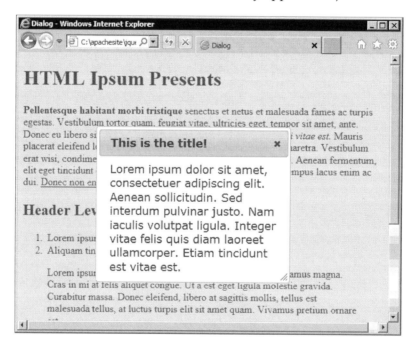

Adding buttons

The `button` option accepts an object literal that is used to specify the different `<button>` elements that should be present on the dialog. Each `property:value` pair represents a single button. Let's add a couple of `<button>` elements to our dialog. Modify the final `<script>` element in `dialog5.html` so that it appears as follows:

```
<script>
  (function($){
    var execute = function() { },
    cancel = function() { },
    dialogOpts = {
      buttons: {
        "Ok": execute,
        "Cancel": cancel
      }
    };
    $("#myDialog").dialog(dialogOpts);
  })(jQuery);
</script>
```

Save the file as `dialog6.html`. The key for each property in the `buttons` object is the text that will form the `<button>` label, and the value is the name of the callback function to execute when the button is clicked. The `buttons` option can take either an object, as in this example, or an array of objects. In this example the `execute()` and `cancel()` functions don't do anything; we'll come back to this example shortly and populate them.

The widget will add our new buttons to their own container at the foot of the dialog, and if the dialog is resized then this container will retain its original dimensions. The `<button>` elements are fully themeable and will be styled according to the theme in use. The following screenshot shows how our new `<button>` elements would appear:

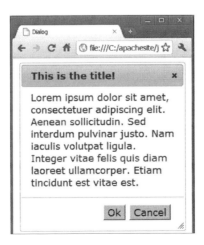

Enabling dialog animations

The dialog provides us with a built-in effect that can be applied to the opening or closing (or both) phases of the widget. There is only a single effect that we can use, which is an implementation of the scale effect (we'll look at this in more detail in *Chapter 13, Sorting*). Change the final `<script>` element in `dialog6.html` to the following:

```
<script>
  (function($){
    var dialogOpts = {
      show: true,
      hide: true
    };
    $("#myDialog").dialog(dialogOpts);
  })(jQuery);
</script>
```

Save this as `dialog7.html`. We set both the `hide` and `show` options to the Boolean value `true`. This enables the built-in effect, which gradually reduces the dialog's size and opacity until it gracefully disappears. The following screenshot shows an effect in motion:

We can enable or disable either the show or hide animations individually using Booleans, as we have in this example, or we may specify the type of animation to be used, by supplying a string specifying the name of the effect to use.

Configuring the dialog's dimensions

There are several options related to the dialog's size, and the minimum and maximum size that it can be resized to. We can add all of these options to the next example as they're all related, to save looking at them individually. Change the configuration object in `dialog7.html` to the following:

```
var dialogOpts = {
  width: 500,
  height: 300,
  minWidth: 150,
  minHeight: 150,
  maxWidth: 600,
  maxHeight: 450
};
```

Save this file as `dialog8.html`. The effect these options have on the widget is simple; the `width` and `height` options define how big the dialog is when it is first opened, while the `min-` and `max-` options define how small or large the dialog can be resized to respectively.

As an additional note, assistive technologies and keyboard users may find the content difficult to navigate if the dialog is made too small. There is a usability tenet that insists dialog boxes should always be non-resizable, whereas windows should always be resizable.

While I don't think this is a black-and-white, set in granite rule, it may be wise to keep small, informational, text-based dialogs at a fixed size, while allowing dialogs richer in content, composed of both images and text, to be resizable.

Stacking

The dialog is made, so that it appears above any of the existing page content, and even provides the `zIndex` option, in case we need to raise it slightly to cover our existing content. But what if we have two dialogs on the page? Do we need to separately define the `zIndex` for each dialog? How is focus taken into consideration?

Let's see if we can answer these questions by looking at another example; change the `<body>` of `dialog8.html`, so that it has two dialog boxes on it:

```
<div id="dialog1" title="Dialog 1">
  Lorem ipsum dolor sit amet, consectetuer adipiscing elit.
    Aenean sollicitudin. Sed interdum pulvinar justo. Nam aculis
    volutpat ligula. Integer vitae felis quis diam laoreet
    ullamcorper. Etiam tincidunt est vitae est.
```

```
    </div>
    <div id="dialog2" title="Dialog 2">
      Lorem ipsum dolor sit amet, consectetuer adipiscing elit. Aenean
        sollicitudin. Sed interdum pulvinar justo. Nam iaculis volutpat
        ligula. Integer vitae felis quis diam laoreet ullamcorper. Etiam
        tincidunt est vitae est.
    </div>
```

Now change the final `<script>` element so that it appears as follows:

```
<script>
  $(function(){
    $("#dialog1, #dialog2").dialog();  });
</script>
```

Save this file as `dialog9.html`. We've added another dialog to the page, which is basically just a clone of the original, with different `id` and `title` attributes. In the `<script>`, we simply call the widget method on both of our underlying dialog containers.

Because the widget method is called last on the second dialog, the second dialog will automatically have a higher `zIndex`, so we don't need to worry about configuring it separately. The order in which the dialogs appear in the underlying markup doesn't matter; it's the order of the widget methods that dictates each dialog's `zIndex`.

Because neither dialog has its position explicitly set, only the second dialog will be visible when our example page loads. However, both are draggable and we can align them so that they overlap slightly, by dragging the second dialog away. If we click on the first dialog box, its `zIndex` will automatically be increased to one higher than the second dialog box.

The `stack` option is set to `true` by default, so all of this behavior is automatically available with no additional configuration from us. If for some reason this behavior is not desired, then we can disable it by supplying `false` as the value of the `stack` option.

Dialog's event model

The dialog widget gives us a wide range of callback options that we can use to execute arbitrary code at different points, in any dialog interaction. The following table lists the options available to us:

Event	Fired when...
beforeclose	The dialog is about to be closed.
close	The dialog is closed.
create	The dialog is initialized.
drag	The dialog is being dragged.
dragStart	The dialog starts being dragged.
dragStop	The dialog stops being dragged.
focus	The dialog receives focus.
open	The dialog is opened.
resize	The dialog is being resized.
resizeStart	The dialog starts to be resized.
resizeStop	The dialog stops being resized.

Some of these callbacks are only available in certain situations, such as the `drag` and `resize` callbacks, which will only be available when the draggable and resizable jQuery UI components are included. We won't be looking at these callback options in this chapter, as they'll be covered in detail later in the book.

Other callbacks such as the `beforeClose`, `create`, `open`, `close`, and `focus` callbacks will be available in any implementation. Let's look at an example in which we make use of some of these callback options.

Remove the second dialog from the page in `dialog9.html`, and add the following new markup directly after the first dialog:

```
<div id="status" class="ui-widget ui-dialog ui-corner-all
  ui-widget-content">
  <div class="ui-widget-header ui-dialog-titlebar
    ui-corner-all">Dialog Status
  </div>
  <div class="ui-widget-content ui-dialog-content">
  </div>
</div>
```

Now change the final `<script>` element, so that it appears as follows:

```
<script>
  (function($){
    var dialogOpts = {
      open: function() {
        $("#status").children(":last").text("The dialog is open");
      },
```

```
        close: function() {
          $("#status").children(":last").text("The dialog is closed");
        },
        beforeclose: function() {
          if ($(".ui-dialog").css("width") > 300) {
            return false;
          }
        }
      };
      $("#dialog1").dialog(dialogOpts);
    })(jQuery);
</script>
```

Save this as `dialog10.html`. The page contains a new status box, which will be used to report whether the dialog is open or closed. We've given the elements that make up the status box of several CSS framework classes, to make them fit with the theme in use.

Our configuration object uses the `open`, `close`, and `beforeclose` options to specify simple callback functions. The `open` and `close` callbacks simply set the text of the status box accordingly. The `beforeclose` callback, which is fired after the close button on the dialog has been clicked but before it is actually closed, is used to determine whether or not to close the dialog.

We use a simple `if` statement to check the width of the dialog; if the dialog is greater than `300 px` wide, we return `false` from the callback and the dialog remains open. This kind of behavior is of course usually a big no in terms of usability, but it does serve to highlight how we can use the `beforeclose` callback to prevent the dialog being closed.

When the page loads and the dialog is shown, the `open` callback will be executed and the status box should display a message. When the dialog is closed, as shown in the following screenshot, a different message is displayed:

One thing I should make clear is that the dialog widget only passes a single object (the original event object) to the callback functions. It does pass a second `ui` object into the handler function, although in this release of the library, this object contains no properties.

Controlling a dialog programmatically

The full list of the methods we can call on a dialog is as follows:

Method	Used to...
close	Close or hide the dialog.
destroy	Permanently disable the dialog. The destroy method for a dialog works in a slightly different way than it does for the other widgets we've seen so far. Instead of just returning the underlying HTML to its original state, the dialog's destroy method also hides it.
disable	Temporarily disable the dialog.
enable	Enable the dialog if it has been disabled.
isOpen	Determine whether a dialog is open or not.
moveToTop	Move the specified dialog to the top of the stack.
open	Open the dialog.
option	Get or set any configurable option after the dialog has been initialized.
widget	Return the outer element that the dialog() widget method is called on.

Toggling the dialog

We first take a look at opening the widget, which can be achieved with the simple use of the `open` method. Let's revisit `dialog3.html`, in which the `autoOpen` option was set to `false`, so that the dialog did not open when the page was loaded. Add the following `<button>` to the page:

```
<button type="button" id="toggle">Toggle dialog!</button>
```

Then add the following click-handler directly after the dialog's widget method:

```
$("#toggle").click(function() {
  if (!$("#myDialog").dialog("isOpen")) {
    $("#myDialog").dialog("open");
  } else {
    $("#myDialog").dialog("close");
  }
});
```

Save this file as `dialog11.html`. To the page, we've added a simple `<button>` that can be used to either open or close the dialog depending on its current state. In the `<script>` element, we've added a click handler for the `<button>` that checks, the return value of the `isOpen` method. If it does not return `true`, the dialog is not open, so we call its `open` method, else we call the `close` method.

The `open` and `close` methods both trigger any applicable events; for example, the `close` method first fires the `beforeclose` and then the `close` events. Calling the `close` method is analogous to clicking the close button on the dialog.

Getting data from the dialog

Because the widget is a part of the underlying page, passing data to and from it is simple. The dialog can be treated as any other standard element on the page. Let's look at a basic example.

We looked at an example earlier in the chapter which added some `<button>` elements to the dialog. The callback functions in that example didn't do anything, but this example gives us the opportunity to use them. Replace the existing dialog markup in `dialog6.html` with the following:

```
<p>Please answer the opinion poll:
</p>
<div id="myDialog" title="Best Widget Library">
  <p>Is jQuery UI the greatest JavaScript widget library?
  </p>
  <label for="yes">Yes!
  </label>
  <input type="radio" id="yes"
    value="yes" name="question" checked="checked"><br>
  <label for="no">No!
  </label>
  <input type="radio" id="no" value="no" name="question">
</div>
```

Now change the final `<script>` element as follows:

```
<script>
  (function($){
    var execute = function(){
      var answer =  $("#myDialog").find("input:checked").val();
      $("<p>").text("Thanks for selecting " + answer).
appendTo($("body"));
      $("#myDialog").dialog("close");
    }
```

```
      var cancel = function() {
        $("#myDialog").dialog("close");
      }
      var dialogOpts = {
        buttons: {
          "Ok": execute,
          "Cancel": cancel
        }
      };
      $("#myDialog").dialog(dialogOpts);
    })(jQuery);
</script>
```

Save this as `dialog12.html`. Our dialog widget now contains a set of radio buttons, some `<label>` elements, and some text. The purpose of the example is to get the result of which radio is selected, and then do something with it, when the dialog closes.

We start the `<script>` by filling out the `execute` function that will be attached as the value of the `Ok` property in the `buttons` object, later in the script. It will therefore be executed each time the **Ok** button is clicked.

In this function, we use the :checked filter to determine which of the radio buttons is selected. We set the value of the `answer` variable to the radio button's value, and then created a short message along with appending it to the `<body>` of the page. The callback mapped to the **Cancel** button is simple; all we do is close the dialog using the `close` method.

The point of this trivial example was to see that getting data from the dialog is as simple as getting data from any other element on the page.

Dialog interoperability

In previous chapters, we've combined multiple widgets so that we can see how well they work together, and this chapter will be no exception. We can easily place other UI widgets into the dialog, such as the accordion widget that we looked at in the previous chapter. In a new file in your text editor, create the following page:

```
<!DOCTYPE html>
<html>
  <head>
    <meta charset="utf-8">
    <title>Dialog
    </title>
```

```
    <link rel="stylesheet"
      href="css/smoothness/jquery-ui-1.8.9.custom.css">
  </head>
  <body>
    <div id="myDialog" title="An Accordion Dialog">
      <div id="myAccordion">
        <h2><a href="#">Header 1</a></h2>
        <div>
          Lorem ipsum dolor sit amet, consectetuer adipiscing elit.
            Aenean sollicitudin.
        </div>
        <h2><a href="#">Header 2</a></h2>
        <div>
          Etiam tincidunt est vitae est. Ut posuere, mauris at so
            dales rutrum, turpis.
        </div>
        <h2><a href="#">Header 3</a></h2>
        <div>
          Donec at dolor ac metus pharetra aliquam. Suspendisse pu
            rus.
          </div>
        </div>
      </div>
      <script src="development-bundle/jquery-1.4.4.js">
      </script>
      <script src="development-bundle/ui/jquery.ui.core.js">
      </script>
      <script src="development-bundle/ui/jquery.ui.widget.js">
      </script>
      <script src="development-bundle/ui/jquery.ui.position.js">
      </script>
      <script src="development-bundle/ui/jquery.ui.dialog.js">
      </script>
      <script
        src="development-bundle/ui/jquery.ui.accordion.js">
    </script>
    <script src="development-bundle/ui/jquery.ui.mouse.js">
    </script>
    <script
      src="development-bundle/ui/jquery.ui.draggable.js">
      </script>
      <script
        src="development-bundle/ui/jquery.ui.resizable.js">
      </script>
```

```
    <script>
      (function($){
        $("#myDialog").dialog();
        $("#myAccordion").accordion();
      })(jQuery);
    </script>
  </body>
</html>
```

Save this file as `dialog13.html`. The underlying markup for the accordion widget is placed into the dialog's container element, and we just call each component's widget method in the `<script>`. The combined widget should appear like this:

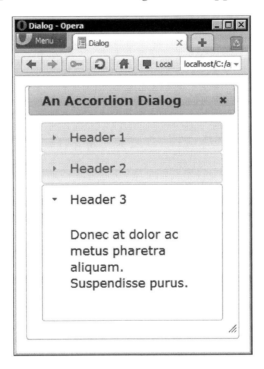

 In this example, we use quite a few separate `<script>` resources. It is worth remembering that for production use, we should use the combined and minified script file, which contains all of the components we selected in the download-builder.

Creating a dynamic image-based dialog

The class behind the dialog widget is compact and caters to a small range of specialized behavior, much of which we have already looked at. We can still have some fun with a dynamic dialog box, which loads different content depending on which element triggers it. The following image shows the kind of page we'll end up with:

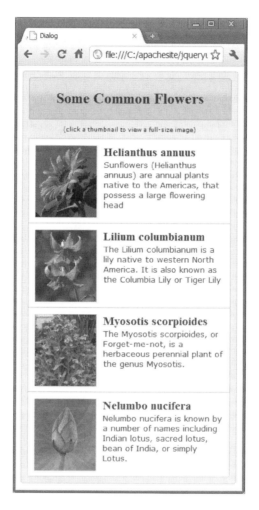

In a new page in your text editor, add the following code:

```
<!DOCTYPE html>
<html>
  <head>
    <meta charset="utf-8">
```

```
    <title>Dialog
    </title>
    <link rel="stylesheet"
      href="css/smoothness/jquery-ui-1.8.9.custom.css">
</head>
<body>
    <div id="thumbs" class="ui-corner-all">
      <div class="ui-widget-header ui-corner-top">
        <h2>Some Common Flowers
        </h2>
      </div>
      <p>(click a thumbnail to view a full-size image)
      </p>
      <div class="thumb ui-helper-clearfix ui-widget-content">
        <a href="img/haFull.jpg" title="Helianthus annuus">
          <img src="img/haThumb.jpg" alt="Helianthus annuus">
        </a>
        <h3>Helianthus annuus
        </h3>
        <p>Sunflowers (Helianthus annuus) are annual plants native to
            the Americas, that possess a large flowering head
        </p>
      </div>
      <div class="thumb ui-helper-clearfix ui-widget-content">
        <a href="img/lcFull.jpg" title="Lilium columbianum">
          <img src="img/lcThumb.jpg" alt="Lilium columbianum">
        </a>
        <h3>Lilium columbianum
        </h3>
        <p>The Lilium columbianum is a lily native to western North
            America. It is also known as the Columbia Lily or Tiger
            Lily
        </p>
      </div>
      <div class="thumb ui-helper-clearfix ui-widget-content">
        <a href="img/msFull.jpg" title="Myosotis scorpioides">
          <img src="img/msThumb.jpg" alt="Myosotis scorpioides">
        </a>
        <h3>Myosotis scorpioides
        </h3>
        <p>The Myosotis scorpioides, or Forget-me-not, is a
          herbaceous perennial plant of the genus Myosotis.
        </p>
      </div>
```

```
      <div class="thumb ui-helper-clearfix ui-widget-content last">
        <a href="img/nnFull.jpg" title="Nelumbo nucifera">
          <img src="img/nnThumb.jpg" alt="Nelumbo nucifera">
        </a>
        <h3>Nelumbo nucifera
        </h3>
        <p>Nelumbo nucifera is known by a number of names including;
          Indian lotus, sacred lotus, bean of India, or simply lotus.
        </p>
      </div>
    </div>
    <div id="ajaxDialog">
    </div>
    <script src="development-bundle/ui/jquery.ui.core.js">
    </script>
    <script src="development-bundle/ui/jquery.ui.widget.js">
    </script>
    <script src="development-bundle/ui/jquery.ui.position.js">
    </script>
    <script src="development-bundle/ui/jquery.ui.dialog.js">
    </script>
    <script
      src="development-bundle/ui/jquery.ui.accordion.js">
    </script>
    <script src="development-bundle/ui/jquery.ui.mouse.js">
    </script>
    <script src="development-bundle/ui/jquery.ui.draggable.js">
    </script>
    <script src="development-bundle/ui/jquery.ui.resizable.js">
    </script>
  </body>
</html>
```

Save this file as `dialog14.html`. The page is relatively straightforward—we've got an outer container which encloses everything and an element which we've given the class name `ui-widget-header`. We've used the latter in order to pick up some of the default styling from the theme in use.

Following this, we have some explanatory text followed by a series of containers. Several classnames are given to these containers, some of which are so that we can style them, and others (such as `ui-helper-clearfix`), in order to pick up framework or theme styles.

Within each of these containers is an image, wrapped in an anchor, a subheading, and some descriptive text. After the outer container becomes the empty, <div> element is used for the dialog. In this example, we don't use the resizable feature.

Each of the thumbnail images is wrapped in a link, in order for the page to function even with JavaScript disabled. The dialog widget won't work in this situation, but the visitor will still be able to see a full-sized version of each image. Progressive enhancement such as this is essential in this kind of application.

Now add the following <script> block directly before the closing </body> tag:

```
<script>
  (function($){
    var filename,
    titleText,
    dialogOpts = {
      modal: true,
      width: 388,
      height: 470,
      autoOpen: false,
      open: function() {
        $("#dialog").empty();
        $("<img />", {
          src: fileName
        }).appendTo("#dialog");
        $("#dialog").dialog("option", "title", titleText);
      }
    };
    $("#dialog").dialog(dialogOpts);
    $("#thumbs").find("a").click(function(e) {
      e.preventDefault();
      filename = $(this).attr("href");
      titleText = $(this).attr("title");
      $("#dialog").dialog("open");
    });
  })(jQuery);
</script>
```

The first thing we do is define three variables; the first variable is used to add the path to the full-sized image of whichever thumbnail was clicked, the second is to store the image title to use, as the text for the widget's title, and the third is the configuration object for the dialog. We've seen all of the configuration options in action already, so I won't go over most of them in much detail.

The `open` callback, called directly before the dialog is opened, is where we add the full-sized image to the dialog. We first empty the dialog, then create a new `<img>` element, and set its `src` to the value of the filename variable. The new `<img>` is then appended to the inner content area of the dialog.

We then use the `option` method to set the `title` option to the value of the `titleText` variable. Once the `open` callback has been defined, we then call the dialog's widget method as normal.

We can use the wrapper `<a>` elements as the triggers to open the dialog. Within our click-handler, we set the contents of our `filename` and `titleText` variables using the `href` and `title` attributes of the link that was clicked. We then call the dialog's `open` method to display the dialog, which in turn triggers the callback function specified in the `open` option.

We'll also need a new style sheet for this example. In a new page in your text editor, add the following code:

```
#thumbs {
  width:342px; padding:10px 0 10px 10px;
  border:1px solid #ccc; background-color:#eee;
}
#thumbs p {
  width:330px; font-family:Verdana; font-size:9px;
  text-align:center;
}
.thumb {
  width:310px; height:114px; padding:10px;
  border:1px solid #ccc; border-bottom:none;
}
.last { border-bottom:1px solid #ccc; }
.thumb img {
  border:1px solid #ccc; margin-right:10px; float:left;
  cursor:pointer;
}
.thumb h3 { margin:0; float:left; width:198px; }
#thumbs .thumb p {
  width:310px; margin:0; font-family:Verdana; font-size:13px;
  text-align:left;
}
#thumbs .ui-widget-header { width:330px; text-align:center; }
```

Many of these styles have been used in previous examples, but adding some new rules for the other page elements lets us see the dialog in real-world context. Save this as `dialogTheme.css` in the `css` folder. We also use some images in this example, which can be found in the `img` folder in the accompanying code download for this book.

This should now give us the page that we saw in the previous screenshot and when a thumbnail is clicked, the full size version of the same image will be displayed:

Summary

The dialog widget is specialized and caters to the display of a message or question in a floating panel that sits above the page content. Advanced functionality such as dragging and resizing, are directly built-in and require just the inclusion of an additional script file for each feature. Other features such as the excellent modality and overlay are easy to configure.

We started out by looking at the default implementation, which is as simple as with the other widgets we have looked at so far. We then examined the range of configurable options exposed by the dialog's API. We can make use of them to enable or disable built-in behavior such as modality, or set the dimensions of the widget. It also gives us a wide range of callbacks that allow us to hook into custom events fired by the widget during an interaction.

We then took a brief look at the built-in opening and closing effects that can be used with the dialog, before moving on to see the basic methods we can invoke, in order to make the dialog do things, such as `open` or `close`.

In the next chapter, we'll move on to look at the slider widget, which allows us to create an interactive form widget used to select from a predefined range of values.

6
The Slider Widget

The slider component allows us to implement an engaging and easy-to-use widget that our visitors should find attractive and intuitive to use. Its basic function is simple. The slider background represents a series of values that are selected by dragging the thumb along the background.

In this chapter, we will cover the following topics:

- The default slider implementation
- Custom styling for sliders
- Changing configuration options
- Creating a vertical slider
- Setting minimum, maximum, and default values
- Enabling multiple handles and ranges
- The slider's built-in event callbacks
- Slider methods

Before we roll up our sleeves and begin creating a slider, let's look at the different elements that it is made from. The following screenshot shows a typical slider widget:

It's a simple widget, as you can see, comprised of just two main elements—the slider handle, also called the thumb, and the slider background, also called the track.

Implementing a slider

Creating the default, basic slider takes no more code than any of the other widgets that we have looked at so far. The underlying HTML markup required is also minimal. Let's create a basic one now. In a new page in your text editor, add the following code:

```html
<!DOCTYPE html>
<html>
  <head>
    <meta charset="utf-8">
    <link rel="stylesheet"
      href="css/smoothness/jquery-ui-1.8.9.custom.css">
    <title>Slider
    </title>
  </head>
  <body>
    <div id="mySlider">
    </div>
    <script src="development-bundle/jquery-1.4.4.js">
    </script>
    <script src="development-bundle/ui/jquery.ui.core.js">
    </script>
    <script src="development-bundle/ui/jquery.ui.widget.js">
    </script>
    <script src="development-bundle/ui/jquery.ui.mouse.js">
    </script>
    <script src="development-bundle/ui/jquery.ui.slider.js">
    </script>
    <script>
      (function($){
        $("#mySlider").slider();
      })(jQuery);
    </script>
  </body>
</html>
```

Save this file as `slider1.html` and view it in your browser. On the page is a simple container element; this will be transformed by the widget into the slider track. In the `<script>` at the end of the `<body>`, we select this element and call the `slider` method on it. The `<a>` element that is used for the slider handle will be automatically created by the widget.

When we run this page in a browser, we should see something similar to the previous screenshot. We've used several library resources for the default implementation, including the following files:

- `jquery-ui-x.x.x.custom.css`
- `jquery-x.x.x.js`
- `jquery.ui.core.js`
- `jquery.ui.widget.js`
- `jquery.ui.mouse.js`
- `jquery.ui.slider.js`

The default behavior of a basic slider is simple but effective. The thumb can be moved horizontally along any pixel of the track on the x-axis by dragging the thumb with the mouse pointer, or using the *left/down* or *right/up* arrow keys of the keyboard. Clicking anywhere on the track with the left or right mouse button will instantly move the handle to that position.

Custom styling

Because of its simplicity, the slider widget is extremely easy to create a custom theme for. Using ThemeRoller is the recommended method of theming, but to completely change the look and feel of the widget, we can easily create our own theme file. In your text editor create the following style sheet:

```css
. background-div {
  height:50px; width:217px; padding:36px 0 0 24px;
  background:url(../img/slider_outerbg.gif) no-repeat;
}
#mySlider {
  width:184px; height:23px; border:none; position:relative;
  left:4px; top:4px;
  background:url(../img/slider_bg.gif) no-repeat;
}
#mySlider .ui-slider-handle {
  width:14px; height:30px; top:-4px;
  background:url(../img/slider_handle.gif) no-repeat;
}
```

Save this file as `sliderTheme.css` in the `css` directory. In `slider1.html`, add a link to the style sheet in the `<head>` of the page (after the jQuery UI style sheet), and wrap the underlying slider element in a new container:

```
<div class="background-div">
  <div id="mySlider">
  </div>
</div>
```

Resave the file as `slider2.html`. With a minimum of CSS and a few images (these can be found in the code download), we can easily but considerably modify the widget's appearance, as shown in the following screenshot:

Of course, this example is completely arbitrary, and was intended purely to show how to override the default theme.

Configurable options

Additional functionality, such as vertical sliders, multiple handles, and stepping can also be configured using an object literal, passed into the widget method when the slider is initialized. The options that can be used in conjunction with the slider widget are listed in the following table:

Option	Default value	Used to...
animate	false	Enable a smooth animation of the slider handle when the track is clicked.
disabled	false	Disable the widget when it is initialized.
max	100	Set the maximum value of the slider.
min	0	Set the minimum value of the slider.
orientation	auto	Set the axis along which the slider thumb is moved. This can accept the strings `vertical` or `horizontal`.

Option	Default value	Used to...
range	false	Create a style-able range element between them.
step	1	Set the distance of the step the handle will take along the track. The max value must be equally divisible by the supplied number.
value	0	Set the value of the slider thumb when the widget is initialized.
values	null	Accept an array of values. Each supplied integer will become the value of a slider handle.

Creating a vertical slider

To make a vertical slider, all we need to do is set the orientation option to vertical; the widget will do the rest for us.

In slider1.html, change the final <script> element so that it appears as follows:

```
<script>
  (function($){
    var sliderOpts = {
      orientation: "vertical"
    };
    $("#mySlider").slider(sliderOpts);
  })(jQuery);
</script>
```

Save the new file as slider3.html. We just need to set this single option to put the slider into vertical mode. When we launch the page, we see that the slider operates exactly as it did before, except that it now moves along the y-axis, as in the following screenshot:

The widget defaults to 100 px in height, if we don't provide our own CSS height rule for the slider track.

Minimum and maximum values

By default, the minimum value of the slider is 0 and the maximum value is 100, but we can change these values easily using the min and max options. Change the configuration object in slider3.html to the following:

```
var sliderOpts = {
  min: -50,
  max: 50
};
```

Save this as slider4.html. We simply specify the integers that we'd like to set as the starting and end values. Because the value option is set to 0 by default, when we run this file, the slider thumb will start in the middle of the track, half way between -50 and 50.

When the slider handle, in this example, is at the minimum value, the value method (see the *methods* section) will return -50, as we would expect.

Slider steps

The step option refers to the number and position of steps along the track that the slider's handle jumps, when moving from the minimum to the maximum positions on the track. The best way to understand how this option works is to see it in action, so change the configuration object in slider4.html to the following:

```
var sliderOpts = {
  step: 25
};
```

Save this version as slider5.html. We set the step option to 25 in this example. We haven't set the min or max options, so they will take the default values of 0 and 100 respectively. Hence, by setting step to 25, we're saying that each step along the track should be a quarter of the track's length, because 100 (the maximum) divided by 25 (the step value) is 4. The thumb will therefore take four steps along the track, from beginning to end.

The max value of the slider should be equally divisible by whatever value we set as the step option, other than that, we're free-to-use whatever value we wish. This is a useful option for confining the value selected by visitors, to one of a set of predefined values.

If we were to set the value of the step option, in this example, to 27 instead of 25, the slider would still work, but the points along the track that the handle stepped to, would not be equal.

Slider animation

The slider widget comes with a built-in animation that moves the slider handle smoothly to a new position, whenever the slider track is clicked. This animation is disabled by default, but we can easily enable it by setting the `animate` option to `true`. Change the configuration object in `slider5.html`, so that it is as follows:

```
var sliderOpts = {
   animate: true
}
```

Save this version as `slider6.html`. The difference this option makes to the overall effect of the widget is extraordinary. Instead of the slider handle just moving instantly to a new position when the track is clicked, it smoothly slides there.

If the `step` option is configured to a value other than `1`, and the `animate` option is enabled, the thumb will slide to the nearest step mark on the track. This may mean that the slider thumb moves past the point that was clicked.

Setting the slider's value

The `value` option, when set to `true` in a configuration object, determines the starting value for the slider thumb. Depending on what we want the slider to represent, the starting value of the handle may not be `0`. If we wanted to start at half-way across the track instead-of at the beginning, we could use the following configuration object:

```
var sliderOpts = {
   value: 50
}
```

Save this file as `slider7.html`. When the file is loaded in a browser, we see that the handle starts halfway along the track instead of at the beginning, exactly as it did when we set the `min` and `max` options earlier on. We can also set this option after initialization, to programmatically set a new value.

Using multiple handles

I mentioned earlier that a slider may have multiple handles; additional handles can be added using the `values` option. It accepts an array, where each item in the array is a starting point for a handle. We can specify as many items as we wish, up to the `max` value (taking `step` into account):

```
var sliderOpts = {
   values: [25, 75]
};
```

Save this variation as `slider8.html`. This is all we need to do; we don't need to supply any additional underlying markup. The widget has created both new handles for us, and as you'll see, they both function exactly as a standard single handle does. The following screenshot shows our dual-handled slider:

When a slider has two or more handles, each handle may move past the other handle(s) without issue.

The range element

When working with multiple handles, we can set the `range` option to `true`. This adds a styled range element between two handles. In `slider8.html`, change the configuration object to this:

```
var sliderOpts = {
  values: [25, 75],
  range: true
};
```

Save this page as `slider9.html`. When the page loads, we should see that a styled `<div>` element now connects our two handles, as in the following screenshot:

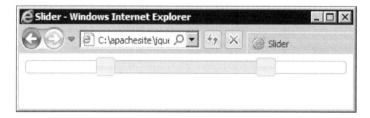

A maximum of two handles can be used in conjunction with the `range` option, but we can also enable it with a single handle as well; change the configuration object in the previous example to the following:

```
var sliderOpts = {
  range: "min"
};
```

Save this as `slider10.html`. Along with the Boolean value `true`, we can also supply one of the string values `"min"` or `"max"`, but only when a single handle is in use.

In this example, we set it to `"min"`, so when we move the slider handle along the track, the range element will stretch from the start of the track to the slider handle. If we set the option to `"max"`, the range will stretch from the handle to the end of the track.

When using two handles and a range, the two handles may not cross each other on the track.

Using slider's event API

In addition to the options we saw earlier, there are another four options used to define functions that are executed at different times during a slider interaction. Any callback functions that we use, are automatically passed by the standard event object and an object representing the slider. The following table lists the event options we can use:

Event	Fired when...
change	The slider's handle stops moving, and its value has changed.
slide	The slider's handle moves.
start	The slider's handle starts moving.
stop	The slider's handle stops moving.

Hooking into these built-in callback functions is extremely easy. Let's put a basic example together to see. Change the configuration object in `slider10.html`, so that it appears as follows:

```
var sliderOpts = {
  start: function() {
    $("#tip").fadeOut(function() {
      $(this).remove();
    });
  },
  change: function(e, ui) {
    $("<div></div>", {
      "class": "ui-widget-header ui-corner-all",
      id: "tip",
      text: ui.value + "%",
      css: {
        left: e.pageX - 35
```

```
        }
    }).appendTo("#mySlider");
    }
};
```

Save this as `slider11.html`. We use two of the callback options in this example—
`start` and `change`. In the `start` function, we select the tool tip element if it exists,
and fade it out with jQuery's `fadeOut()` method. Once hidden from view, it is
removed from the page.

The `change` function will be executed each time the value of the slider handle
changes; when the function is called, we create the tool tip and append it to the
slider. We position it so that it appears above the center of the slider handle and give
it some of the framework classnames in order to style it with the theme in use.

In several places, we use the second object passed to the callback function, the
prepared `ui` object that contains useful information from the slider. In this example,
we use the `value` option of the object to obtain the new value of the slider handle.

We also need a very small custom style sheet for this example. In a new page in your
text editor, add the following code:

```
#mySlider { margin:60px auto 0; }
#tip {
   position:absolute; display:inline; padding:5px 0;
   width:50px; text-align:center; font:bold 11px Verdana;
}
```

Save this file as `sliderTheme2.css` in the `css` folder, and link to it from the `<head>`
of `slider11.html`. When displayed, our tool tip should appear as shown in the
following screenshot:

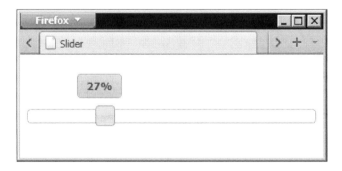

When all of the event options are used together, the events will be fired in the following order:

- `start`
- `slide`
- `stop`
- `change`

The `slide` callback can be quite an intensive event as it is fired on every mouse-move while the handle is selected, but it can also be used to prevent a slide in certain situations by returning `false` from the callback function. When using the `stop` and `change` callbacks together, the `change` callback may override the `stop` callback.

As with all library components, each of these events can also be used with jQuery's `bind()` method by prefixing the word `slider` to the event name, for example, `sliderstart`.

Slider methods

The slider is intuitive and easy-to-use, and like the other components in the library, it comes with a range of methods that are used to programmatically control the widget after it has been initialized. The methods specific to the slider are shown in the following table:

Method	Used to...
`value`	Set a single slider handle to a new value. This will move the handle to the new position on the track automatically. This method accepts a single argument which is an integer representing the new value.
`values`	Set the specified handle to move to a new value when multiple handles are in use. This method is exactly the same as the `value` method, except that it takes two arguments—the index number of the handle followed by the new value.

The methods `destroy`, `disable`, `enable`, `option`, and `widget` are common to all components, and work in the same way with slider that we would expect them to.

The `value` and `values` methods are exclusive to the slider, and are used to get or set the value of single or multiple handles. Of course, we can also do this using the `option` method, so these two methods are merely shortcuts to cater for common implementational requirements. Let's take a look at them in action. First of all, let's see how the `value` method can be used.

In `slider11.html`, remove the `<link>` to `sliderTheme2.css` and add a new `<button>` element to the page, directly after the slider container:

```
<button type="button" id="setMax">Set to max value</button>
```

Now, change the final `<script>` element so that it is as follows:

```
<script>
  (function($){
    $("#mySlider").slider();
    $("#setMax").click(function() {
      var maxVal = $("#mySlider").slider("option", "max");
      $("#mySlider").slider("value", maxVal);
    });
  })(jQuery);
</script>
```

Save this file as `slider12.html`. We add a click handler for our new `<button>`; whenever it is clicked, this method will first determine what the maximum value for the slider is, by setting a variable to the result of the `option` method, specifying `max` as the option we'd like to get. We don't need a configuration object in this example.

Once we have the maximum value, we then call the `value` method, passing in the variable that holds the maximum value as the second argument; our variable will be used as the new value. Whenever the button is clicked, the slider handle will instantly move to the end of the track.

Working with multiple handles is just as easy, but involves a slightly different approach. Remove the `setMax` button in `slider12.html`, and add these two buttons directly after the slider element:

```
<button type="button" class="preset" id="low">Preset 1 (low)
</button>
<button type="button" class="preset" id="high">Preset 2 (high)
</button>
```

Now change the final `<script>` element at the end of the `<body>` to the following:

```
<script>
  $(function(){

    var sliderOpts = {
      values: [25, 75]
    };

    $("#mySlider").slider(sliderOpts);
    $(".preset").click(function() {
```

```
        if (this.id === "low") {
          $("#mySlider").slider("values", 0, 0);
          $("#mySlider").slider("values", 1, 25);
        } else {
          $("#mySlider").slider("values", 0, 75);
          $("#mySlider").slider("values", 1, 100);
        }
      });
    });
  </script>
```

Save this file as `slider13.html`. To trigger multiple handles, we specify the values of two handles in our configuration object. When either of the two `<button>` elements on the page are clicked, we work out which button was clicked and then set the handles to either low values or high values, depending on which button was clicked.

The `values` method takes two arguments. The first argument is the index number of the handle we'd like to change, and the second argument is the value that we'd like the handle to be set to. Notice that we have to set each handle individually and that we can't chain the two methods together. This is because the method returns the new value and not a jQuery object (this is fixed in an upcoming version of the library).

The following screenshot shows how the page should appear after the second button is clicked:

Practical uses

An HTML5 element that may lend itself particularly well to implementations of the slider widget, is the `<audio>` element. This element will automatically add controls that enable the visitor to play, pause, and adjust the volume of the media being played.

The default controls, however, at this point anyway, do not appear to be style-able, so if we wish to change their appearance, we need to create our own controls. The slider widget of course, makes an excellent substitution for the default volume control.

Create the following new page in your text editor:

```
<!DOCTYPE html>
<html>
  <head>
    <link rel="stylesheet"
      href="css/smoothness/jquery-ui-1.8.9.custom.css">
    <meta charset="utf-8">
    <title>Slider
    </title>
  </head>
  <body>
    <audio id="audio"
      src="http://upload.wikimedia.org/wikipedia/
      en/7/77/Jamiroquai_-_Snooze_You_Lose.ogg">
      Your browser does not support the <code>audio</code>
        element.
    </audio>
    <div id="volume">
    </div>
    <script src="development-bundle/jquery-1.3.2.js">
    </script>
    <script src="development-bundle/ui/jquery.ui.core.js">
    </script>
    <script src="development-bundle/ui/jquery.ui.widget.js">
    </script>
    <script src="development-bundle/ui/jquery.ui.mouse.js">
    </script>
    <script src="development-bundle/ui/jquery.ui.slider.js">
    </script>
    <script>
      (function($){
        var audio = $("audio")[0],
        sliderOpts = {
          value: 5,
          min: 0,
          max: 10,
          orientation: "vertical",
          change: function() {
            var vol = $(this).slider("value") / 10;
```

```
            audio.volume = vol;
        }
    };
    audio.volume = 0.5;
    audio.play();
    $("#volume").slider(sliderOpts);
}) (jQuery);
</script>
</body>
</html>
```

Save this as `slider14.html`. On the page, we have the `<audio>` tag, which has its `src` attribute set to a copyright-free audio clip hosted on Wikipedia. We also have the empty container element for our volume control.

 This example uses a hosted OGG file as the source for the audio player. The OGG codec is supported in Firefox 3.5+, Chrome 3+, and Opera 11+.

In the script we first select the `<audio>` element using the standard jQuery syntax and retrieve the actual DOM element from the jQuery object, so that we can call methods from the `<audio>` API.

Next, we define the configuration object for our slider; we set the initial minimum and maximum values, and set the slider to `vertical`. We then add a handler for the `change` event, which is used to change the volume of the currently playing audio track, using the `volume` property and `play()` method. Whenever the value of the slider is changed, we get the new value and convert it to the required format for the `volume` option, by dividing it by `10`.

Once our variables are defined, we set the volume of the audio clip and begin playing the clip immediately with the `play()` method.

When we run this example in a supporting browser, the only thing visible on the page will be the volume slider, but we should also be able to hear the audio clip. Whenever the slider handle is moved, the volume of the clip should increase or decrease.

A color slider

A fun implementation of the slider widget, which could be very useful in certain applications, is the color slider. Let's put what we've learned about this widget into practice to produce a basic color choosing tool. The following screenshot shows the page that we'll be making:

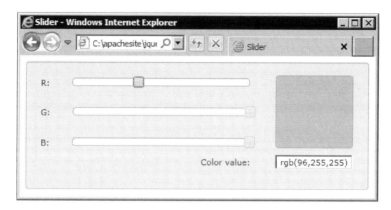

In a new file in your text editor, create the following page:

```
<!DOCTYPE html>
<html>
  <head>
    <meta charset="utf-8">
    <link rel="stylesheet"
      href="css/smoothness/jquery-ui-1.8.9.custom.css">
    <link rel="stylesheet" href="css/sliderTheme3.css">
    <title>Slider</title>
  </head>
  <body>
    <div id="container" class="ui-widget ui-corner-all ui-
      widget-content ui-helper-clearfix">
      <label>R:</label>
      <div id="rSlider"></div><br>
      <label>G:</label>
      <div id="gSlider"></div><br>
      <label>B:</label>
      <div id="bSlider"></div>
      <div id="colorBox" class="ui-corner-all ui-widget-
        content">
      </div>
      <input id="output" type="text" value="rgb(255,255,255)">
      <label for="output" id="outputLabel">Color value:</label>
```

```
    </div>
    <script src="development-bundle/jquery-1.4.4.js">
    </script>
    <script src="development-bundle/ui/jquery.ui.core.js">
    </script>
    <script src="development-bundle/ui/jquery.ui.widget.js">
    </script>
    <script src="development-bundle/ui/jquery.ui.mouse.js">
    </script>
    <script src="development-bundle/ui/jquery.ui.slider.js">
    </script>
    <script>
      $(function(){
        var sliderOpts = {
          min:0,
          max: 255,
          value: 255,
          slide: function() {
            var r = $("#rSlider").slider("value"),
            g = $("#gSlider").slider("value"),
            b = $("#bSlider").slider("value");
            var rgbString = ["rgb(", r, ",", g, ",", b, ")"]
              .join("");
            $("#colorBox").css({
              backgroundColor: rgbString
            });
            $("#output").val(rgbString);
          }
        };
        $("#rSlider, #gSlider, #bSlider").slider(sliderOpts);
      })(jQuery);
    </script>
  </body>
</html>
```

Save this as `slider15.html`. The page itself is simple enough. We've got some elements used primarily for displaying the different components of the color slider, as well as the individual container elements, which will be transformed into slider widgets. We use three sliders for our color chooser, one for each RGB channel.

We'll need some CSS as well to complete the overall appearance of our widget. In a new page in your text editor, create the following style sheet:

```css
#container {
    width:426px; height:146px; padding:20px 20px 0;
    position:relative; font-size:11px; background:#eee;
}
#container label {
    float:left; text-align:right; margin:0 30px 26px 0;
    clear:left;
}
.ui-slider { width:240px; float:left; }
.ui-slider-handle { width:15px; height:27px; }
#colorBox {
    width:104px; height:94px; float:right; margin:-83px 0 0 0;
    background:#fff;
}
#container #outputLabel {
    float:right; margin:-14px 34px 0 0;
}
#output {
    width:100px; text-align:center; float:right; clear:both;
    margin-top:-17px;
}
```

Save this as `colorSliderTheme.css` in the `css` folder.

In our script, we give various elements such as the container and color box elements, classnames from the CSS framework, so that we can take advantage of effects like the rounded corners, and so that we can cut down on the amount of CSS we need to write ourselves.

The JavaScript is as simple as the underlying markup. We first set the configuration object. As RGB color values range from 0 to 255, we set the `max` option to 255 and the `value` option to 255 as well, so that the widget handles start in the correct location (the color box will have a white background on page load).

The `slide` callback is where the action happens. Every time a handle is moved, we update each of the r, g, and b variables, by using the `value` method in `getter` mode, and then construct a new RGB string from the values of our variables. This is necessary, as we can't pass the variables directly into jQuery's `css()` method. We also update the value in the `<input>` field.

When we run the example, we should find that everything works as expected. As soon as we start moving any of the slider handles, the color box begins to change color and the <input> updates.

 The slide event is a potentially intensive event that may cause issues in older browsers or on slow computers. Care should be taken when used in a production environment.

Summary

In this chapter, we looked at the slider widget and saw how quickly and easily it can be put on the page. It requires minimal underlying markup and just a single line of code to initialize.

We looked at the different options that we can set, in order to control how the slider behaves and how it is configured once it's initialized. It can be fine-tuned to suit a range of implementations.

We also saw the rich event model that can easily be hooked into, and reacted to, with up to four separate callback functions. This allows us to execute code at important times, during an interaction.

Finally, we looked at the range of methods that can be used to programmatically interact with the slider, including methods for setting the value of the handle(s), or getting and setting configuration options after initialization.

These options and methods turn the widget into a useful and highly functional interface tool that adds an excellent level of interactivity to any page.

In the next chapter, we look at the datepicker widget, which has the biggest, most feature-packed API of any widget in the library, and includes full internationalization.

7
The Datepicker Widget

The jQuery UI datepicker widget is probably the most refined and documented widget found in the library. It has the biggest API and probably provides the most functionality out of all the widgets. It not only works completely out-of-the-box, but is also highly configurable and robust.

Quite simply, the datepicker widget provides an interface that allows visitors to your site or application to select dates. Wherever a form field is required that asks for a date to be entered, the datepicker widget can be added. This means your visitors get to use an attractive and engaging widget, and you get dates in the format in which you expect them. It's easy for everyone, and that's the attraction.

In this section, we will look at the following topics:

- The default datepicker implementation
- Exploring the configurable options
- Implementing a trigger button
- Configuring alternative animations
- The `dateFormat` option
- Easy internationalization
- Multiple month datepickers
- Date range selection
- Datepicker's methods
- Using AJAX with the datepicker

Additional functionality built into the datepicker includes automatic opening and closing animations along with the ability to navigate the interface of the widget using the keyboard. While holding down the *Ctrl* key (or Command key on the Mac), the arrows on the keyboard can be used to choose a new day cell, which can then be selected using the *Return* key.

While easy to create and configure, the datepicker is a complex widget made up of a wide range of underlying elements, as shown in the following screenshot:

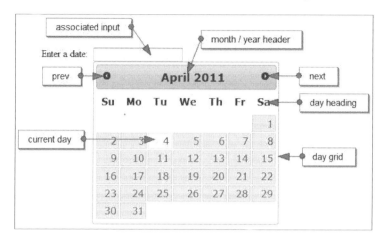

Despite this complexity, we can implement the default datepicker with just a single line of code, much like the other widgets in the library that we have covered so far.

The default datepicker

To create the default datepicker, add the following code to a new page in your text editor:

```
<!DOCTYPE html>
<html>
  <head>
    <meta charset = "utf-8">
    <link rel="stylesheet"
      href = "development-bundle/themes/smoothness/ui.all.css">
    <title>Datepicker
    </title>
  </head>
<body>
    <label for="date">Enter a date:
    </label>
    <input id="date">
    <script src="development-bundle/jquery-1.4.4.js">
    </script>
    <script src="development-bundle/ui/jquery.ui.core.js">
```

```
    </script>
    <script src="development-bundle/ui/jquery.ui.datepicker.js">
    </script>
    <script>
      (function($){
        $("#date").datepicker();
      })(jQuery);
    </script>
  </body>
</html>
```

Save this as `datePicker1.html` in the `jqueryui` project folder. All we have on the page is a `<label>` and a standard text `<input>` element. We don't need to specify any empty container elements for the datepicker widget to be rendered into. All of the markup required to create the widget is automatically added by the library.

When you run the page in your browser and focus on the `<input>` element, the default datepicker should appear below the input and will look like the screenshot at the start of the chapter. Along with an `<input>`, the datepicker can also be attached to a `<div>` element.

Apart from looking great, the default datepicker also comes with a lot of built-in functionality. When the datepicker opens, it is smoothly animated from zero to full size, and it will automatically be set to the present date. Selecting a date will automatically add the date to the `<input>` and close the calendar (again with a nice animation).

With no additional configuration and a single line of code, we now have a perfectly usable and attractive widget that makes date selection easy. If all you want is to let people pick a date, then this is all that you need. The source files required for the default datepicker are the following:

- `jquery-x.x.x.js`
- `jquery.ui.core.js`
- `jquery.ui.datepicker.js`

Configurable options of the datepicker

The datepicker has a large range of configurable options (currently 46 to be exact). The following table lists the basic options, their default values, and gives a brief description of their usage:

Option	Default value	Usage
altField	""	Specifies a CSS selector for an alternative `<input>` field to which the selected date is also added.
altFormat	""	Specifies an alternative format for the date added to the alternative `<input>`. See the `dateFormat` option in the later section for clarification on the value this option takes.
appendText	""	Adds text after the datepicker `<input>` to show the format of the selected date.
autoSize	false	Automatically sets the width of the `<input>` element so that it can accommodate a date according to the specified dateFormat.
buttonImage	""	Specifies a path to the image to use for the trigger `<button>`.
buttonImageOnly	false	Sets to `true` to use an image instead of a trigger button.
buttonText	"..."	Provides text to display on a trigger `<button>` (if present).
calculateWeek	$.datepicker. iso8601Week	Accepts a function, used to calculate the week of the year for a specified date.
changeMonth	false	Show the month change drop-down.
changeYear	false	Show the year change drop-down.
constrainInput	true	Constrains the `<input>` to the format of the date, specified by the widget.

Option	Default value	Usage
defaultDate	null	Sets the date that will be highlighted when the datepicker opens and the `<input>` is empty.
disabled	false	Disables the datepicker.
duration	"normal"	Sets the speed at which the datepicker opens.
gotoCurrent	false	Sets the current day link to move the datepicker to the currently selected date instead of today.
hideIfNoPrevNext	false	Hides the prev/next links when not needed, instead of disabling them.
maxDate	null	Sets the maximum date that can be selected. Accepts a date object or a relative number. For example: +7, or a string such as "+6m".
minDate	null	Sets the minimum date that can be selected. Accepts a number, date object, or string.
navigationAsDateFormat	false	Allows us to specify month names using the prev, next, and current links.
numberOfMonths	1	Sets the number of months shown on a single datepicker.
selectOtherMonths	false	Allows days in previous or next months that are shown on the current month's panel (see the showOtherMonths option) to be selected.
shortYearCutoff	"+10"	Determines the current century when using the y year representation; numbers less than this are deemed to be in the current century.
showAnim	"show"	Sets the animation used when the datepicker is displayed.

Option	Default value	Usage
showButtonPanel	false	Shows a panel of buttons for the datepicker, consisting of close and current links.
showCurrentAtPos	0	Sets the position of the current month in multiple-month datepickers.
showOn	"focus"	Sets the event that triggers displaying the datepicker.
showOptions	{}	It's an object literal containing options to control the configured animation.
showOtherMonths	false	Shows the last and first days of the previous and next months.
showWeek	false	Displays a column showing the week of the year. The week is determined using the calculateWeek option.
stepMonths	1	Sets how many months are navigated with the previous and next links.
yearRange	"-10:+10"	Specifies the range of years in the year drop-down.

Basic options

Change the final <script> element in datepicker1.html to the following:

```
<script>
  (function($){
    var pickerOpts = {
      appendText: "mm/dd/yy",
      defaultDate: "+5",
      showOtherMonths: true
    };
    $("#date").datepicker(pickerOpts);
  })(jQuery);
</script>
```

Save this as `datePicker2.html`. The following image shows how the widget will look after configuring these options:

We've used a number of options in this example because there are simply so many options available—the appearance of the initial page, before the datepicker is even shown, can be changed using the `appendText` option. This adds the specified text string using a `<span>` element directly after the `<input>` field, which is associated with the picker. This helps visitors to clarify the format that will be used for the date.

For styling purposes, we can target the new `<span>` element using the `.ui-datepicker-append` classname.

The `defaultDate` option sets which date is highlighted in the datepicker, when it opens initially and the `<input>` is empty. We've used the relative `"+5"` string in this example, so when the datepicker opens initially, the date five days from the current date is selected. Pressing the *Enter* key on the keyboard will select the highlighted date.

Along with a relative string, we can also supply `null` as the value of `defaultDate` to set it to the current date (today subjectively), or a standard JavaScript date object.

As we can see in the previous screenshot, the styling of the datepicker date for the current date is different from the styling used to show the default date. This will vary between themes, but for reference, the current date is shown in a light yellow color, while the default date has a darker border than normal dates with the default theme.

Once a date has been selected, subsequent openings of the datepicker will show the selected date as the default date, which again has different styling (a preselected date with the smoothness theme will be white).

By setting the `showOtherMonths` option to `true`, we've added grayed-out (non-selectable) dates from the previous and next months to the empty squares that sit at the beginning and end of the date grid, before and after the current month. These are visible in the previous screenshot and are rendered in a much lighter color than selectable dates.

Minimum and maximum dates

By default, the datepicker will go forward or backward infinitely, there are no upper or lower boundaries. If we want to restrict the selectable dates to a particular range, we can do it easily using the `minDate` and `maxDate` options. Change the configuration object in `datePicker2.html` to the following:

```
var pickerOpts = {
  minDate: new Date(),
  maxDate: "+10"
};
```

Save this as `datePicker3.html`. In this example, we supply a standard, unmodified JavaScript date object to the `minDate` option, which will set the minimum date to the current date. This will make any dates in the past un-selectable.

For the `maxDate` option, we use a relative text string of `"+10"`, which will make only the current date and the next 10 dates selectable. You can see how these options affect the appearance of the widget in the following screenshot:

The `minDate` and `maxDate` options can also take strings such as `"+6w"`, `"-10m"`, or `"1y"`, which represent weeks, months, and years respectively.

Changing the elements in the datepicker UI

The datepicker API exposes a number of options directly related to adding or removing additional UI elements within the datepicker. To show `<select>` elements that allow the visitor to choose the month and year, we can use the `changeMonth` and `changeYear` configuration options:

```
var pickerOpts = {
  changeMonth: true,
  changeYear: true
};
```

Save this as `datePicker4.html`. Using the month and year `<select>` elements, gives the user a much quicker way to navigate to dates that may be far in the past or future. The following screenshot shows how the widget will appear with these two options enabled:

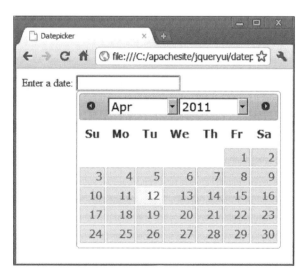

By default, the year select box will include the previous and next 10 years, covering a total range of 20 years. We can navigate further than this using the prev/next arrow links, but if we know beforehand that visitors may be choosing dates very far in the past or future, we can change the range of years using the yearRange option:

```
var pickerOpts = {
  changeMonth: true,
  changeYear: true,
  yearRange: "-25:+25"
};
```

Save this as datePicker5.html. This time when we run the page, we should find that the year range now covers 50 years in total.

Another change we can make to the UI of the datepicker is to enable the button panel, which adds two buttons to the footer of the widget. Let's see it in action. Change the configuration object in datepicker5.html, so that it appears as follows:

```
var pickerOpts = {
  showButtonPanel: true
};
```

Save this as datePicker6.html. The buttons added to the foot of the widget appear exactly as the buttons in a dialog widget, as you can see in the following screenshot:

The **Today** button will instantly navigate the datepicker back to the month showing the current date, while the **Done** button will close the widget without selecting a date. We can change the **Today** button, so that it goes to the selected date instead of the current date using the **gotoCurrent** option.

Adding a trigger button

By default, the datepicker is opened when the `<input>` element that it is associated with, receives focus. However, we can change this very easily, so the datepicker opens when a button is clicked instead. The most basic type of `<button>` can be enabled with just the `showOn` option. Change the configuration object in `datePicker6.html`, so that it is as follows:

```
var pickerOpts = {
  showOn: "button"
};
```

Save this as `datePicker7.html`. Setting the `showOn` option to `true` in our configuration object will automatically add a simple `<button>` element directly after the associated `<input>` element. We can also set this option to both, so that it opens when the `<input>` is focused as well as when the `<button>` is clicked.

The datepicker will now open only when the `<button>` is clicked, rather than when the `<input>` is focused. This option also accepts the string value both, which opens the widget when the `<input>` is focused and when the `<button>` is clicked. The new `<button>` is shown in the following screenshot:

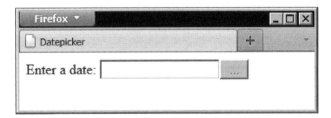

The default text shown on the `<button>` (an ellipsis) can easily be changed by providing a new string as the value of the `buttonText` option; change the previous configuration object to this:

```
var pickerOpts = {
  showOn: "button",
  buttonText: "Open Picker"
};
```

Save this as `datePicker8.html`. Now, the text on the `<button>` should match the value that we set as the `buttonText` option:

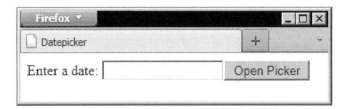

Instead of using text as the label of the `<button>` element, we can use an image. This is configured using the `buttonImage` option:

```
var pickerOpts = {
    showOn: "button",
    buttonText: "Open Picker"
    buttonImage: "img/cal.png",
};
```

Save this as `datePicker9.html`. The value of the `buttonImage` option is a string, consisting of the path to the image that we'd like to use on the button. Notice that we also set the `buttonText` option in this example too; the reason for this is that the value of the `buttonText` option is automatically used as the `title` and `alt` attributes of the `<img>` element that is added to the `<button>`. Our trigger button should now look as shown in the following screenshot:

We don't need to use a button at all if we don't want to; we can replace the `<button>` element with an `<img>` element instead. Change the configuration object in `datePicker9.html`, so that it appears as follows:

```
var pickerOpts = {
    showOn: "button",
    buttonImage: "img/date-picker/cal.png",
    buttonText: "Open Picker",
    buttonImageOnly: true
};
```

Save this as `datePicker10.html`. This should give you a nice image-only button, as illustrated in the following screenshot:

Configuring alternative animations

The datepicker widget comes with an attractive built-in opening animation that makes the widget appear to grow from nothing to full size. Its flexible API also exposes several options related to animations. These are the `duration`, `showAnim`, and `showOptions` configuration options.

The simplest animation configuration that we can set is the speed at which the widget opens and closes. To do this, all we have to do is change the value of the `duration` option. This option requires a simple string that can take a string value of either `slow`, `normal` (the default), or `fast`, or a number representing a duration in milliseconds.

Change the configuration object in `datePicker10.html` to the following:

```
var pickerOpts = {
   duration: "fast"
};
```

Save this variation as `datePicker11.html`. When we run this page in a browser, we should find that the opening animation is visibly faster.

Along with changing the speed of the animation, we can also change the animation itself using the `showAnim` option. The default animation used is a simple show animation, but we can change this so that it uses any of the other show/hide effects included with the library (refer to *Chapter 13, Sorting*). Change the configuration object from the previous example to the following:

```
var pickerOpts = {
   showAnim: "drop",
   showOptions: {direction: "up"}
};
```

Save this as `datePicker12.html`. We also need to use two new `<script>` resources to use alternative effects. These are the `jquery.effects.core.js` and the source file of the effect we wish to use, in this example, `jquery.effects.drop.js`. We'll look at both of these effects in more detail in *Chapter 14, UI Effects*, but they are essential for this example to work. Make sure you add these to the file, directly after the source file for the datepicker:

```
<script src="development-bundle/ui/jquery.ui.datepicker.js">
</script>
<script src="development-bundle/ui/jquery.effects.core.js">
</script>
<script src="development-bundle/ui/jquery.effects.drop.js">
</script>
```

Our simple configuration object configures the animation to drop, using the `showAnim` option, and sets the `direction` option of the effect using `showOptions`, which is required due to the datepicker's absolute positioning. When you now run this example, the datepicker should drop-down into position instead of opening. Other effects can be implemented in the same way.

Multiple months

So far, all of our examples have looked at single-month datepickers, where only one month was shown at a time. However, we can easily adjust this to show a different number of months, if we wish using a couple of configuration options. Remove the effect source files before the configuration object in `datePicker12.html`, and change the configuration object so that it appears as follows:

```
var pickerOpts = {
  numberOfMonths: 3

};
```

Save this as `datePicker13.html`. The `numberOfMonths` option takes an integer representing the number of months that we would like to be displayed in the widget at any point. Our datepicker should now appear like this:

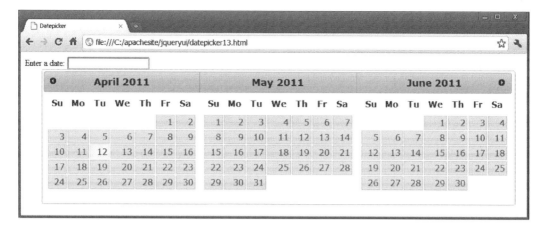

 There is no upper limit to the number of months that will be displayed; however, the performance of the widget decreases with each additional month shown. There is also a noticeable lag between focusing the `<input>` and the widget being displayed.

Also, the individual month panels are floated side-by-side, and due to their size, they will soon overflow the viewport causing a horizontal scrollbar to appear. However, as-soon-as the scrollbar is used, the datepicker will close, making any months that go beyond the boundary of the screen unusable. For these reasons, it's best to keep the number of months displayed to a minimum.

There are several other configuration options related to multiple-month datepickers. The `stepMonths` option controls how many months are changed when the previous or next links are used.

The defau lt value of `stepMonths` is 1, so in our previous example, the widget starts with the current month displayed first and the next two months after it. Each time the `Previous` or **Next** icons are clicked, the panels move one space left or right.

If we set `stepMonths` to 3, the same as the number of months shown, each month will move three spaces left or right when the previous or next links are clicked, so entirely new panels are shown on each click.

The `showCurrentAtPos` option specifies where the current month is shown when the datepicker is displayed. In our previous example, the current month is shown as the first month panel. Each month panel has a zero-based index number, so if we want the current month to be in the middle of the widget, then we would set this option to 1 instead.

Changing the date format

The dateFormat option is one of the localization options at our disposal for advanced datepicker locale configuration. Setting this option allows you to quickly and easily set the format of selected dates (as displayed in the <input>), using a variety of short-hand references. The format of dates can be a combination of any of the following characters (they are case-sensitive):

- d: day of month (single digit where applicable)
- dd: day of month (two digits)
- m: month of year (single digit where applicable)
- mm: month of year (two digits)
- y: year (two digits)
- yy: year (four digits)
- D: short day name
- DD: full day name
- M: short month name
- MM: long month name
- '...': any literal text string
- @: UNIX timestamp (milliseconds since 01/01/1970)

We can use these shorthand codes to quickly configure our preferred date format, as in the following example. Change the configuration object in datePicker13.html to the following:

```
var pickerOpts = {
    dateFormat:"d MM yy"
};
```

Save the new file as datePicker14.html. We use the dateFormat option to specify a string containing the shorthand date code for our preferred date format. The format we set is the day of the month (using a single digit if possible) with d, the full name of the month with MM, and the full four-digit year with yy.

When dates are selected and added to the associated <input>, they will be in the format specified in the configuration object, as in the following screenshot:

Note that dates returned programmatically through the `getDate` method (see *Datepicking methods* section) are in the default GMT date-and-time standard. In order to change the format of the date returned by the API, the `$.datepicker.formatDate()` utility method should be used.

When using a string as the value of this option to configure dates, we can also specify whole strings of text. However, if we do and any letters in the string are those used as shorthand, they will need to be escaped using single quotes.

For example, to add the string `Selected:` to the start of the date, we would need to use the string `Selecte'd':` to avoid having the lowercase d picked up as the short day of month format:

```
var pickerOpts = {
    dateFormat:"Selecte'd': d MM yy"
};
```

Save this change as `datePicker15.html`. Notice how we escape the lowercase d in the string `Selected` by wrapping it in single quotes. Now when a date is selected, our text string is prefixed to the formatted date:

There are also a number of built-in preconfigured date formats that correspond to common standards or RFC notes. These formats are added to the components as constants and can be accessed via the `$.datepicker` object. As an example, let's format the date according to the ATOM standard:

```
var pickerOpts = {
    dateFormat: $.datepicker.ATOM
};
```

Save this as `datePicker16.html`. When a date is selected in this example, the value entered into the `<input>` should be in the format as shown in the following screenshot:

The complete set of predefined date formats is listed in the following table:

Option value	Short-hand	Formatted as...
`$.datepicker.ATOM`	`"yy-mm-dd"`	`2011-04-13`
`$.datepicker.COOKIE`	`"D, dd M y"`	`Wed, 13 Apr 2011`
`$.datepicker.ISO_8601`	`"yy-mm-dd"`	`2011-04-13`
`$.datepicker.RFC_822`	`"D, d M y"`	`Wed, 13 Apr 11`
`$.datepicker.RFC_850`	`"DD, dd-M-y"`	`Wednesday, 13-Apr-11`
`$.datepicker.RFC_1036`	`"D, d M y"`	`Wed, 13 Apr 11`
`$.datepicker.RFC_1123`	`"D, d M yy"`	`Wed, 13 Apr 2011`
`$.datepicker.RFC_2822`	`"D, d M yy"`	`Wed, 13 Apr 2011`
`$.datepicker.RSS`	`"D, d M y"`	`Wed, 13 Apr 11`
`$.datepicker.TIMESTAMP`	`@ (UNIX timestamp)`	`1302649200000`
`$.datepicker.W3C`	`"yy-mm-dd"`	`2011-04-13`

Updating an additional input element

There may be times when we want to update two `<input>` elements with the selected date, perhaps to show a different date format. The `altField` and `altFormat` options can be used to cater to this requirement. Add a second `<input>` element to the page in `date-Picker16.html` with an `id` attribute of `alt`, and then change the configuration object to the following:

```
var pickerOpts = {
  altField: "#alt",
  altFormat: $.datepicker.TIMESTAMP
};
```

Save this as `datePicker17.html`. The `altField` option accepts a standard jQuery selector as its value, and allows us to select the additional `<input>` element that is updated when the main `<input>` is updated. The `altFormat` option can accept the same formats as the `dateFormat` option. The following screenshot shows how the page should appear, once a date has been selected using the datepicker:

Localization

In addition to the options already listed, there are also a range of regionalization options. They can be used easily to provide custom locale support in order to easily display a datepicker with all the text shown in an alternative language, or to change the default values of words in English.

Those options that are used specifically for localization are listed in the following table:

Option	Default	Usage
closeText	"Close"	Text to display on the close button.
currentText	"Current"	Text to display on the current link.
dateFormat	"mm/dd/yy"	The format selected dates should take when added to the `<input>`.
dayNames	["Sunday", "Monday", "Tuesday", "Wednesday", "Thursday", "Friday", "Saturday"]	An array of names of days in a week.
dayNamesMin	["Su", "Mo", "Tu", "We", "Th", "Fr", "Sa"]	An array of two-letter names of days in a week.

Option	Default	Usage
dayNamesShort	["Sun", "Mon", "Tue", "Wed", "Thu", "Fri", "Sat"]	An array of abbreviated names of days in a week.
firstDay		Specify the first column of days in the datepicker.
isRTL	false	Set the calendar to right-to-left format.
monthNames	["January", "Febru-ary", "March", "April", "May", "June", "July, "August", "September", "October", "November", "December"]	An array of month names.
monthNamesShort	["Jan", "Feb", "Mar", "Apr", "May", "Jun", "Jul", "Aug", "Sep", "Oct", "Nov", "Dec"]	An array of abbreviated month names.
nextText	"Next"	Text to display on the next link.
prevText	"Prev"	Text to display on the prev link.
showMonthAfterYear	false	Shows the month after the year in the header of the widget.
yearSuffix	""	An additional text string to display after the year in the month header.

A wide range of different translations have already been provided and reside within the i18n folder in the development-bundle/ui directory. Each language translation has its own source file and to change the default language, all we have to do is include the source file of the alternative language.

In datePicker1.html, add the following new <script> element directly after the link to jquery.ui.datepicker.js:

```
<script
  src="development-bundle/ui/i18n/jquery.ui.datepicker-fr.js">
</script>
```

Save this as `datePicker18.html` and view the results in a browser:

With just a single link to one new resource, we've changed all of the visible text in the datepicker to an alternative language, and we don't even need to set any configuration options. If we wanted to truly internationalize the datepicker, there is even a roll-up file containing all of the alternative languages, which we can link to.

Custom localization is also very easy to implement. This can be done using a standard configuration object containing the configured values for the options from the previous table. In this way, any alternative language, not included in the roll-up file can be implemented.

For example, to implement a Lolcat datepicker, change the configuration object of `datePicker6.html` to the following:

```
var pickerOpts = {
    closeText: "Kthxbai",
    currentText: "Todai",
    nextText: "Fwd",
    prevText: "Bak",
    monthNames: ["January", "February", "March", "April", "Mai", "Jun",
        "July", "August", "Septembr", "Octobr", "Novembr", "Decembr"],
    monthNamesShort: ["Jan", "Feb", "Mar", "Apr", "Mai", "Jun", "Jul",
        "Aug", "Sep", "Oct", "Nov", "Dec"],
    dayNames: ["Sundai", "Mondai", "Tuesdai", "Wednesdai", "Thursdai",
        "Fridai", "Katurdai"],
    dayNamesShort: ["Sun", "Mon", "Tue", "Wed", "Thu", "Fri", "Kat"],
```

```
    dayNamesMin: ["Su", "Mo", "Tu", "We", "Th", "Fr", "Ka"],
    dateFormat: 'dd/mm/yy',
    firstDay: 1,
    isRTL: false,
    showButtonPanel: true
};
```

Save this change as `datePicker19.html`. Most of the options are used to provide simple string substitutions. However, the `monthNames`, `monthNamesShort`, `dayNames`, `dayNamesShort`, and `dayNamesMin` options require arrays.

Note that the `dayNamesMin` and other day-related arrays should begin with `Sunday` (or the localized equivalent). We've set `Monday` to appear first in this example using the `firstDay` option. Our datepicker should now appear like this:

Callback properties

The final set of configuration options are related to the event model exposed by the widget. It consists of a series of callback functions that we can use to specify the code to be executed at different points during an interaction with the datepicker. These are listed in the following table:

Event	Fired when...
beforeShow	The datepicker is about to open.
beforeShowDay	Each individual date is rendered in the datepicker. Can be used to determine whether the date should be selectable or not.

Event	Fired when...
onChangeMonthYear	The current month or year changes.
onClose	The datepicker is closed.
onSelect	A date is selected.

To highlight how useful these callback properties are, we can extend the previous internationalization example to create a page that allows visitors to choose any available language found in the i18n roll-up file.

When using the roll-up file, the language displayed by the datepicker will be whichever language happens to appear last in the source file, which at the time of writing is Taiwanese. We can change this by setting the regional utility of the datepicker.

In datePicker19.html, add the following new <select> box to the page with the following <option> elements:

```
<select id="language">
  <option id="en-GB">English</option>
  <option id="ar">Arabic</option>
  <option id="ar-DZ">Algerian Arabic</option>
  <option id="az">Azerbaijani</option>
  <option id="bg">Bulgarian</option>
  <option id="bs">Bosnian</option>
  <option id="ca">Catalan</option>
  <option id="cs">Czech</option>
  <option id="da">Danish</option>
  <option id="de">German</option>
  <option id="el">Greek</option>
  <option id="en-AU">English/Australia</option>
  <option id="en-NZ">English/New Zealand</option>
  <option id="en-US">English/United States</option>
  <option id="eo">Esperanto</option>
  <option id="es">Spanish</option>
  <option id="et">Estonian</option>
  <option id="eu">Euskarako</option>
  <option id="fa">Farsi</option>
  <option id="fi">Finnish</option>
  <option id="fo">Faroese</option>
  <option id="fr">French</option>
  <option id="fr-CH">Swiss-French</option>
  <option id="gl">Galician</option>
  <option id="he">Hebrew</option>
  <option id="hr">Croatian</option>
```

```
    <option id="hu">Hungarian</option>
    <option id="hy">Armenian</option>
    <option id="id">Indonesian</option>
    <option id="is">Icelandic</option>
    <option id="it">Italian</option>
    <option id="ja">Japanese</option>
    <option id="ko">Korean</option>
    <option id="kz">Kazakh</option>
    <option id="lt">Lithuanian</option>
    <option id="lv">Latvian</option>
    <option id="ml">Malayalam</option>
    <option id="ms">Malaysian</option>
    <option id="nl">Dutch</option>
    <option id="no">Norwegian</option>
    <option id="pl">Polish</option>
    <option id="pt-BR">Brazillian</option>
    <option id="pt">Portuguese</option>
    <option id="rm">Romansh</option>
    <option id="ro">Romanian</option>
    <option id="ru">Russian</option>
    <option id="sk">Slovakian</option>
    <option id="sl">Slovenian</option>
    <option id="sq">Albanian</option>
    <option id="sr-SR">Serbian</option>
    <option id="sv">Swedish</option>
    <option id="ta">Tamil</option>
    <option id="th">Thai</option>
    <option id="tr">Turkish</option>
    <option id="uk">Ukrainian</option>
    <option id="vi">Vietnamese</option>
    <option id="zh-CN">Chinese</option>
    <option id="zh-HK">Chinese</option>
    <option id="zh-TW">Taiwanese</option>
</select>
```

Next link to the i18n.js roll-up file as follows:

```
<script src="development-bundle/ui/i18n/jquery-ui-i18n.js">
</script>
```

Now change the final `<script>` element so that it appears as follows:

```
<script>
  (function($){
    var pickerOpts = {
      beforeShow: function() {
        var lang = $(":selected", $("#language")).attr("id");
        $.datepicker.setDefaults($.datepicker.regional[lang]);
      }
    };
    $("#date").datepicker(pickerOpts);
    $.datepicker.setDefaults($.datepicker.regional['']);
  })(jQuery);
</script>
```

Save this file as `datePicker20.html`. We use the `beforeShow` callback to specify a function that is executed each time the datepicker is displayed on the screen. Within this function, we obtain the `id` attribute of the selected `<option>` element and then pass this to the `$.datepicker.regional` option. This option is set using the `$.datepicker.setDefaults()` utility method.

When the page first loads, the `<select>` element won't have a selected `<option>` child, and because of the order of the i18n roll-up file, the datepicker will be set to Taiwanese. In order to set it to default English, we can set the regional utility to an empty string after the datepicker has been initialized.

The following screenshot shows the datepicker after an alternative language has been selected in the `<select>` element:

Utility methods

We used one of the utility methods available in a datepicker in the previous example—setDefaults is used to set configuration options on all datepicker instances. In addition to this, there are several other utility methods that we can use; these are shown in the following table:

Utility	Used to...
formatDate	Transform a date object into a string in a specified format. When using the dateFormat option, dates are returned in this specified format using the formatDate method. This method accepts three arguments—the format to convert the date to (see dateFormat in configurable options of the picker), the date object to convert, and an optional configuration object containing additional settings. The following options can be provided: dayNamesShort dayNames monthNamesShort monthNames
iso8601Week	Return the week number that a specified date falls on according to the ISO 8601 date-and-time standard. This method accepts a single argument—the date to show the week number.
noWeekends	Make weekend dates unselectable. It can be passed to the beforeShowDay event.
parseDate	Do the opposite of formatDate, converting a formatted date string into a date object. It also accepts three arguments—the expected format of the date to parse, the date string to parse, and an optional settings object containing the following options: shortYearCutoff dayNamesShort dayNames monthNamesShort monthNames
regional	Set the language of the datepicker.
setDefaults	Set configuration options on all datepickers. This method accepts an object literal containing the new configuration options.

All of these methods are called on the singleton instance of the $.datepicker manager object, which is created automatically by the widget on initialization and used to interact with instances of the datepicker.

Date picking methods

Along with the wide range of configuration options at our disposal, there are also a number of useful methods defined that make working with the datepicker a breeze. The datepicker API exposes the following unique methods:

Method	Used to...
dialog	Open the datepicker in a dialog widget.
getDate	Get the currently selected date.
hide	Programmatically close a datepicker.
isDisabled	Determine whether a datepicker is disabled.
refresh	Redraw the datepicker.
setDate	Programmatically select a date.
show	Programmatically show a datepicker.

The widget can also use the shared API methods discussed in *Chapter 1, Introducing jQuery UI*: destroy, disable, enable, option, and widget.

Selecting a date programmatically

There may be times when we want to be able to set a particular date from within our program logic, without the visitor using the datepicker widget in the usual way. Let's look at a basic example.

Remove the <select> element in datePicker20.html and directly after the <input> element add the following <button>:

```
<button id="select">Select +7 Days</button>
```

Now change the final <script> element so that it appears like this:

```
<script>
  (function($){
    $("#date").datepicker();
      $("#select").click(function() {
      $("#date").datepicker("setDate", "+7");
    });
  })(jQuery);
</script>
```

Save this as `datePicker21.html`. The `setDate` function accepts a single argument, which is the date to set. Like with the `defaultDate` configuration option, we can supply a relative string (as we do in this example), or a date object.

Showing the datepicker in a dialog box

The `dialog` method produces the same highly usable and effective datepicker widget, but it displays it in a floating dialog box. The method is easy to use, but makes some aspects of using the widget non-autonomous, as we shall see.

Remove the `<button>` from the page and change the final `<script>` element in `datePicker21.html` to the following:

```
<script>
  (function($){
    function updateDate(date) {
      $("#date").val(date);
    }
    $("#date").focus(function() {
      $(this).datepicker("dialog", null, updateDate);
    });
  })(jQuery);
</script>
```

Save this as `datePicker22.html`. First we define a function called `updateDate`. This function will be called whenever a date is selected in the datepicker. All we do within this function is assign the date that is selected, which will be passed to the function automatically, to our `<input>` element on the page.

We use the `focus` event to call the `dialog` method, which takes two arguments. In this example, we've supplied `null` as the first argument, so the datepicker defaults to the current date.

The second argument is a callback function to execute when a date is selected, which is mapped to our `updateDate` function.

We can also supply additional third and fourth arguments; the third is the configuration object for the datepicker, the fourth is used to control the position of the dialog containing the datepicker. By default, it will render the dialog in the centre of the screen.

An AJAX datepicker

For our final datepicker example, we'll work a little AJAX magic into the mix and create a datepicker, which will communicate with a server to see if there are any dates that cannot be selected.

Change the `<body>` of `datepicker22.html`, so that it contains the following mark-up:

```html
<div id="bookingForm" class="ui-widget ui-corner-all">
  <div class="ui-widget-header ui-corner-top">
    <h2>Booking Form</h2>
  </div>
  <div class="ui-widget-content ui-corner-bottom">
    <label>Appointment date:</label><input id="date">
  </div>
<div>
```

Save this as `datepicker23.html`. Our simple example form is made from a series of container elements and a simple `<input>`. Each of the containers has classnames from the CSS framework, which allow us to take advantage of the styling offered by the theme in use, helping the elements and the widget to appear consistent.

Now we can add the script that will configure and control the widget; this should go directly before the `</body>` tag:

```html
<script>
  (function($){
    var months = [],
    days = [];
    $.getJSON(
      "http://www.danwellman.co.uk/bookedDates.php?jsoncallback=?",
function(data) {
        for (var x = 0; x < data.dates.length; x++) {
          months.push(data.dates[x].month);
          days.push(data.dates[x].day);
        }
      }
    );
    function addDates(date){
      if (date.getDay() == 0 || date.getDay() == 6) {
        return [false, ""];
      }
      for (var x = 0; x < days.length; x++) {
        if (date.getMonth() == months[x] - 1 &&
          date.getDate() == days[x]) {
            return [false, "preBooked_class"];
```

```
        }
      }
      return [true, ""];
    }
    var pickerOpts = {
      beforeShowDay: addDates,
      minDate: "+1"
    };
    $("#date").datepicker(pickerOpts);
  })(jQuery);
</script>
```

The first part of our script initially declares two empty arrays, and then performs an AJAX request to obtain the JSON object from a PHP file. The JSON object contains a single option called `dates`. The value of this option is an array, where each item is also an object.

Each of these sub-objects contain `month` and `day` properties, representing one date that should be made unselectable. The `months` or `days` array are populated with the values from the JSON object for use later in the script.

Next, we define the `addDates` callback function that is invoked on the `beforeShowDay` event. This event occurs once for each of the 35 individual day squares in the datepicker. Even the empty squares.

This function has passed the date of the current day square and must return an array containing up to two items. The first is a Boolean indicating whether the day is selectable, and the second is optionally a classname to give the date.

Our function first checks to see whether the day portion of the current date is equal to either `0` (for Sunday) or `6` (for Saturday). If it is, we return `false` as the first item in the array to make weekends unselectable.

 There is a built-in function of the manager object, `$.datepicker.noWeekends()` that automatically makes weekends unselectable. This is specified as the value of the `beforeShowDay` option when used, but we cannot use it in this example as we are providing our own callback function.

We then loop through each item in our `months` and `days` arrays to see if any of the dates passed to the callback function match the items in the arrays. If both the `month` and `day` items match a date, then the array returns with `false` and a custom classname as its items. If the date does not match, we return an array containing `true` to indicate that the day is selectable. This allows us to specify any number of dates that cannot be selected in the datepicker.

Finally we define a configuration object for the datepicker. The properties of the object are simply the callback function to make the dates specified in the JSON object unselectable, and the `minDate` option, which will be set to the relative value `+1`, as we don't want people to select dates in the past, or on the current day.

In addition to the HTML page, we'll also need a little custom styling. In a new page in your editor, create the following style sheet:

```css
#bookingForm { width:503px; }
#bookingForm h2 { margin-left:20px; }
#bookingForm .ui-widget-content {
  padding:20px 0; border-top:none;
}
label {
  margin:4px 20px 0; font-family:Verdana; font-size:80%;
  float:left;
}
#date { width:302px; }
.ui-datepicker .preBooked_class { background:none; }
.ui-datepicker .preBooked_class span {
  color:#ffffff;
  background:url(../img/date-picker/red_horizon.gif) no-repeat;
}
```

Save this as `datepickerTheme.css` in the `css` folder. We use PHP to provide the JSON object in response to the AJAX request made by our page. If you don't want to install and configure PHP on your web server, you can use the file that I have placed at the URL specified in the example. For anyone that is interested, the PHP used is as follows:

```php
<?php
  header('Content-type: application/json');
  $dates = "({
    'dates':[
      {'month':12,'day':2},
      {'month':12,'day':3},
      etc
    ]
  })";
  $response = $_GET["jsoncallback"] . $dates;
  echo $response;
?>
```

This can be saved as `bookedDates.php` in the main `jqueryui` project folder. The pre-booked dates are just hardcoded into the PHP file. Again, in a proper implementation, you'd probably need a more robust way of storing these dates, such as in a database.

When we run the page in a browser and open the datepicker, the dates specified by the PHP file should be styled according to our `preBooked_class`, and should also be completely non-responsive, as shown in the following screenshot:

Summary

We looked at the datepicker widget in this chapter that is supported by one of the biggest APIs in the jQuery UI library. This gives us a huge number of options to work with and methods to receive data from. We first looked at the default implementation and how much behavior is added to the widget automatically.

We looked at the rich API exposed by the datepicker, which includes more configurable options than any other component. We also saw how we can use the utility functions that are unique to the datepicker manager object.

We saw how easy the widget makes implementing internationalization. We also saw that there are 34 additional languages the widget has been translated into. Each of these are packed into a module that is easy to use in conjunction with the datepicker for adding support for alternative languages. We also saw how we create our own custom language configuration.

We covered some of the events that are fired during a datepicker interaction, and looked at the range of methods available for working with and controlling the datepicker from our code.

In the next chapter, we'll take a look at the progressbar widget, which allows us to show a determinate progress bar indicating the time remaining for a given process.

8

The Progressbar Widget

The progressbar widget is used to show the percentage complete for any arbitrary process. It's a simple and easy-to-use component with an extremely compact API, which provides excellent visual feedback to visitors.

We'll look at the following aspects of the widget during this chapter:

- The default implementation
- The configurable options
- The event API exposed by the widget
- The single unique method exposed by the progressbar
- Some real-world examples

In the current version of the component, the progressbar is purely determinate, so we or the system must explicitly tell the widget the current amount of progress. An indeterminate progressbar is planned for a future release.

The widget is made up of just two nested `<div>` elements—an outer container `<div>`, and an inner `<div>`, which is used to highlight the current progress. The following screenshot shows a progressbar that is 50 percent complete:

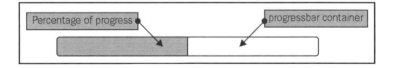

The default progressbar implementation

Let's take a look at the most basic progressbar implementation. In a new file in your text editor, create the following file:

```html
<!DOCTYPE html>
<html>
  <head>
    <meta charset="utf-8">
    <title>Progressbar
    </title>
    <link rel="stylesheet"
      href="css/smoothness/jquery-ui-1.8.9.custom.css">
  </head>
  <body>
    <div id="myProgressbar">
    </div>
    <script src="development-bundle/jquery-1.4.4.js">
    </script>
    <script src="development-bundle/ui/jquery.ui.core.js">
    </script>
    <script src="development-bundle/ui/jquery.ui.widget.js">
    </script>
    <script
      src="development-bundle/ui/jquery.ui.progressbar.js">
    </script>
    <script>
      (function($){
        $("#myProgressbar").progressbar();
      })(jQuery);
    </script>
  </body>
</html>
```

Save this as `progressbar1.html` in the `jqueryui` project folder. With no configuration, the progressbar is of course empty. Our example should appear like the first screenshot, but without any progress displayed (the container is empty).

The progress bar depends on the following components:

- `jquery-ui-x.x.x.custom.css`
- `jquery-x.x.x.js`
- `jquery-ui.core.js`
- `jquery-ui.progressbar.js`

All we need on the page is a simple container element. In this case, we've used a `<div>` element, but other block-level elements, such as a `<p>`, for example, can also be used. The widget will add a nested `<div>` element to the specified container element at initialization, which represents the value of the progressbar.

This widget, like some of the other widgets, such as the accordion, will naturally fill the width of its container. Both the container and the inner `<div>` are given a series of attributes and classnames by the component. The classnames pick up styling from the theme file in use, and the component is fully ThemeRoller-ready.

The additional attributes added to the widget are ARIA-compliant, making the widget fully accessible to visitors using assisted technologies.

Progressbar's configuration options

The progressbar has just two configuration options at the time of writing:

Option	Default Value	Used to...
disabled	false	Disable the widget
Value	0	Set the value (in percent) of the widget

Setting progressbar's value

Change the final `<script>` element in `progressbar1.html`, so that it appears as follows:

```
<script>
  (function($) {
    var progressOpts = {
      value: 50
    };
    $("#progress").progressbar(progressOpts);
  })(jQuery);
</script>
```

Save this as `progressbar2.html`. The `value` option takes an integer and sets the width of the inner `<div>` of the widget to the corresponding percentage. This change will make the widget appear as it did in the first screenshot of this chapter, with the progressbar half-filled.

Progressbar's event API

The progressbar exposes three custom events:

Event	Fired when...
create	The widget is initialized
change	The widget's value changes
complete	The value of the widget reaches 100 percent

As with the other widgets, we can supply an anonymous callback function as the value of these events in a configuration object, and the component will automatically call the function for us, each time the event fires.

To see this event in action, add the following <button> to the page in progressbar2.html:

```
<button id="increase">Increase by 10%</button>
```

Next, change the final <script> block to the following:

```
<script>
  (function($) {
    var progress = $("#myProgressbar"),
    progressOpts = {
      change: function() {
        var val = $(this).progressbar("option", "value");
        if (!$("#value").length) {
          $("<span />", {
            text: val + "%",
            id: "value",
            css: {
              float: "right",
              marginTop: -28,
              marginRight: 10
            }
          }).appendTo(""progress);
        } else {
          $("#value").text(val + "%");
        }
      }
    };
    progress.progressbar(progressOpts);
    $("#increase").click(function() {
      var currentVal = progress.progressbar("option", "value"),
```

```
        newVal = currentVal + 10;
        progress.progressbar("option", "value", newVal);
      });
    });
</script>
```

Save this file as `progressbar3.html`. We first cache the selector for the progressbar, then define an event handler for the `change` event. Within this callback function, we first obtain the current value of the progressbar, which will correspond to the value after its last update. We can select the progressbar using `$(this)`, when inside the event handler.

Provided the value is less than or equal to 100 (percent), we check whether there is already an element with an `id` of `value` on the page. If there isn't, we create a new `<span>` element and set its text to the current value. We also give it an `id` attribute and position it, so that it appears inside the progressbar. If the element already exists, we just update its text to the new value.

We also add a click-handler for the button that we added to the page. Whenever the button is clicked, we first get the current value of the progressbar by using the `option` method in `getter` mode. We then add `10` to the value, before using the `option` method in `setter` mode to increase the value of the inner `<div>` by `10` percent. The value is added to a `<span>` element to indicate the progress.

The following screenshot shows the result of clicking the button:

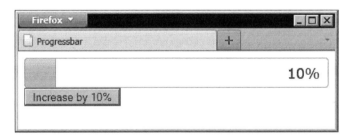

In this example, we set the value of the progressbar manually whenever the button is clicked; we use the standard `option` method, common to all UI library components, to retrieve information about the current state of the progressbar.

Don't forget that like the other library components, this event can be used with jQuery's `bind()` method by prefixing the name of the widget onto the event name, for example, `progressbarchange`.

Progressbar methods

In addition to the common API methods that are exposed by all library components, such as destroy, disable, enable, and option, the slider API also exposes the value method, which is a short-cut for using the option method to set the value of the progressbar.

We can do exactly the same as we did in the last example, but with less code, using the value method. Change the final <script> element in progressbar3.html, so that it is as follows:

```
<script>
  (function($) {
    var progress = $("#myProgressbar");
    progress.progressbar();
    $("#increase").click(function() {
      var currentVal = progress.progressbar("option", "value"),
      newVal = currentVal + 10;
      progress.progressbar("value", newVal);
      if (!$("#value").length) {
        $("<span></span>", {
          text: newVal + "%",
          id: "value",
          css: {
            float: "right",
            marginTop: -28,
            marginRight: 10
          }
        }).appendTo(progress);
      } else {
        $("#value").text(val + "%");
      }
    });
  })(jQuery);
</script>
```

Save this as progressbar4.html. We lose the configuration object in this example as it isn't required. The logic for increasing the value using the value method has been moved into the click handler for the <button> element.

User initiated progress

At its most basic level, we can manually update the progressbar in response to user interaction. For example, we could specify a wizard-style form, which has several steps to complete. In this example, we'll create a form as shown in the following screenshot:

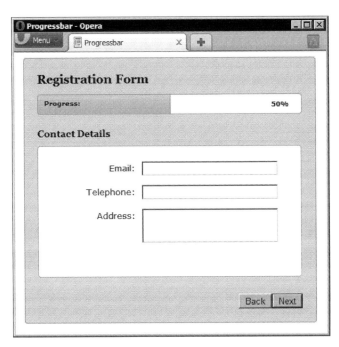

During each step, we can increment the progressbar manually to let the user know how far through the process they are. In `progressbar4.html`, replace the progressbar container and button with the following code:

```
<div class="form-container ui-helper-clearfix ui-corner-all">
  <h1>Registration Form</h1>
  <p>Progress:</p>
  <div id="progress"></div>\
  <label id="amount">0%</label>
  <form action="serverScript.php">
    <div class="form-panel">
      <h2>Personal Details</h2>
      <fieldset class="ui-corner-all">
        <label>Name:</label>
        <input type="text">
        <label>D.O.B:</label>
```

```
        <input type="text">
        <label>Choose password:</label>
        <input type="password">
        <label>Confirm password:</label>
        <input type="password">
      </fieldset>
    </div>
    <div class="form-panel ui-helper-hidden">
      <h2>Contact Details</h2>
      <fieldset class="ui-corner-all">
        <label>Email:</label>
        <input type="text">
        <label>Telephone:</label>
        <input type="text">
        <label>Address:</label>
        <textarea rows="3" cols="25"></textarea>
      </fieldset>
    </div>
    <div class="form-panel ui-helper-hidden">
      <h2>Registration Complete</h2>
      <fieldset class="ui-corner-all">
        <p>Thanks for registering!</p>
      </fieldset>
    </div>
    <button id="next">Next</button>
    <button id="back" disabled="disabled">Back</button>
  </form>
</div>
```

Save this as `progressbar5.html`. In the `<head>` section, we link to the framework theme files, as we have done with the other examples in this chapter, and will need to link to a custom style sheet that we'll add in a moment:

```
<link rel="stylesheet" href="css/progressTheme.css">
```

The `<body>` of the page contains a few layout elements and some text nodes, but the main elements are the container for the progressbar and the `<form>`. The `<form>` is separated into several different sections using `<div>` and `<fieldset>` elements. The reason for this is so that we can hide parts of the form to make it appear as if it spans several pages.

We've added a paragraph and a `<label>` next to the progressbar. We'll position these so that they appear inside the widget. The paragraph contains a simple text string. The label will be used to show the current progress value.

The outer container is given several classnames; the first is so that we can apply some custom styling to the element, but the next two are to target different features of the CSS framework. The `ui-helper-clearfix` class is used to automatically clear floated elements and is a great way of reducing the clutter of additional and unnecessary clearing `<div>` elements. Don't forget to make explicit use of this and other framework classes when creating your own widgets.

The `ui-corner-all` class is used to give the container element (as well as the progressbar itself, which has them automatically, and our `<fieldset>` elements) rounded corners, using several proprietary style rules. These are now supported by most modern browsers. We also have a **next** `<button>` to move forward through each panel, and a **back** `<button>` which is disabled by default.

We use another class from the CSS framework, within the form. Several panels need to be hidden when the page first loads; we can therefore make use of the `ui-helper-hidden` class to ensure that they are set to `display:none`. When we want to show them, all we have to do is remove this classname.

Now let's add the JavaScript; change the final `<script>` element at the bottom of the page, so that it appears as follows:

```
(function($) {
  var prog = $("#myProgressbar"),
  progressOpts = {
    change: function() {
      prog.next()
      .text(prog.progressbar("value") + "%");
    }
  };
  prog.progressbar(progressOpts);
  $("#next, #back").click(function() {
    $("button").attr("disabled", true);
    if (this.id == "next") {
      prog.progressbar("option", "value",
        prog.progressbar("option", "value") + 50);
      $("form").find("div:visible").fadeOut()
      .next().fadeIn(function(){
        $("#back").attr("disabled", false);
        if (!$("form").find("div:last").is(":visible")) {
          $("#next").attr("disabled", false);
        }
      });
    } else {
      prog.progressbar("option", "value",
        pro.progressbar("option", "value") - 50);
      $("form").find("div:visible").not(".buttons")
```

```
              .fadeOut().prev().fadeIn(function() {
                $("#next").attr("disabled", false);
                if (!$("form").find("div:first").is(":visible")) {
                  $("#back").attr("disabled", false);
                }
              });
          }
      });
  })(jQuery);
```

We first cache a selector for the progressbar and define our configuration object, making use of the change event to specify an anonymous callback function. Each time the event is fired, we'll grab the current value of the progressbar using the value method, and set it as the text of the <label> directly after the progressbar element. The event is fired after the change takes place, so the value we obtain will always be the new value.

Once the progressbar is initialized, we add a click handler for the buttons after the form. Within this handler function, we first disable both of the buttons to prevent the form from breaking, if a <button> is repeatedly clicked. We then use an if statement to run slightly different code branches, depending on which <button> was clicked.

If the next <button> was clicked, we increase the value of the progressbar by 50 percent by setting the value option to the current value plus 50 percent. We then fade-out the currently visible panel and fade-in the next panel. We use a callback function as an argument to the fadeIn() method, which will be executed once the animation ends.

Within this function, we re-enable the **back** <button> (as it was **next** that was clicked, it is not possible for the first panel to be visible, so this <button> should be enabled) and determine whether to enable the **next** <button>, which can be done, provided the last panel is not visible.

The second branch of the outer if statement deals with the **back** <button> being clicked. In this case, we reduce the progressbar by 50 percent, enable the **next** <button>, and check whether the **back** <button> should be enabled.

This is now all of the JavaScript that we'll need. All we have to do now is add some basic CSS to lay the example out; in a new file in your text editor add the following code:

```
h1, h2 { font-family:Georgia; font-size:140%; margin-top:0; }
h2 { margin:20px 0 10px; font-size:100%; text-align:left; }
p {
  margin:0; font-size:75%; position:absolute; left:30px;
  top:60px; font-weight:bold;
```

```
  }
#amount {
    position:absolute; right:30px; top:60px; font-size:80%;
    font-weight:bold;
}
#thanks { text-align:center; }
#thanks p {
    margin-top:48px; font-size:160%; position:relative; left:0;
    top:0;
}
form { height:265px; position:relative; }
.form-container {
    width:400px; margin:0 auto; position:relative;
    font-family:Verdana; font-size:80%; padding:20px;
    background-color:#e0e3e2; border:1px solid #abadac;
}
.form-panel {
    width:400px; height:241px; position:absolute; top:0; left:0; }
fieldset {
    width:397px; height:170px; margin:0 auto; padding:22px 0 0;
    border:1px solid #abadac; background-color:#ffffff;
}
label {
    width:146px; display:block; float:left; text-align:right;
    padding-top:2px; margin-right:10px;
}
input, textarea {
    float:left; width:200px; margin-bottom:13px;
}
button { float:right; }
```

Save this as `progressTheme.css` in the `css` directory. We should now have a working page with a wired-up progressbar. When we run the page, we should find that we can navigate through each panel of the form, and the progressbar will update itself accordingly.

We're still relying on user interaction to set the value of the progressbar in this example, which is driven by the visitor navigating through each of the panels.

Rich uploads with progressbar

Instead of relying on user interaction to increase the value of the progressbar and therefore the completion of the specified task, we can instead rely on the system to update it; deterministic means simply that something must be able to update it accurately.

In our final progressbar example, we can incorporate the HTML5 file API, in order to upload a file asynchronously, and can use the `onprogress` event to update the progressbar, while the file is uploading.

Although the `onprogress` event is defined as part of an official W3C specification, it has only been implemented by Firefox and webkit. This example however, will only work in Firefox 3.5+, as webkit browsers do not implement the `getAsBinary()` method that we use on file objects.

This example will also only work correctly using a full web server with PHP installed and configured. We won't be looking at the server-side part of the upload process in this example; we're not interested in what happens to the file once it's been uploaded, only in updating the progressbar based on feedback received from the system, while it is uploading.

Change the `<body>` in `progressbar5.html`, so that it contains the following elements:

```
<h2>AJAX File Upload</h2>
<input type="file" id="file" />
<div id="myProgressbar"></div>
```

On the page, we have an `<input>` of the type `file`, followed by the container for the progressbar as usual. Next, let's add the script; change the final `<script>` element at the end of the `<body>` to the following:

```
(function($) {
  var prog = $("#myProgressbar"),
  inputFile = $("#file"),
  progressOpts = {
    complete: function() {
      $("#filename").text("Complete!");
    }
  }
  inputFile.change(function() {
    prog.progressbar(progressOpts);
    var files = inputFile.attr("files"),
    file = files[0],
    xhr = new XMLHttpRequest();
    xhr.upload.onprogress = function updateProgress(e) {
      var loaded = (e.loaded / e.total);
      prog.progressbar("value", Math.round(loaded * 100));
    }
    xhr.upload.onload = function() {
      prog.progressbar("value", 100);
```

```
      }
      $("<span />", {
          id: "filename",
          text: file.fileName
      }).insertAfter(prog);
      xhr.open("POST", "progressUpload.php");
      xhr.sendAsBinary(file.getAsBinary());
    });
  })(jQuery);
```

Save this file as `progressbar6.html`. First of all, we cache some selectors and define a configuration object for the progressbar. Within this object, we configure the `complete` option, so that the callback function updates the filename string to the string `Complete!`.

Next, we add an anonymous function that hooks into the `change` event of the `<input>` element, which will be triggered when a file is selected (after clicking the `Browse` button that is automatically added next to the `<input>`).

Within this callback, we first need to get the file that has been selected, which will be available through the `files` attribute of the `<input>`. Multiple files can be selected, but this example doesn't cover that, so we just get the first file from the `files` collection.

Next, we create a new `XMLHttpRequest` object and then set an anonymous callback function as the value of the `input.onprogress` property. The function will be executed each time the event is fired. Within this function, we calculate the percentage of upload by dividing the amount uploaded so far by the total amount to upload. These details are available through the event object (`e`), which is automatically passed to the function.

Once we've established what the percentage of upload is, we can update the value of the progressbar using the `value` method. The value stored in the `loaded` variable will be a number between `0` and `1`, so we need to multiply it by `100` to get the correct percentage. We can also round the number to the nearest decimal point using `JavaSript's Math.round` method.

Next, we display the filename of the file being uploaded next to the progressbar. We don't need to do this, but it's a good example of how the `file` object can to used to obtain information about the selected file before the upload has even taken place.

We also add a handler for the `upload.onload` event, which is fired once when the request has completed. We use this function to set the value of the progressbar to `100` percent, as the `onprogress` event does not also fire at the end of the request.

Finally, we can open a POST connection to the server, and send the file to the server. Using the `file` API, we can send the file as a binary file using the `getAsBinary` and `sendAsBinary` methods. The PHP file is not necessary for the example to work, but even saving an empty PHP of the same name in the directory will prevent 404 errors, when the example runs.

We also need a tiny bit of CSS for this example; in a new file add the following code:

```
#file { float:left; }
#myProgressbar.ui-progressbar {
   height:1em; width:221px; margin:3px 0 0 4px; float:left;
}
#filename {
   float:left; margin:4px 0 0 10px; font-family:Verdana;
   font-size:12px;
}
```

This can be saved in the `css` folder as `progressTheme2.css`. Mostly the styles just position the various elements and set the width of the progressbar.

When we run this file in Firefox, we should see that once a file has been selected, it will automatically begin to upload, and the progressbar will begin to fill-up. If testing locally, it will be pretty quick, so it's best tested with reasonably large files. The following screenshot shows the page once the upload has completed:

Summary

Despite its compact API, the progressbar widget makes a great addition to the library, providing essential visitor feedback when processes are in progress. The component is useful in any situation where the percentage complete of the process can reliably be updated by the system.

After looking at the default implementation, we moved on to take a look at the `value` option and how it can be used; we can set the value prior to initialization using a configuration object, and we can set it after initialization using the `option` method.

Next, we looked at the `change` event, which is fired by the widget whenever its value is changed. Using the standard way of hooking into the event with an anonymous callback function within our configuration object, we can easily react to the amount of progress changing, or the process completing using the `complete` event.

We saw that in addition to the standard API methods such as `destroy`, the widget also exposes the `value` method, which can be used as a shortcut to setting the value using the `option` method.

Although the current version of this widget is purely deterministic, a future release will include support for an indeterminate progress indicator, for use when the current status of the process cannot be accurately determined. This is currently quite a young widget compared to some of the other components, so its API is sure to mature and grow in forthcoming releases.

In the next chapter, we'll look at two of the most recent additions to the library, the button widget and the autocomplete widget.

9
The Button and Autocomplete Widgets

The button and autocomplete widgets are the newest two widgets in the library, and were released in version 1.8. The autocomplete widget has actually been resurrected, having been included in a pre-ThemeRoller 1.6 release, retired in 1.7, and then brought back transformed in the 1.8 release.

Traditionally, it has been tricky to style form elements consistently across all browsers and platforms, and to confound this, most browsers and platforms render form controls uniquely. Both of the widgets covered in this chapter are used to improve some of the traditional form elements that are used on the web.

The button widget allows us to create visually appealing, ThemeRoller-ready, and highly configurable buttons from elements including <button>, <input>, and <a> elements. Types of the <input> element that are supported include submit, radio, and checkbox. Additional features, such as icons, button sets, and split buttons can be used to further enhance the underlying controls.

The autocomplete widget is attached to a standard text <input> and is used to provide a menu of contextual selections. When the visitor begins typing in the <input>, the suggestions which match the characters entered into the control are displayed.

Autocomplete is fully accessible through the keyboard input, allowing the list of suggestions to be navigated with the arrow keys, a selection made with the *Enter* key, and the menu closed with the *Esc* key. When the arrow keys are used to navigate the list of suggestions, each suggestion will be added to the <input> before a selection is made. If the *Esc* key is used to close the menu after the list has been navigated, the value of the <input> will revert to the text entered by the visitor.

In this chapter, we will cover the following topics:

- Standard button implementations
- Configurable options
- Adding icons
- Button events
- Buttonsets
- Button methods
- Using local data sources with autocomplete
- The configurable options of the autocomplete
- Autocomplete events
- Unique methods of the autocomplete
- Using remote data sources with autocomplete
- Using HTML in the autocomplete suggestions menu

The button widget

The button widget is used to provide a consistent, fully-themed styling to a range of elements and input types. The widget can be created from several different elements and the resulting DOM of the widget, as well as the features that can be used, will vary slightly depending on which element is used.

A standard button widget, built from either a `<button>`, or an `<a>` element, or an `<input>` with a type of `button`, `submit`, or `reset` will appear as follows:

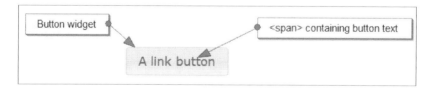

Standard implementations

Because the button can be built from several different elements, there are some minor variations of the underlying code that we can use. When creating buttons using `<a>` or `<button>` elements, a `<span>` element will be created automatically by the widget and nested within the underlying element. This new `<span>` will contain the text label of the button.

To create a link button, use the following page:

```
<!DOCTYPE html>
<html>
  <head>
    <meta charset="utf-8">
    <title>Button</title>
    <link rel="stylesheet"
      href="css/smoothness/jquery-ui-1.8.9.custom.css">
  </head>
  <body>
    <a href="some_other_page.html" id="myButton">A link button</a>
    <script src="development-bundle/jquery-1.4.4.js"></script>
    <script src="development-bundle/ui/jquery.ui.core.js"></script>
    <script src="development-bundle/ui/jquery.ui.widget.js"></script>
    <script src="development-bundle/ui/jquery.ui.button.js"></script>
  </body>
</html>
```

Save this page as `button1.html`. An `<input>` element is not allowed to contain children, so a `<span>` is not used for the text when creating button widgets from this element. It is imperative that the `type` attribute of the element is set in this case, so that the appearance of the button matches that of other buttons created from other underlying elements. For a standard, single button widget, the `type` attribute can be set to either `submit`, `reset`, or `button`.

The script required to create a button, when using an `<a>` element as the underlying HTML can be as simple as this, which should be added after the last `<script>` element in the previous code:

```
<script>
  (function($){
    $("#myButton").button();
  })(jQuery);
</script>
```

In this case, no special behavior is added to the resulting button; the `<a>` element will simply send the visitor to the new page or anchor specified in the `href` attribute of the anchor. In this case, the widget is simply themed consistently with other jQuery UI widgets that we may be using in the page or site.

Creating a button from a `<button>` element is identical to the previous code (except that we don't add a `href` attribute to the `<button>`):

```
<button id="myButton">A &lt;button&gt; button</button>
```

Creating a button from an `<input>` element is also very similar, except that we use the `value` attribute to set the text on the button instead of adding text content to the `<input>`:

```
<input id="myButton" value="An &lt;input&gt; button">
```

The button widget requires the following library resources:

- `jquery-ui-x.x.x-custom.css`
- `jQuery-x.x.x.js`
- `jquery.ui.core.js`
- `jquery.ui.widget.js`
- `jquery.ui.button.js`

Theming

Like all widgets, the button has a variety of classnames added to it, which contribute to its overall appearance. Of course, we can use the theme classnames in our own style sheets to override the default appearance of the theme in use, if we wish to provide custom styling. ThemeRoller is still usually the best tool for theming buttons.

Configurable options

The button widget has the following configuration options:

Option	Default Value	Used to...
disabled	false	Disable the button instance
icons	{primary: null, secondary: null}	Set the icons for the button instance
label	The content of the underlying element or value attribute	Set the text of the button instance
text	true	Hide the text of the button when using an icon-only instance

In our first example, the text content of the `<a>` element was used as the button's label. We can easily override this using the `label` option. Change the final `<script>` element in `button1.html`, so that it appears as follows:

```
(function($){
  var buttonOpts = {
    label: "A configured label"
  };
```

```
    $("#myButton").button(buttonOpts);
})(jQuery);
```

Save this file as `button2.html`. As we'd expect, when we run this page in a browser, we see that the `<span>` within the button widget takes the configured text as its label, instead of the text content of the `<a>` element.

Button icons

We can easily configure our buttons, so that they have up to two icons in most cases. Whenever an `<a>` or `<button>` element is used as the underlying element for the button, we can use the `icons` configuration option to specify one or two icons.

To see icons in action, change the configuration object in `button2.html`, so that it appears as follows:

```
var buttonOpts = {
  icons: {
    primary: "ui-icon-disk",
    secondary: "ui-icon-triangle-1-s"
  }
};
```

Save this version as `button3.html`. The `icons` property accepts an object with up to two keys; `primary` and `secondary`. The values of these options can be any of the `ui-icon-` classes found in the `jquery.ui.theme.css` file. The icons that we set are displayed as follows:

The icons are added to the widget using additional `<span>` elements, which are automatically created and inserted by the widget. The `primary` icon is displayed to the left of the button text, while the `secondary` icon is displayed to the right of the text.

To generate an icon-only button that has no text label, change the configuration object in `button3.html` to the following:

```
var buttonOpts = {
  icons: {
    primary: "ui-icon-disk",
    secondary: "ui-icon-triangle-1-s"
  },
  text: false
};
```

Save this as `button4.html`. When we view this variation in a browser, we see that the button displays only our two icons:

Input icons

As child `<span>` elements are used to the display the specified icons, we cannot use icons when using an `<input>` element as the underlying markup for a button instance. We can easily add our own icons when using `<input>` elements, however, by adding an extra container, the required `<span>` elements, and some custom CSS.

Change the `<body>` of `button4.html`, so that it contains the following elements:

```
<div
  class="iconic-input ui-button-text-icons ui-state-default ui-
    corner-all">
  <span class="ui-button-icon-primary ui-icon ui-icon-disk"></span>
  <input id="myButton" type = "button" value="Input icons"
    class="ui-button-text">
  <span class="ui-button-icon-secondary ui-icon ui-icon-triangle-
    1-s"></span>
</div>
```

Save this as `button5.html`. We'll also need to override some of the button's styling for this example. Create a new style sheet and add to it the following basic styles:

```
.iconic-input { display:inline-block; position:relative; }
.ui-icon { z-index:2; }
.iconic-input input { border:none; margin:0; }
```

In older versions of Internet Explorer, the `display: inline-block` style will not be applied. To prevent the button taking up the full width of its container, we would need to float it, or set a width explicitly.

Save this in the `css` directory as `buttonTheme.css`. Don't forget to link to the new style sheet from the `<head>` of our page (after the link to the standard jQuery UI style sheet):

```
<link rel="stylesheet" href="css/buttonTheme.css">
```

Visually our custom `<input>`-based widget is complete, but behaviorally it's not quite there—the icons do not pick up the correct hover states (the reason for this is because the widget has applied the required classnames to the underlying `<input>` instead of our custom container). We can add the required behavior, like we have added the container and `<span>` elements, manually. Change the code in the final `<script>` element, so that it appears as follows:

```
(function($) {
    $("#myButton").button().hover(function() {
        $(this).parent().addClass("ui-state-hover");
    }, function() {
        $(this).parent().removeClass("ui-state-hover");
    });
})(jQuery);
```

Now our button should work as intended. As this example shows, although it's technically feasible to manually add the elements, the styling, and the behavior required to add icons to a button built from an `<input>` element, in most cases it will be easier and more efficient to simply use an `<a>` or `<button>` element.

Button events

Buttons built from `<a>` elements will work as intended with no further intervention from us—the browser will simply follow the `href` as we would expect. Provided `<button>` or `<input>` elements are within a `<form>` and have the relevant `type` attribute set, these elements will submit the form data in the standard way.

If more modern AJAX submission of any `<form>` data is required, or if the button is to trigger some other action or process, we can use standard jQuery click event-handlers to react to the button being clicked.

In the next example, we use the following underlying markup for the button widget:

```
<button type="button" id="myButton">A button</button>
```

The button widget exposes a single event, the `create` event, which is fired when the button instance is initially created. We could use this event to run additional code each time a button instance is created; for example, if we wanted the button to be initially hidden from view (in order to display later, after something else has occurred), we could use the following configuration object:

```
var buttonOpts = {
  create: function() {
    $(this).css("display", "none")
  }
};
```

Save this page as `button6.html`. Within the event handler, this refers to the button instance, which is hidden from view using jQuery's `css()` method.

In order for the button to fulfill its primary purpose, that is, to do something when clicked, we should attach a handler to the button manually. We might want to collect some registration information from our visitors, for example, and use a button to send this information to the server.

Replace the `<button>` in `button6.html`, with the following markup:

```
<form method="post" action="serverscript.php">
  <label for="name">Name:
    <input type="text" id="name" name="name">
  </label>
  <label for="email">Email:
    <input type="text" id="email" name="email">
  </label>
  <button type="submit" id="myButton">Register</button>
</form>
```

Change the final `<script>` element to the following:

```
(function($){
  $("#myButton").button().click(function(e) {
    e.preventDefault();
    var form = $("form"),
    formData = {
      name: form.find("#name").val(),
      email: form.find("#email").val()
    };
    $.post("register.php", formData, function() {
```

```
        $("#myButton").button("option", "disabled", true);
        form.find("label").remove();
        $("<label />", {
          text: "Thanks for registering!"
        }).prependTo(form);
      });
    });
  })(jQuery);
```

Save this page as `button7.html`. The underlying `<button>` element is now part of a simple `<form>`, which simply provides text inputs for the visitor, their name, and an e-mail address. In the script, we chain a click-handler on to the `button()` method, which first prevents the default action of the browser, which would be to post the form in a traditional non-AJAX way.

We then collect the name and e-mail address entered into the fields, and post the data to the server asynchronously using jQuery's `post()` method. In the success handler for the request, we use the widget's `option` method to disable the button, then create and display a thanks message.

We're not interested in the server side of things in this example, and we don't include any validation, but you can see how easy it is to react to the button being clicked using standard jQuery functionality. To see the example work, we'll need to run the page through a web server, and should add a PHP file of the name specified in the request in the same directory as the page. The following screenshot shows how the page should appear after the button has been clicked:

Buttonsets

The button widget can also be used in conjunction with radio buttons and checkboxes. The button component is unique in jQuery UI, in that it has not one but two widget methods. It has the `button()` method that we have already looked at, and it has the `buttonset()` method, which is used to create groups of buttons based on radio buttons and checkboxes.

Checkbox buttonsets

Change the `<body>` of `button7.html`, so that it contains the following markup:

```
<div id="buttons">
  <h2>Programming Languages</h2>
  <p>Select all languages you know:</p>
  <label for="js">JavaScript</label>
  <input id="js" type="checkbox">
  <label for="py">Python</label>
  <input id="py" type="checkbox">
  <label for="cSharp">C#</label>
  <input id="cSharp" type="checkbox">
  <label for="jv">Java</label>
  <input id="jv" type="checkbox">
</div>
```

Now change the final `<script>` element, so that it appears as follows:

```
(function($){
  $("#buttons").buttonset();
})(jQuery);
```

Save this page as `button8.html`. All we need to do is call the `buttonset()` method on the container in which the `<label>` and `<input>` elements reside.

When we run this page in a browser, we see that the checkboxes are hidden from view and the `<label>` elements are converted into buttons and grouped visually in a horizontal set:

Although the actual checkboxes themselves are hidden from view behind the buttons, whenever a button is selected, the underlying checkbox will have its `checked` attribute updated, so we can still harvest the states from script with ease.

When a checkbox button is selected, it will have a selected state applied to it by the widget, so that the visitor can easily see that it has been selected. As we would expect, multiple buttons may be selected at once.

There are a couple of rules that we need to adhere to when creating buttons from checkboxes. In HTML5, it is common to nest form controls within their associated `<label>` elements (we did this in an earlier example), but this is not allowed when using the button widget. Using the `for` attribute with the `<label>` is required.

Radio buttonsets

Buttons based on radio buttons are visually the same as those based on checkboxes; they differ only in their behavior. In `button8.html`, change the elements in the `<body>` to the following:

```
<div id="buttons">
  <h2>Programming Languages</h2>
  <p>Select your most proficient languages:</p>
  <label for="js">JavaScript</label>
  <input id="js" type="radio" name="lang">
  <label for="py">Python</label>
  <input id="py" type="radio" name="lang">
  <label for="cSharp">C#</label>
  <input id="cSharp" type="radio" name="lang">
  <label for="jv">Java</label>
  <input id="jv" type="radio" name="lang">
</div>
```

Save this page as `button9.html`. The script to initialize radio buttons is the same; we simply call the `buttonset()` method on the container. The only difference to the underlying markup, other than specifying `radio` as the type, is that these `<input>` elements must have the `name` attribute set.

Button methods

The button widget comes with the default `destroy`, `disable`, `enable`, `widget`, and `option` methods common to all widgets. In addition to these methods, the button widget exposes one custom method, which is the `refresh` method. This method is used for changing the state of checkbox and radio buttons, if they are changed programmatically. By combining some of the previous examples, we can see this method in action.

Change the `<body>` of `button8.html`, so that it includes two new `<button>` elements as shown below:

```
<div id="buttons">
  <h2>Programming Languages</h2>
  <p>Select all languages you know:</p>
  <label for="js1">JavaScript</label>
```

```
<input id="js1" type="checkbox">
<label for="py1">Python</label>
<input id="py1" type="checkbox">
<label for="cSharp1">C#</label>
<input id="cSharp1" type="checkbox">
<label for="jv1">Java</label>
<input id="jv1" type="checkbox">
</div>
<br>
<button type="button" id="select">Select All</button>
<button type="button" id="deselect">Deselect All</button>
```

In this example, we have reverted to the checkboxes, so that we can programmatically select or deselect them as a group. Now change the final `<script>` element, so that it appears as follows:

```
$("#buttons").buttonset();
$("#select").button().click(function() {
  $("#buttons").find("input").attr("checked", true).button("refresh");
});
$("#deselect").button().click(function() {
  $("#buttons").find("input").attr("checked", false).
button("refresh");
});
```

Save this file as `button10.html`. In this example, we have a **Select all** button and a **Deselect all** button; when the **Select all** button is clicked, we set the `checked` attribute of the checkboxes to `true`. This will check the underlying (and hidden) check boxes, but it won't do anything to the `<label>` elements that are styled to appear as buttons. To update the state of these buttons, so that they appear selected, we call the `refresh` method.

The **Deselect all** button sets the **checked** attribute to `false`, and then calls the `refresh` method again to remove the selected states from each button.

The autocomplete widget

The autocomplete widget is back, and looking better than ever. This is one of my favorite widgets in the library, and although it doesn't yet have the full set of behavior that it had in its first incarnation, it still provides a rich set of functionality to enhance simple text inputs that expect data from a predefined range.

A good example is cities; you have a standard `<input type="text">` on the page, which asks for the visitor's city. When they begin typing in the `<input>`, all of the cities that contain the letter that the visitor has typed, are displayed. The range of cities that the visitor can enter is finite and constrained to the country in which the visitor lives (this is either assumed by the developer or has already been selected previously by the visitor).

The following screenshot shows how this widget appears:

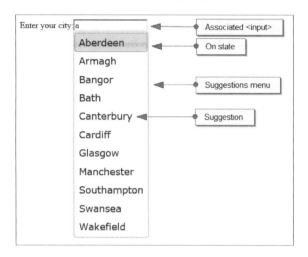

Like other widgets, a range of elements and classnames are added programmatically when the widget is initialized.

Working with local data sources

To implement a basic autocomplete with a local array as its data source, create the following new page:

```
<!DOCTYPE html>
<html>
  <head>
    <meta charset="utf-8">
    <title>Autocomplete</title>
    <link rel="stylesheet" href="css/smoothness/jquery-ui-
      1.8.9.custom.css">
  </head>
  <body>
    <label>Enter your city:</label>
    <input id="city">
    <script src="development-bundle/jquery-1.4.4.js"></script>
    <script src="development-bundle/ui/jquery.ui.core.js"></script>
```

```
    <script src="development-bundle/ui/jquery.ui.widget.js"></script>
    <script src="development-bundle/ui/jquery.ui.position.js">
</script>
    <script src="development-bundle/ui/jquery.ui.autocomplete.js">
</script>
  </body>
</html>
```

All we need on the page is a standard `<input>` element of the type `text`. The initialization required for autocomplete is slightly larger than that required for other components; add the following `<script>` element, after the autocomplete source file:

```
<script>
  (function($){
    var autoOpts = {
      source: [
        "Aberdeen", "Armagh", "Bangor", "Bath", "Canterbury",
        "Cardiff",
        "Derby", "Dundee", "Edinburgh", "Exeter", "Glasgow",
        "Gloucester",
        "Hereford", "Inverness", "Leeds", "London", "Manchester",
        "Norwich",
        "Newport", "Oxford", "Plymouth", "Preston", "Ripon",
        "Southampton",
        "Swansea", "Truro", "Wakefield", "Winchester", "York"
      ]
    };
    $("#city").autocomplete(autoOpts);
  })(jQuery);
</script>
```

Save this page as `autocomplete1.html`. In our configuration object for the autocomplete, we use the `source` option to specify a local array of strings. The `source` option is mandatory and must be defined. The object is then passed to the `widget` method, which is called on the `<input>` that the autocomplete is to be associated with.

When we run this page in a browser, we should find that as we begin to type into the `<input>`, a list of the cities defined in our source array that contain the letter(s) that we have typed is displayed in a drop-down menu attached to the `<input>`.

The autocomplete widget requires the following files in order to function:

- `jquery-ui-x.x.x.custom.css`
- `jquery-x.x.x.js`
- `jquery.ui.core.js`
- `jquery.ui.widget.js`

- `jquery.ui.position.js`
- `jquery.ui.autocomplete.js`

Using an array of objects as the data source

In addition to providing an array of strings, we can also supply an array of objects as the data source, which gives us more flexibility over the text added to the `<input>` when a suggestion from the menu is selected. Change the configuration object in `autocomplete1.html`, so that it appears as follows:

```
var autoOpts = {
  source: [
    { value: "AB", label: "Aberdeen" },
    { value: "AR", label: "Armagh" },
    { value: "BA", label: "Bangor" },
    { value: "BA", label: "Bath" },
    { value: "CA", label: "Canterbury" },
    { value: "CD", label: "Cardiff" },
    { value: "DE", label: "Derby" },
    { value: "DU", label: "Dundee" },
    { value: "ED", label: "Edinburgh" },
    { value: "EX", label: "Exeter" },
    { value: "GL", label: "Glasgow" },
    { value: "GO", label: "Gloucester" },
    { value: "HE", label: "Hereford" },
    { value: "IN", label: "Inverness" },
    { value: "LE", label: "Leeds" },
    { value: "LO", label: "London" },
    { value: "MA", label: "Manchester" },
    { value: "NO", label: "Norwich" },
    { value: "NE", label: "Newport" },
    { value: "OX", label: "Oxford" },
    { value: "PL", label: "Plymouth" },
    { value: "PR", label: "Preston" },
    { value: "RI", label: "Ripon" },
    { value: "SO", label: "Southampton" },
    { value: "SW", label: "Swansea" },
    { value: "TR", label: "Truro" },
    { value: "WA", label: "Wakefield" },
    { value: "WI", label: "Winchester" },
    { value: "YO", label: "York" }
  ]
};
```

Save this page as `autocomplete2.html`. Each item in the array that we are using as the data source is now an object, instead of a simple string. Each object has two keys: `value` and `label`. The value of the `value` key is the text that is added to the `<input>` when a suggestion is selected from the list. The value of `label` is what is displayed in the suggestion list. Other keys, which store custom data, can also be used.

If each object in the array contains only a single property ,the property will be used as both the `value` and `label`. In this case, we might as well use an array of strings instead of an array of objects, but it is worth noting the alternative format of the local data.

Configurable autocomplete options

The following options can be set in order to modify the behavior of the widget:

Option	Default Value	Used to...
appendTo	"body"	Specify which element to append the widget to.
autofocus	false	Focus the first suggestion in the list when displaying the list of suggestions.
delay	300	Specify the number of milliseconds the widget should wait before displaying the list of suggestions, after the visitor has started typing in the `<input>`.
disabled	false	Disable the widget.
minLength	1	Specify the number of characters the visitor needs to enter in the `<input>` before the list of suggestions is displayed. Can be set to `0` to make the widget display all suggestions in the menu.
position	{ my: "left top", at: "left bottom", collision: "none" }	Specify how the list of suggestions should be positioned relative to the `<input>` element. This option is used in the exact same way, and accepts the same values as the `position` utility that we looked at earlier in the book.
source		Specify the data source used to fill the list of suggestions. This option is mandatory and must be configured. It accepts an array, string, or function as its value.

Configuring minimum length

The `minLength` option allows us to specify the minimum number of characters that need to be typed into the associated `<input>` element before the list of suggestions is displayed. By default, the suggestions that are displayed by the widget only contain the letters typed into the `<input>`, rather than just those starting with the entered letters, which can result in many more suggestions being displayed than is necessary.

Setting the `minLength` option to a number higher than the default value of 1 can help narrow the list of suggestions, which may be much more important when dealing with large remote data sources.

Change the configuration object that we used in `autocomplete1.html` (we'll revert to using an array of strings as the data source for the time being), so that it appears as follows:

```
var autoOpts = {
  minLength: 2,
  source: [
    "Aberdeen", "Armagh", "Bangor", "Bath",         "Canterbury",
"Cardiff",
    "Derby", "Dundee", "Edinburgh", "Exeter", "Glasgow", "Gloucester",
    "Hereford", "Inverness", "Leeds", "London", "Manchester",
"Norwich",
    "Newport", "Oxford", "Plymouth", "Preston", "Ripon",
"Southampton",
    "Swansea", "Truro", "Wakefield", "Winchester", "York"
  ]
};
```

Save this file as `autocomplete3.html`. The `minLength` option accepts an integer specifying the number of characters that must be typed in the `<input>`. When we run this page in a browser, we should find that we need to type two characters into the `<input>`, and only cities that contain the characters in consecutive order are displayed, which vastly reduces the number of suggestions.

Although the benefits are not obvious in this basic example, this can drastically reduce the data returned by a remote data source.

Appending the suggestion list to an alternative element

By default, the suggestion list is appended to the `<body>` of the page and the `position` utility is used to position the list, so that it appears to be attached to the `<input>` it is associated with. We can change this and specify that the list should be added to another element on the page, instead of using the `appendTo` option.

Wrap the underlying `<label>` and `<input>` in a container `<div>` in autocomplete3.html:

```
<div id="container">
  <label>Enter your city:</label>
  <input id="city">
</div>
```

Then change the configuration object in the final `<script>` element to the following:

```
var autoOpts = {
  appendTo: "#container",
  source: [
    "Aberdeen", "Armagh", "Bangor", "Bath",        "Canterbury",
"Cardiff",
    "Derby", "Dundee", "Edinburgh", "Exeter", "Glasgow", "Gloucester",
    "Hereford", "Inverness", "Leeds", "London", "Manchester",
"Norwich",
    "Newport", "Oxford", "Plymouth", "Preston", "Ripon",
"Southampton",
    "Swansea", "Truro", "Wakefield", "Winchester", "York"
  ]
};
```

Save this page as autocomplete4.html. Usually, the suggestion list is added right at the bottom of the `<body>` of the page. The `appendTo` option accepts a jQuery selector or an actual DOM element as its value.

In this example, we see that the list is appended to our container `<div>` instead of the `<body>`, which we can verify using Firebug, or another DOM explorer.

Autocomplete events

The autocomplete widget exposes a range of unique events that allow us to react programmatically to the widget being interacted with. These events are listed below:

Event	Fired when...
change	A suggestion from the list is selected. This event is fired once the list has closed and the `<input>` has lost focus.
close	The suggestion list is closed.
create	An instance of the widget is created.
focus	The keyboard is used to focus a suggestion in the list.
open	The suggestion menu is displayed.
search	The request for the suggestions is about to be made.
select	A suggestion from the list is selected.

The `select` event is useful when we are working with an array of objects as the data source and have additional data other than the `label` and `value` properties that we used earlier. For the next example, remove the container `<div>` that we used in the last example and then change the configuration object, so that it appears as follows:

```
var autoOpts = {
  source: [
    { value: "AB", label: "Aberdeen", population: 212125 },
    { value: "AR", label: "Armagh", population: 54263 },
    { value: "BA", label: "Bangor", population: 21735 },
    { value: "BA", label: "Bath", population: 83992 },
    { value: "CA", label: "Canterbury", population: 43432 },
    { value: "CD", label: "Cardiff", population: 336200 },
    { value: "DE", label: "Derby", population: 233700 },
    { value: "DU", label: "Dundee", population: 152320 },
    { value: "ED", label: "Edinburgh", population: 448624 },
    { value: "EX", label: "Exeter", population: 118800 },
    { value: "GL", label: "Glasgow", population: 580690 },
    { value: "GO", label: "Gloucester", population: 123205 },
    { value: "HE", label: "Hereford", population: 55700 },
    { value: "IN", label: "Inverness", population: 56660 },
    { value: "LE", label: "Leeds", population: 443247 },
    { value: "LO", label: "London", population: 7200000 },
    { value: "MA", label: "Manchester", population: 483800 },
    { value: "NO", label: "Norwich", population: 259100 },
    { value: "NE", label: "Newport", population: 137011 },
    { value: "OX", label: "Oxford", population: 149300 },
    { value: "PL", label: "Plymouth", population: 256700 },
    { value: "PR", label: "Preston", population: 114300 },
    { value: "RI", label: "Ripon", population: 15922 },
    { value: "SO", label: "Southampton", population: 236700 },
    { value: "SW", label: "Swansea", population: 223301 },
    { value: "TR", label: "Truro", population: 17431 },
    { value: "WA", label: "Wakefield", population: 76886 },
    { value: "WI", label: "Winchester", population: 41420 },
    { value: "YO", label: "York", population: 182000 }
  ],
  select: function(e, ui) {
    if ($("#pop").length) {
      $("#pop").text(ui.item.label + "'s population is: " + ui.item.
population);
    } else {
      $("<p></p>", {
        id: "pop",
```

```
            text: ui.item.label + "'s population is: " + ui.item.
population
        }).insertAfter("#city");
    }
  }
};
```

Save this file as `autocomplete5.html`. We've added an extra property to each object in our array data source—the population of each city. We use the `select` event to obtain the `label` and our extra property, and write them to the page whenever a city is selected.

The event handler that we pass to the `select` event accepts the `event` object and the object from the data source that was selected. We can access any property defined within our object in the standard way.

Once a city has been selected, the page should appear as follows:

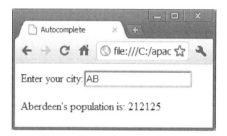

Autocomplete methods

In addition to the standard methods that all widgets share, the autocomplete gives us two unique methods that allow us to initiate certain actions. The unique methods are listed below:

Method	Used to...
close	Close the suggestion menu
search	Request the list of suggestions from the data source, specifying the search term as an optional argument

The `close` method is extremely easy-to-use, we simply call the autocomplete `widget` method and specify `close` as an argument:

```
$("#associated_input").autocomplete("close");
```

This will cause the suggestions menu to be closed, and the `close` event to be triggered.

The `search` method is slightly more complex, in that it can accept an additional argument, although this is not mandatory. If the `search` method is called without passing an argument (which is likely to be the default behaviour), the value of the associated `<input>` is used as the search term. Alternatively, the term can be provided to the method as the argument.

Working with remote data sources

So far in this example, we've worked with a rather small local array of data. The autocomplete widget really comes into its own when working with remote data sources, which is the recommended way of using the widget when the data source is large.

Using a string as the value of the source option

In the next example, we'll use a web service to retrieve the list of UK cities instead of using our local array. Change the `<input>` in `autocomplete5.html`, so that it appears as follows:

```
<label>Enter your country:</label>
<input id="country">
```

Then change the final `<script>` element, so that the configuration object is defined like this:

```
var autoOpts = {
    source: "http://danwellman.co.uk/countries.php?callback=?"
};
```

Save this file as `autocomplete6.html`. We changed the `<input>` in this example, as we are requesting the visitor's country instead of a city. It is not important that we are looking for countries now, instead of cities.

We have specified a string as the value of the `source` configuration object in this example. When a string is supplied to this option, the string should contain a URL that points to a remote resource. The widget assumes that the resource will output JSON data, and it assumes that the JSON data will be in the format that we saw earlier when using an array of objects as the source.

Therefore, when using a simple string as the value of the `source` option, the data that is returned should be an array of objects, where each object contains at least a key called `label`. The data can be in JSON or JSONP format for cross-domain requests. The widget will automatically add the query string `term=`, followed by whatever was typed into the `<input>`.

In this example, I have specified a URL of my own website. The resource at this URL will output data in the correct format, so you can run this example from your desktop computer (without even needing a web server) and see the correct behavior:

One important point that I should make is that the PHP file, which I have used, will only return entries from the database that start with the letter(s) typed into the `<input>`, and does not contain the letters as is the default for the widget. I wanted to clarify that this is a change that I implemented at the server-level, not behavior exhibited by the widget.

So, using a string as the value of the `source` option is useful and convenient when we have a data source that outputs data in the exact format we require, which is usually when we are in control of the web service that returns the data, as well as the data itself. This may not be the case if we are trying to extract data from a public web service over which we have no control. In these situations, we will need to use a function as the value of the `source` option and parse out the data manually.

Using a function as the value of the source option

Passing a function to the `source` option, instead of a local array or a string, is the most powerful way of working with the widget. In this scenario, we have complete control over the request and how the data is processed before being passed to the widget to display in the suggestion menu.

In this example, we'll use a different PHP file that returns different data, which is not in the format that autocomplete expects. We'll use the function to request and process the data before passing it to the widget. The context of the example will be the front-end for a messaging system similar to Facebook's, in which people to send the message to are suggested, but can also be removed after they have been selected and added to the `<input>`. The page we will end up with will appear as in the following screenshot:

To start with, change the `<body>` of `autocomplete6.html`, so that it contains the following markup:

```
<div id="formWrap">
  <form id="messageForm" action="#" method="post">
    <fieldset>
      <legend>New message form</legend>
      <span>New Message</span>
      <div class="inner-form ui-helper-clearfix">
        <label for="toList">To:</label>
        <div id="toList" class="ui-helper-clearfix">
          <input id="to" type="text">
          <input id="emails" type="hidden">
        </div>
        <label for="message">Message:</label>
        <textarea id="message" name="message" rows="2" cols="50">
        </textarea>
      </div>
      <div class="buttons ui-helper-clearfix">
        <button type="submit">Send</button>
        <a href="#" title="Cancel">Cancel</a>
      </div>
    </fieldset>
  </form>
</div>
```

Then change the final `<script>` element, so that it appears as follows:

```
(function($){
  var autoOpts = {
    source: function(req, resp){
```

```
          $.getJSON("http://danwellman.co.uk/contacts.php?callback=?",
req,
          function(data) {
          var suggestions = [];
          $.each(data, function(i, val){
            var obj = {};
            obj.value = val.name;
            obj.email = val.email;
            suggestions.push(obj);
          });
          resp(suggestions);
        });
      },
      select: function(e, ui) {
        var emailList = $("#emails"),
        emails = emailList.val().split(","),
        span = $("<span></span>", {
          text: ui.item.value
        }),
        a = $("<a></a>", {
          "class": "remove",
          href: "#",
          title: "Remove",
          text: "x"
        }).appendTo(span);
        span.insertBefore("#to");
        emails.push(ui.item.email);
        emailList.val(emails.join(","));
        $("#to").remove();
        $("<input/>", {
          id: "to"
        }).insertBefore("#emails").autocomplete(autoOpts);
      }
    };
    $("#to").autocomplete(autoOpts);
    $("#toList").click(function(){
      $("#to").focus();
    });
    $("#toList").delegate("a", "click", function(){
      var email = $(this).parent().data("email"),
      emails = $("#emails").val().split(",");
      $(this).parent().remove();
      $.each(emails, function(i, val) {
        if (val === email) {
```

```
            emails.splice(i, 1);
        }
    });
        $("#emails").val(emails);
    });
}) (jQuery);
```

Save this page as `autocomplete7.html`. On the page, we've got some basic markup for a form and the necessary elements to recreate the Facebook-style message dialog. We use a `<div>` element that is styled to look just like an `<input>`, with a totally unstyled actual `<input>` within this.

The actual `<input>` is needed, so that the visitor can type into it and so that it can be associated with the autcomplete. We use the `<div>` because we can't insert the `<span>` elements that will make up each contact into the `<input>`. We also have a hidden `<input>`, which will be used to store the actual e-mail addresses.

In the script, we use a function as the value of the `source` option; this function is called every time the text in the `<input>` is updated. The function accepts two arguments; the first, `req`, will contain a property called `term`, which is the text entered into the `<input>`. The second, `resp`, is a callback function, which we should call in order to display the suggestion menu. This callback must be passed for the list of suggestions to display.

The first thing we do within the `source` function is make a JSON request to the data source. Within the callback for this request, we create an empty array and then iterate over each item in the JSON object, returned by the request. As before, the PHP file only returns matching entries from the database, so we don't need to do any pattern matching.

We process each item in the returned data using jQuery's `each()` method, which executes the anonymous function for each item in the data set. Within this function, we create a new object and add to it `value` and `email` properties. The widget will display the `value` properties within the suggestion menu and we will make use of the `email` property later in the script.

Each newly created object is added to the `suggestions` array, and once each item in the returned data has been processed, the `suggestions` array is passed to the `resp` callback function, passed to the `source` function as the second argument.

The autocomplete will now function as intended using our non-standard remote data source. However, we still want to post-process the items when they are selected. We can use the `select` configuration option to do this and specify a function as the value of this option. This function receives two arguments: the `event` object and a special `ui` object prepared by the widget.

Within this function, we first cache the selector for the hidden `<input>` and then create an array from its contents by splitting the text on any commas, which we'll use to separate the e-mail address when we add them to this field.

We then create a new `<span>` element and set its text to the value of the item selected from the suggestion menu, which is available under `ui.item.value`. We also create a new `<a>` element and append it to the new `<span>`. This element will be used to remove the `<span>` from the list of recipients. We also add the e-mail address as `data` on the `<span>`, so that each recipient name can be associated with its e-mail address.

We then insert the new `<span>` into the `<div>` element, styled to look like an `<input>`, and then add the `email` property from the selected item (available under `ui.item.email`) to the array of e-mails extracted from the hidden `<input>`. Once this is done, we join the array of e-mail addresses into a single string, specifying a comma as the separator, and then write the text string back to the hidden `<input>`.

In order to stop the selected item being added to the unstyled `<input>` that the autocomplete is attached to, we remove this `<input>` from the page, and then create a new version of it, giving it the same `id` attribute and re-attaching the autocomplete to it.

The remainder of the code deals with initially attaching the autocomplete to the original unstyled `<input>`, focusing this `<input>` whenever the `<div>` element that is styled to look like the `<input>` is clicked, and handling removing a recipient from the list. When this happens, we also remove the e-mail address from the hidden `<input>` element, which we do by splitting the contents of the hidden `<input>` into an array and using the `data` that we stored on the `<span>` earlier to remove the matching e-mail address.

We'll also need a style sheet to go with this example; add the following CSS to a new file:

```
#formWrap {
  padding:10px; position:absolute; background-color:#000;
  background:rgba(82,82,82,0.7); border-radius:8px;
  font:bold 14px "lucida grande",tahoma,verdana,arial,sans-serif;
}
#formWrap a:hover { color:#ff0000; }
#messageForm {
  width:467px; border:1px solid #666; background-color:#eee;
}
#messageForm fieldset {
  padding:0; margin:0; position:relative; border:none #CCC;
  background-color:#fff;
}
#messageForm legend { visibility:hidden; height:0; }
```

```css
#messageForm span {
  display:block; width:467px; padding:10px 0; background-
color:#6D84B4;
  border:#3B5998 #3B5998; color:#fff; text-indent:20px;
}
.inner-form { padding:20px; }
#toList {
  width:349px; min-height:27px; padding:3px 3px 0 3px;
  border:1px solid #6D84B4; margin-bottom:8px; float:left;
  background-color:#fff; cursor:text;
}
#messageForm #to {
  width:10px; padding:0; position:relative; top:4px; float:left;
  border:none;
}
#messageForm input, #messageForm textarea {
  display:block; width:349px; padding:3px; border:1px solid #6D84B4;
  float:left; outline:none;
}
#messageForm textarea { resize:vertical; }
#messageForm label {
  width:60px; margin:7px 10px 0 0; float:left; color:#666;
  font-size:11px; text-align:right;
}
.buttons { padding:10px 20px; background-color:#f2f2f2; }
.buttons a {
  margin:3px 10px 0 0; float:right; font-size:11px; color:#6D84B4;
}
.buttons button { float:right; }
#toList span {
  width:auto; margin:0 3px 3px 0; padding:3px 20px 4px 8px;
  border:1px solid #9DACCC; border-radius:3px; position:relative;
  float:left; font-size:11px; font-weight:normal; text-indent:0;
  background-color:#E2E6F0; color:#1C2A47;
}
#toList span a {
  position:absolute; right:7px; top:1px; color:#666;
  font-weight:bold; font-size:12px; text-decoration:none;
}
.ui-menu .ui-menu-item { white-space:nowrap; padding:0 10px 0 0; }
```

Save this file as `autocompleteTheme.css` in the `css` folder, and link to the new file from the `<head>` of our new page:

```html
<link rel="stylesheet" href="css/autocompleteTheme.css">
```

When we run the page in a browser, we should find that we can type into the `<input>`, select a name from the suggestions menu, and get a nicely formatted and styled name added to the fake input. The actual e-mail address should be added to the hidden text field, which we can see using Firebug or some other DOM explorer:

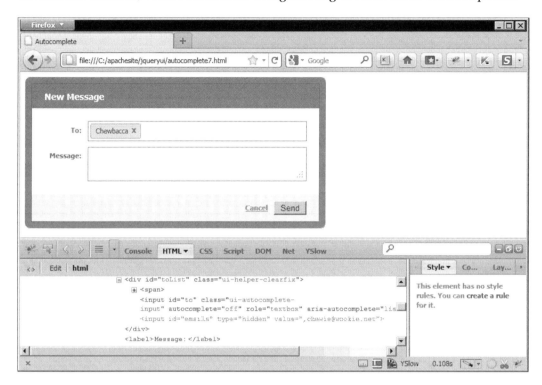

Displaying HTML in the list of suggestions

By default, the autocomplete widget will only display plain text for each suggestion in the list. Of course, this plain text is within HTML elements created by the widget, but nevertheless, if we try to use HTML within our data source, then it will be stripped out and ignored. However, Scott González has written an extension that allows us to use HTML for each suggestion in the list instead of plain text, if the need arises.

This could be handy if we wanted to highlight to the visitor the parts of the suggestion that matched what they had typed in the `<input>`. We will need the extension for this example, which can be found at `https://github.com/scottgonzalez/jquery-ui-extensions/blob/master/autocomplete/jquery.ui.autocomplete.html.js`.

The file can be saved in our local `js` directory and should be linked to from the page after the source file for the autocomplete:

```
<script src="js/jquery.ui.autocomplete.html.js"></script>
```

Change the final `<script>` element in `autocomplete7.html`, so that it appears as follows:

```
(function($){
  var data = [
    { value: "Aberdeen", label: "Aberdeen" },
    { value: "Armagh", label: "Armagh" },
    { value: "Bangor", label: "Bangor" },
    { value: "Bath", label: "Bath" },
    { value: "Canterbury", label: "Canterbury" },
    { value: "Cardiff", label: "Cardiff" },
    { value: "Derby", label: "Derby" },
    { value: "Dundee", label: "Dundee" },
    { value: "Edinburgh", label: "Edinburgh" },
    { value: "Exeter", label: "Exeter" },
    { value: "Glasgow", label: "Glasgow" },
    { value: "Gloucester", label: "Gloucester" },
    { value: "Hereford", label: "Hereford" },
    { value: "Inverness", label: "Inverness" },
    { value: "Leeds", label: "Leeds" },
    { value: "London", label: "London" },
    { value: "Manchester", label: "Manchester" },
    { value: "Norwich", label: "Norwich" },
    { value: "Newport", label: "Newport" },
    { value: "Oxford", label: "Oxford" },
    { value: "Plymouth", label: "Plymouth" },
    { value: "Preston", label: "Preston" },
    { value: "Ripon", label: "Ripon" },
    { value: "Southampton", label: "Southampton" },
    { value: "Swansea", label: "Swansea" },
    { value: "Truro", label: "Truro" },
    { value: "Wakefield", label: "Wakefield" },
    { value: "Winchester", label: "Winchester" },
    { value: "York", label: "York" }
  ],
  autoOpts = {
    html: true,
    source: function(req, resp) {
      var suggestions = [],
      regEx = new RegExp("^" + req.term, "i");
      $.each(data, function(i, val){
        if (val.label.match(regEx)) {
          var obj = {};
```

```
            obj.value = val.value;
            obj.label = val.label.replace(regEx, "<span>" + req.term +
              "</span>");
            suggestions.push(obj);
          }
        });
        resp(suggestions);
      }
    };
    $("#city").autocomplete(autoOpts);
  })(jQuery);
```

Save this file as `autocomplete8.html`. In this example, we've gone back to using a local array of objects, but we've moved it out of the configuration object for the autocomplete into its own variable called `data`. Both the `value` and `label` properties in each object hold the same data to begin with.

In our configuration object, we specify a new option `html`, which is used in conjunction with the html extension. We set the value of this option to `true`.

As before, we use a function as the value of the `source` option in this example. Within the function provided as the value of `source`, we first create a new empty array and define a new regular expression object, which will case-insensitively match whatever is typed into the `<input>`, at the start of a string.

We then iterate over each object in our data array and test whether our regular expression matches any of the `label` values in the objects in our array. If any items do match, we create a new object and give it `value` and `label` properties; the `value` (which is added to the `<input>` when a suggestion is selected) is simply the corresponding value from our data array, and the `label` (what is displayed in the suggestion menu) is a new string that contains a `<span>` element wrapping the text entered into the `<input>`.

Finally, we call the `resp` callback, passing in the newly constructed suggestions array. We should always ensure that this callback is called, as this is required by the widget. It doesn't matter if the suggestions array is empty, the important thing is that the callback is called.

So now, each item in the suggestions menu will have a `<span>` element, wrapping the text that was typed into the `<input>`. We can use it to style this text slightly differently, such as with the following `<style>` (added to the `<head>` of the page):

```
<style>
  span { color:green !important; }
</style>
```

This should now make the suggestion menu appears like this:

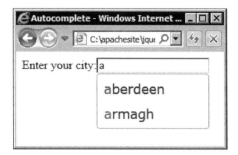

Summary

We covered two widgets in this chapter; both of them are new to the library and both work with `<form>` elements of some description. The button widget can be used to turn `<a>`, `<button>`, and `<input>` (of type `button`, `submit`, or `reset`) into attractively and consistently styled-rich widgets.

The autocomplete widget is attached to an `<input>` of the type text and is used to show a list of suggestions when the visitor begins typing into the `<input>`. The widget is preconfigured to work with a local array of data or a URL that outputs data in the expected format. It can also be configured to work with data that is not output in the expected format, provided we process the data prior to it being passed to the widget, in order to be displayed in the suggestions menu, making this an extremely versatile and powerful widget.

This now brings us to the end of the section covering the visible widgets we see and interact with on the page. In the next few chapters, we'll look at the interaction helpers, which add different types of behavior to the elements on our pages, starting with the draggable and droppable components.

10
Drag and Drop

So far in this book, we've covered the complete range of fully released interface widgets, and over the next four chapters, we're going to shift our focus to the core interaction helpers. These components of the library differ from those that we've already looked at, in that they are not physical objects or widgets that exist on the page.

These are low-level interaction components as opposed to the high-level widgets that we looked at in the first part of this book. They help the elements used on your pages to be more engaging and interactive for your visitors, which adds value to your site and can help make your web applications appear more professional. They also help to blur the distinction between the browser and the desktop, and provide greater usability to make web applications more efficient, effective, and natural.

In this chapter, we'll be covering two very closely related components—**draggables** and **droppables**. The draggables API transforms any specified element into something that your visitors can pick up with the mouse pointer and drag around the page. Methods that are exposed allow you to restrict the draggables movement, make it return to its starting point after being dropped, and much more.

In this chapter, we will cover the following topics:

- How to make elements draggable
- The options available for configuring draggable objects
- How to make an element return to its starting point once the drag ends
- How to use event callbacks at different points in an interaction
- The role of a drag helper
- Containing draggables
- How to control draggability with the component's methods
- Turning an element into a drop target

- Defining accepted draggables
- Working with droppable classnames
- Defining drop tolerance
- Reacting to interactions between draggables and droppables

The droppables API allows you to define a region of the page or a container of some kind, for people to drop the draggables on to, in order to make something else happen, for example, to define a choice that is made, or add a product to a shopping basket. A rich set of events are fired by the droppable that lets us react to the most interesting moments of any drag interaction.

The deal with drag and droppables

Dragging-and-dropping as behaviors go hand-in-hand with each other. Where one is found, the other is invariably close by. Dragging an element around a web page is all very well and good, but if there's nowhere for that element to be dragged to, the whole exercise is usually pointless.

You can use the `draggable` class independently from the `droppable` class, as pure dragging for the sake of dragging can have its uses, such as with the dialog component. However, you can't use the `droppable` class without the `draggable`. You don't need to make use of any of draggable's methods of course, but using droppables without having anything to drop on to them is of no value whatsoever.

Like with the widgets, it is possible, however, to combine some of the interaction helpers; draggables and droppables go together obviously. But draggables can also be used with sortables, as we'll see in *Chapter 12, Selecting*, as well as resizables.

Draggables

The draggables component is used to make any specified element or collection of elements draggable, so that they can be **picked up** and moved around the page by a visitor. Draggability is a great effect, and is a feature that can be used in numerous ways to improve the interface of our web pages.

Using jQuery UI means that we don't have to worry about all of the tricky differences between browsers that originally made draggable elements on web pages a nightmare to implement and maintain.

A basic drag implementation

Let's look at the default implementation by first making a simple `<div>` element draggable. We won't do any additional configuration. Therefore, all that this code will allow you to do is pick up the element with the mouse pointer and drag it around the viewport.

In a new file in your text editor, add the following code:

```html
<!DOCTYPE html>
<html>
  <head>
    <meta charset="utf-8">
    <title>Draggable</title>
    <link rel="stylesheet" href="css/draggable.css">
  </head>
  <body>
    <div id="drag"></div>
      <script src="development-bundle/jquery-1.4.4.js">
      </script>
      <script src="development-bundle/ui/jquery.ui.core.js">
      </script>
      <script src="development-bundle/ui/jquery.ui.widget.js">
      </script>
      <script src="development-bundle/ui/jquery.ui.mouse.js">
      </script>
      <script src="development-bundle/ui/jquery.ui.draggable.js">
      </script>
      <script>
        (function($){
          $("#drag").draggable();
        })(jQuery);
      </script>
  </body>
</html>
```

Save this as `draggable1.html` in your `jqueryui` folder. As with the widget-based components of jQuery UI, the draggable component can be enabled using a single line of code. This invokes the draggable's constructor method `draggable` and turns the specified element into a drag object.

We need the following files from the library to enable draggability on an element:

- `jquery-x.x.x.js`
- `jquery.ui.core.js`
- `jquery.ui.widget.js`
- `jquery.ui.mouse.js`
- `jquery.ui.draggable.js`

We're using a plain `<div>` with a background image specified in the CSS file that we're linking to in the `<head>` of the page. Use the following style sheet for the drag element:

```
#drag {
  width:114px; height:114px; cursor:move;
  background:url(../img/draggable.png) no-repeat;
}
```

Save this as `draggable.css` in the `css` folder. When you view the page in a browser, you'll see that the image can be moved around to your heart's content, as shown in the following screenshot:

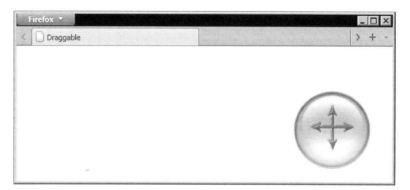

Configuring draggable options

The draggable component has a wide range of configurable options, giving us a very fine degree of control over the behavior that it adds. The following table lists the options that we can manipulate to configure and control our drag elements:

Option	Default value	Used to...
addClasses	true	Add the `ui-draggable` class to the drag object. Set to `false` to prevent this class being added.
appendTo	"parent"	Specify a container element for drag objects with a helper attached.
axis	false	Constrain drag objects to one axis of motion. Accepts the strings x and y as values, or the Boolean `false`.
cancel	":input, option"	Prevent certain elements from being dragged, if they match the specified element selector.
connectToSortable	false	Allow the drag object to be dropped on to a sortable list and become one of the sort elements.
containment	false	Prevent drag objects from being dragged out of the bounds of its parent element.
cursor	"auto"	Specify a CSS `cursor` to be used while the pointer is over the drag object.
cursorAt	false	Specify a default position at which the cursor appears relative to the drag object, while it is being dragged.
delay	0	Specify a time in milliseconds that the start of the drag interaction should be delayed by.
disabled	false	Disable dragging on the draggable.
distance	1	Specify the distance in pixels that the pointer should move with the mouse button held down on the drag object, before the drag begins.
grid	false	Make the drag object snap to an imaginary grid on the page. Accepts an array containing x and y pixel values of the grid.
handle	false	Define a specific area of the drag object that is used to hold the pointer on, in order to drag.
helper	"original"	Define a pseudo-drag element that is dragged instead of the drag object. Can accept the string values `original` or `clone`, or can accept a function that returns the helper element.

Option	Default value	Used to...
iframeFix	false	Stop all <iframe> elements on the page from capturing mouse events, while a drag is in progress.
opacity	false	Set the opacity of the helper element.
refreshPositions	false	Calculate the positions of all drop objects while the drag is in progress.
revert	false	Make the drag object return to its start position once the drag ends, when set to true. Can also accept the strings valid and invalid, where the revert is only applied if the drag object is dropped on a valid drop object or vice-versa, respectively.
revertDuration	500	Set the number of milliseconds it takes for the drag object to return to its starting position.
scope	"default"	Set the scope of the drag object with respect to the drop objects that are valid for it.
scroll	true	Make the viewport automatically scroll when the drag object is moved within the threshold of the viewport's edge.
scrollSensitivity	20	Define how close in pixels the drag object should get to the edge of the viewport, before scrolling begins.
scrollSpeed	20	Set the speed at which the viewport scrolls.
snap	false	Cause drag objects to snap to the edges of specified elements.
snapMode	"both"	Specify which edges of the element the drag object will snap to. Can be set to either inside, outside, or both.
snapTolerance	20	Set the distance from snapping elements that drag objects should reach, before snapping occurs.
stack	false	Ensure that the current drag object is always on top of other drag objects in the same group. Accepts an object containing group and/or min properties.
zIndex	false	Set the zIndex of the helper element.

Using the configuration options

Let's put some of these options to use. They can be configured in exactly the same way as the options exposed by the widgets that we looked at in previous chapters, and also usually have both getter and setter modes.

In the first example a moment ago, we used CSS to specify that the `move` cursor should be used when the pointer hovers over our draggable `<div>`. Let's change this and use the `cursor` option of the draggables component instead.

Remove `cursor:move` from `draggable.css`, and resave it as `draggableNoCursor.css`. Also change the `<link>` tag in `draggable1.html`, to reference the new file:

```
<link rel="stylesheet" href="css/draggableNoCursor.css">
```

Then change the final `<script>` element to the following:

```
<script>
  (function($) {
    var dragOpts = {
      cursor: "move"
    };
    $("#drag").draggable(dragOpts);
  })(jQuery);
</script>
```

Save this as `draggable2.html`, and try it out in your browser. An important point to note about this option is that the `move` cursor that we have specified is not applied until we actually start the drag. When using this option in place of simple CSS, we should perhaps provide some other visual cue that the element is draggable.

Let's look at a few more of draggable's many configuration options. Change the configuration object in `draggable2.html` to the following:

```
var dragOpts = {
  cursor: "move",
  axis: "y",
  distance: "30",
  cursorAt: {
    top: 0,
    left: 0
  }
};
```

This can be saved as `draggable3.html`. The first new option that we've configured is the `axis` option, which has restricted the draggable to moving only upwards or downwards in the page, but not side-to-side across it.

Next, we've specified `30` as the value of the `distance` option. This means that the cursor will have to travel `30` pixels across the drag object, with the mouse button held down, before the drag will begin.

The final option, `cursorAt`, is configured using an object literal, whose properties can be `top`, `right`, `bottom`, or `left`. The values supplied to the properties that we choose to use are the values relative to the drag object that the cursor will assume when a drag occurs.

However, you'll notice in this example that the value for the `left` option seems to be ignored. The reason for this is that we have configured the `axis` option. When we begin the drag, the drag object will automatically move, so that the cursor is at `0` pixels from the top of the element, but it will not move, so that the cursor is `0` pixels from the left edge as we have specified, because the drag object cannot move left.

Let's look at some more of draggable's options in action. Change `draggable3.html`, so that the configuration object appears as follows:

```
var dragOpts = {
  delay: 500,
  grid: [100,100]
};
```

Save the file as `draggable4.html`. The `delay` option, which takes a value in milliseconds, specifies the length of time that the mouse button must be held down with the cursor over the drag object, before the drag will begin.

The `grid` option is similar in usage to the `steps` option of the slider widget. It is configured using an array of two values representing the number of pixels along each axis that the drag element should jump, when it is dragged. This option can be used safely in conjunction with the `axis` option.

Resetting dragged elements

It is very easy to configure drag objects to return to their original starting position on the page once they've been dropped, and there are several options that can be used to control this behavior. Change the configuration object that we used with `draggable4.html`, so that it appears as follows:

```
var dragOpts = {
  revert: true
};
```

Save this as `draggable5.html`. By supplying `true` as the value of the `revert` option, we've caused the drag object to return to its starting position at the end of any drag interaction. However, you'll notice that the drag element doesn't just pop back to its starting position instantly. Rather, it's smoothly animated back, with no additional configurations required.

Another revert-related option is the `revertDuration` option, which we can use to control the speed of the revert animation. Change the configuration object in `draggable5.html`, so that it appears as follows:

```
var dragOpts = {
    revert: true,
    revertDuration: 100
};
```

Save this as `draggable6.html`. The default value for the `revertDuration` is `500` milliseconds, so by lowering it to `100`, the relative speed of the animation is considerably increased.

The actual speed of the animation will always be determined on the fly, based on the distance from the drop point to the starting point. The `revertDuration` option simply defines a target for the animation length in time.

Drag handles

The `handle` option allows us to define a region of the drag object that can be used to drag the object. All other areas cannot be used to drag the object. A simple analogy is the dialog widget. You can drag the dialog around only if you click and hold on the title bar. The title bar is the drag handle.

In the following example, we'll add a simple drag handle to our drag object. Put a new empty `<div>` element inside the drag element:

```
<div id="drag"><div id="handle"></div></div>
```

Then, change the configuration object to the following:

```
var dragOpts = {
    handle: "#handle"
};
```

Save this as `draggable7.html`. We've given the new `<div>` an `id` attribute and then specified this `id` as the value of the `handle` option in our configuration object.

The handle is styled with a few simple style rules. Add the following new styles to draggableNoCursor.css:

```
#handle {
   width:30px; height:30px; border-bottom:2px solid #ff0000;
   border-left:2px solid #ff0000; position:absolute;
   right:10px; top:10px; cursor:move;
}
```

Save this as dragHandle.css in the css folder. Don't forget to link to the new style sheet from the <head> of draggable7.html:

```
<link rel="stylesheet" href="css/draggableHandle.css">
```

When we run the page in a browser, we see that the original drag object is still draggable, but only when the handle is selected with the pointer as seen in the following screenshot:

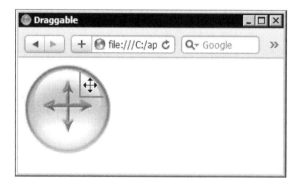

Helper elements

Several configuration options are directly related to drag helpers. A helper is a substitute element that is used to show where the object is on screen, while the drag is in progress, instead of moving the actual draggable.

A helper can be a very simple object in place of the actual drag object. This can help cut-down on the intensity of the drag operation, lessening the load on the visitor's processor. Once the drag has completed, the actual element can be moved to the new location.

Let's look at how helpers can be used in the following example. Remove the
`<div>` we used for the handle and revert back to the `draggable.css` style sheet
in `draggable7.html`, then change the configuration object to the following:

```
var dragOpts = {
    helper: "clone"
};
```

Save this file as `draggable8.html`. The value `clone` for the `helper` option causes
an exact copy of the original drag object to be created and used as the draggable.
Therefore, the original object stays in its starting position at all times.

This also causes the `clone` object to revert back to its starting position, an effect
which cannot be changed, even by supplying `false` as the value of the `revert`
option. The following screenshot shows the `clone` option in action:

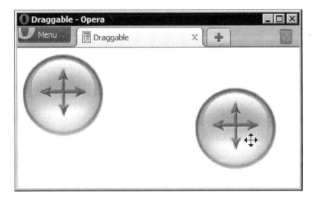

In addition to the string `clone` and the default `original`, we can also use a function
as the value of this option. This allows us to specify our own custom element to use
as the helper.

Change the final `<script>` element in `draggable8.html` to the following:

```
<script>
  (function($) {
    function helperMaker() {
      return $("<div />", {
        css: {
          border: "4px solid #ccc",
          opacity: 0.5,
          height: 110,
          width: 120
        }
      });
```

```
    }
    var dragOpts = {
      helper: helperMaker
    };
    $("#drag").draggable(dragOpts);
  })(jQuery);
</script>
```

Save this file as `draggable9.html`. Our `helperMaker()` function creates a new `<div>` element using standard jQuery functionality, and then sets some CSS properties on it to define its physical appearance. It then, importantly, returns the new element. When supplying a function as the value of the `helper` option, the function must return an element (either a jQuery object, as in this example, or an actual DOMNode).

Now when the drag begins, it is our custom helper that becomes the drag object. Because the custom element is much simpler than the original drag object, it can help improve the responsiveness and performance of the application it is used in. The following screenshot shows our custom helper:

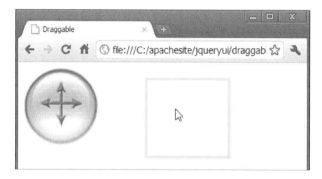

Helper opacity

We used the `css` jQuery method in this example during the creation of the custom helper. However, we can also use the `opacity` option of the drag object to set the opacity of helper elements as a cross-platform solution.

Constraining the drag

Another aspect of drag scenarios is that of containment. In our examples so far, the `<body>` of the page has been the container of the drag object. There are also options that we can configure to specify how the drag object behaves with regard to another container element.

We'll look at these in the following examples, starting with the `container` option, which allows us to specify a container element for the drag object. In the `<head>` of `draggable9.html`, add the following link to the style sheet that we'll be using in this example:

```
<link rel="stylesheet" href="css/draggableContainer.css">
```

Then, wrap the drag element within a container `<div>` as follows:

```
<div id="container">
  <div id="drag">
  </div>
</div>
```

Then, change the configuration object to the following:

```
var dragOpts = {
  containment: "parent"
};
```

Save this variant as `draggable10.html`. On the page, we've added a new `<div>` element as the parent of the existing drag element. In the code, we've used the value `parent` for the `containment` option, so the element that is the direct parent of the drag object (the `<div>` with the `id` of `container` in this example) will be used as the container.

The parent `<div>` needs some basic styling to give it dimensions and so it can be seen on the page. Add the following code to `draggable.css` and resave the file as `draggableContainer.css`. Remember, this string is not the `id` of an element, or a jQuery selector (although selectors are also supported).

```
#container {
  height:250px; width:250px; border:2px solid #ff0000;
}
```

When you run the page in your browser, you'll see that the drag object cannot exceed the boundary of its container.

Along with the string `parent` that we used in this example, we could also specify a selector, for example:

```
var dragOpts = {
  containment: "#container"
};
```

There are three additional options related to drag objects within containers and these are all related to scrolling. However, you should note that these are only applicable when the document is the container.

The default value of the `scroll` option is `true`, but when we drag the `<div>` to the edge of the container, it does not scroll. You may have noticed in previous examples, where the drag object was not within a specified container, the viewport automatically scrolled. We can fix this by setting the CSS `overflow` style to `auto` in a style sheet if necessary.

Snapping

Drag elements can be given an almost magnetic quality by configuring snapping. This feature causes dragged elements to align themselves to specified elements, while they are being dragged.

In the next example, we'll look at the effects that snapping has on the behavior of the drag object. Get rid of the container we added in the previous example, and add a new empty `<div>` element directly after the drag element, as follows:

```
<div id="drag"></div>
<div id="snapper"></div>
```

Then, change the configuration object, so that it appears as follows:

```
var dragOpts = {
  snap: "#snapper",
  snapMode: "inner",
  snapTolerance: 50
};
```

Save this as `draggable11.html`. We also need some additional styles; add the following code to the bottom of `draggable.css`:

```
#snapper {
  width:300px; height:300px; border:1px solid #ff0000;
}
```

Save this file as `draggableSnap.css` in the `css` directory. Don't forget to add a link to the new style sheet in the `<head>` of the page:

```
<link rel="stylesheet" href="css/draggableSnap.css">
```

We've supplied the selector `#snapper` as the value of the `snap` option in our configuration object, and have added a `<div>` element with a matching `id` to the page. Therefore, our drag object will snap to this element on the page, while the object is being dragged.

We also set the `snapMode` option to `inner` (the other possible values are `outer` and `both`), so snapping will occur on the inside edges of our `snapper` element. If we drag the element towards the outer edge of the `snapper` element and get within the tolerance range, the element will snap to the inner edge.

Finally, we've set the `snapTolerance` to `50`, which is the maximum distance (in pixels) the drag object will need to get to the `snapper` element, before snapping will occur. As soon as a drag object is within this range, it will snap to the element.

When we drag the image within `50` pixels of the edge of the snapper element, the drag object will automatically align itself to that edge, as shown in the following screenshot:

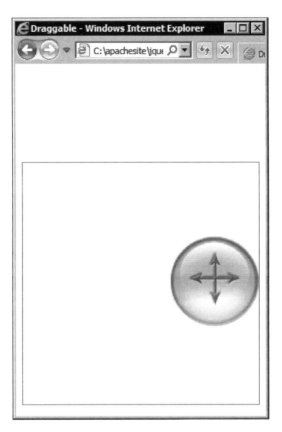

Draggable event callbacks

In addition to the options that we have already looked at, there are three more that can be used as callback functions to execute code after specific custom events occur. These events are listed in the following table:

Event	Fired when...
drag	The mouse is moved while dragging
start	Dragging starts
stop	Dragging stops

When defining callback functions to make use of these events, the functions will always receive two arguments automatically, the original event object as the first argument and a second object containing the following properties:

Property	Usage
helper	A jQuery object representing the helper element
position	A nested object with properties top and left, which is the position of the helper element relative to the original drag element
absolutePosition	A nested object with properties top and left, which is the position of the helper element relative to the page

Using the callbacks and the two objects that are passed as arguments is extremely easy. We can look at a brief example to highlight their usage. Remove the snapper `<div>` in `draggable11.html`, and change the configuration object as follows:

```
var dragOpts = {
  start: function(e, ui) {
    ui.helper.addClass("up");
  },
  stop: function(e, ui) {
    ui.helper.removeClass("up");
  }
};
```

Save this as `draggable12.html`. We also need a new style sheet for this example; add the following code to `draggable.css`:

```
#drag.up {
  width:120px; height:121px;
  background:url(../img/draggable_on.png) no-repeat;
}
```

Save this version of the style sheet as `draggableEvents.css` in the `css` directory, and don't forget to update the link in the `<head>` of the page to point to the new style sheet.

In this example, our configuration object contains just two options — the `start` and `stop` callbacks. We set literal functions as the values of these options. What all the functions do in this example is add or remove a classname respectively.

The classname adds a slightly different background image to the draggable element, which when applied appears as shown in the following before and during screenshot:

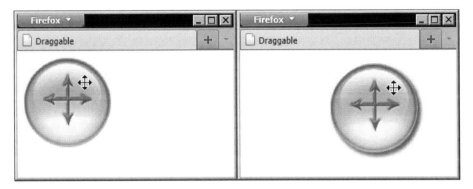

Let's move on to a slightly more complex example where we can make use of the second object passed to our callbacks. We need a couple of new elements on the page; change the `<body>` of the page, so that it contains the following elements:

```
<div id="container">
  <div id="drag"></div>
</div>
<div id="results"></div>
```

Then change the final `<script>` element, so that it appears as follows:

```
<script>
  (function($) {
    var dragOpts = {
      stop: function(e, ui) {
        var rel = $("<p />", {
          text: "The helper was moved " + ui.position.top + "px down,
            and " + ui.position.left + "px to the left of its
            original position."
        }),
        offset = $("<p />", {
```

```
            text: "The helper was moved " + ui.offset.top + "px from
                the top, and " + ui.offset.left + "px to the left
                relative to the viewport."
            });
            $("#results").empty().append(rel).append(offset);
        }
    };
    $("#drag").draggable(dragOpts);
})(jQuery);
</script>
```

Save this as `draggable13.html`. We've defined a callback function as the value of the `stop` option, so it will be executed each time a drag interaction stops. Our callback function receives the event object (which we don't need but must specify in order to access the second object) and a `ui` object containing useful information about the draggable helper.

All our function needs to do is, create two new `<p>` elements, concatenating the values found in the `ui` object: `ui.position.top`, `ui.position.left`, `ui.offset.top`, and `ui.offset.left`. It then inserts the new elements into the results `<div>`. Here's how the page should look after the draggable has been dragged:

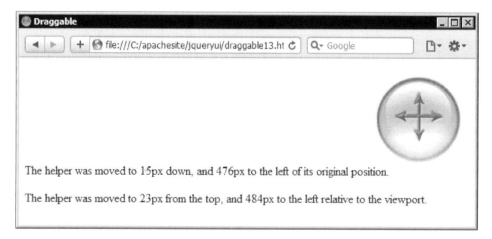

Draggable's methods

The draggable interaction helper does not expose any unique methods of its own, only the common API methods, which are, `destroy`, `disable`, `enable`, `option`, and `widget`.

Droppables

In a nutshell, the droppables component of jQuery UI gives us a place for drag objects to be dropped. A region of the page is defined as a droppable, and when a drag object is dropped onto that region, something else is triggered. You can react to drops on a valid target very easily, using the extensive event model exposed by this component.

Let's start with the default droppable implementation. In a new file in your text editor, add the following page:

```html
<!DOCTYPE html>
<html>
  <head>
    <meta charset="utf-8">
    <title>Droppable</title>
    <link rel="stylesheet" href="css/droppable.css">
  </head>
  <body>
    <div id="drag"></div>
    <div id="target"></div>
    <script src="development-bundle/jquery-1.4.4.js"></script>
    <script src="development-bundle/ui/jquery.ui.core.js">
    </script>
    <script src="development-bundle/ui/jquery.ui.widget.js">
    </script>
    <script src="development-bundle/ui/jquery.ui.mouse.js">
    </script>
    <script src="development-bundle/ui/jquery.ui.draggable.js">
    </script>
    <script src="development-bundle/ui/jquery.ui.droppable.js">
    </script>
    <script>
      (function($){
        $("#drag").draggable();
        $("#target").droppable();
      })(jQuery);
    </script>
  </body>
</html>
```

Save this as `droppable1.html`. The extremely basic style sheet that is linked to, in this example, is simply an updated version of `draggable.css`, and appears as follows:

```
#drag {
    width:114px; height:114px; margin-bottom:5px; z-index:2;
    cursor:move; background:url(../img/draggable.png) no-repeat;
}
#target {
    width:200px; height:200px; border:3px solid #000;
    position:absolute; right:20px; top:20px; z-index:1;
}
```

Save this as `droppable.css` in the `css` folder. When the page is run in a browser, it should look like the following screenshot:

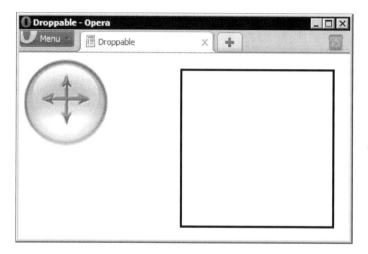

In this example, the droppable is created (we can see this with the class name `ui-droppable` that is added to the specified element when the page loads).

Even though we haven't added any additional logic to our script, events are firing throughout the interaction on both the drag object and the drop target. A little later in the chapter, we'll look at these events in more detail to see how we can hook into them, to react to successful drops.

The files we used for this basic droppable implementation are as follows:

- `jquery-x.x.x.js`
- `jquery.ui.core.js`
- `jquery.ui.widget.js`

- jquery.ui.mouse.js
- jquery.ui.draggable.js
- jquery.ui.droppable.js

As you can see, the droppables component is an extension of draggables, rather than a completely independent component. Therefore, it requires the jquery. ui.draggable.js file in addition to its own source file. The reason our droppable does nothing, is because we haven't configured it, so let's do that next.

Configuring droppables

The droppable class is considerably smaller than the draggable class, and there are fewer configurable options for us to play with. The following table lists those options available to us:

Option	Default	Used to...
accept	"*"	Set the draggable element(s) that the droppable will accept.
activeClass	false	Set the class that is applied to the droppable, while an accepted drag object is being dragged.
addClasses	true	Add the ui-droppable class to the droppable.
disabled	false	Disable the droppable.
greedy	false	Stop drop events from bubbling when a drag object is dropped onto nested droppables.
hoverClass	false	Set the class that is applied to the droppable, while an accepted drag object is within the boundary of the droppable.
scope	"default"	Define sets of drag objects and drop targets.
tolerance	"intersect"	Set the mode that triggers an accepted drag object being considered over a droppable.

Configuring accepted draggables

In order to get a visible result from the droppable, we're going to use a couple of the configurable options together in the following example, which will highlight the drop target when an accepted drag object is interacted with. Change the elements on the page in droppable1.html, so that they appear as follows:

```
<div class="drag" id="drag1"></div>
<div class="drag" id="drag2"></div>
<div id="target"></div>
```

Next, change the final `<script>` element to the following:

```
<script>
  (function($) {
    $(".drag").draggable();
    var dropOpts = {
      accept: "#drag1",
      activeClass: "activated"
    };
    $("#target").droppable(dropOpts);
  })(jQuery);
</script>
```

Save this as `droppable2.html`. The `accept` option takes a selector. In this example, we've specified that only the drag object that has an `id` of `drag1` should be accepted by the droppable.

We've also specified the classname `activated` as the value of the `activeClass` option. This classname will be applied to the droppable when the accepted drag object starts to be dragged. The `hoverClass` option can be used in exactly the same way to add styles, when an accepted drag object is over a droppable.

We need a new style sheet for this example; modify `droppable.css` so that it appears as follows:

```
.drag {
  width:114px; height:114px; margin-bottom:5px; z-index:2;
  cursor:move; background:url(../img/draggable.png) no-repeat;
}
#target {
  width:200px; height:200px; border:3px solid #000;
  position:absolute; right:20px; top:20px; z-index:1;
}
.activated {
  border:3px solid #339900; background-color:#ccffcc;
}
```

Save this file as `droppableActive.css` in the `css` folder, and link to it in the `<head>` of the page:

```
<link rel="stylesheet" href="css/droppableActive.css">
```

When we view this page in a browser, we should find that when we move the first drag object, which is defined as accepted, the droppable picks up the `activated` class and turns green. However, when the second drag object is moved, the drop target does not respond. The following screenshot shows how the page should look, while the first drag object is being dragged:

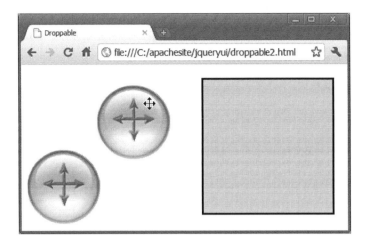

In addition to a string value, the `accept` option can also take a function as its value. This function will be executed once for every drag object that is on the page. The function must return either `true`, to indicate that the drag object is accepted, or `false` to indicate that it's not.

To see the function value of the `accept` option in action, change the final `<script>` element in `droppable2.html` to the following:

```
<script>
  (function($) {
    $(".drag").draggable();
    function dragEnrol(el) {
      return (el.attr("id") === "drag1") ? true : false;
    }
    var dropOpts = {
      accept: dragEnrol,
      activeClass: "activated"
    };
    $("#target").droppable(dropOpts);
  })(jQuery);
</script>
```

Save this variation as `droppable3.html`. On the surface, the page works exactly the same as it did in the previous example. But this time, acceptability is being determined by the JavaScript ternary statement within the `dragEnrol` function, instead of a simple selector.

Note that the function we use with the `accept` option is automatically passed by a jQuery object representing the drag object as an argument, so we can call jQuery methods on this object. This makes it easy to obtain information about it, such as its `id` as in this example. This callback can be extremely useful when advanced filtering beyond a selector is required.

Tolerance

Drop tolerance refers to the way a droppable detects whether a drag object is over it or not. The default value is `intersect`. The following table lists the modes that this option may be configured with:

Mode	Implementation
fit	The drag object must be completely within the boundary of the droppable for it to be considered over it
intersect	At least 25 percent of the drag object must be within the boundary of the droppable before it is considered over it
pointer	The mouse pointer must touch the droppable boundary before the drag object is considered over the droppable
touch	The drag object is over the droppable as soon as an edge of the drag object touches an edge of the droppable

So far, all of our droppable examples have used `intersect`, which is the default value of the `tolerance` option. Let's see what difference the other values for this option make to an implementation of the component. Revert to the `#drag` and `#target` elements from `droppable2.html`, and then use the following configuration object:

```
var dropOpts = {
  hoverClass: "activated",
  tolerance: "pointer"
};
```

Save this as `droppable4.html`. This time we use the `hoverClass` option to specify the classname that is added to the droppable. We then use the `tolerance` option to specify which tolerance mode is used.

The part of the drag object that is over the droppable is irrelevant in this example; it is the mouse pointer that must cross the boundary of the droppable, while a drag is in progress for our `over` class to be activated:

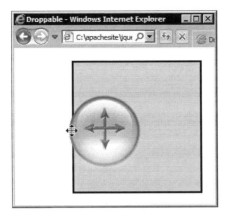

For good measure, the following screenshot shows how the `touch` mode works. Here, the drag element itself need only touch the edge of the droppable, before triggering our `over` class:

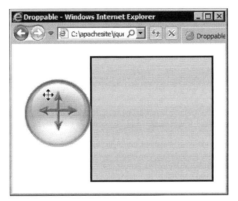

Droppable event callbacks

The options that we've looked at so far configure various operational features of the droppable. In addition to these, there are almost as many callback options, so that we can define functions that react to different things occurring to the droppable and its accepted drag objects. These options are listed in the following table:

Callback option	Invoked when...
activate	An accepted drag object begins dragging
deactivate	An accepted drag object stops being dragged
drop	An accepted drag object is dropped onto a droppable

Callback option	Invoked when...
out	An accepted drag object is moved out of the bounds (including the tolerance) of the droppable
over	An accepted drag object is moved within the bounds (including the tolerance) of the droppable

Let's put together a basic example that makes use of these callback options. We'll add a status bar to our droppable that reports the status of different interactions between the drag object and the droppable. In `droppable4.html`, add the following new element directly after the `target` element:

```
<div id="status"></div>
```

Then, change the final `<script>` element to this:

```
<script>
  (function($) {
    $("#drag").draggable();
    var dropOpts = {
      accept: "#drag",
      activate: eventCallback,
      deactivate: eventCallback,
      drop: eventCallback,
      out: eventCallback,
      over: eventCallback
    },
    eventMessages = {
      dropactivate: "A draggable is active",
      dropdeactivate: "A draggable is no longer active",
      drop: "An accepted draggable was dropped on the droppable",
      dropout: "An accepted draggable was moved off the droppable",
      dropover: "An accepted draggable is over the droppable"
    };
    function eventCallback(e) {
      var message = $("<p />", {
        id: "message",
        text: eventMessages[e.type]
      });
      $("#status").empty().append(message);
    }
    $("#target").droppable(dropOpts);
  })(jQuery);
</script>
```

Save this file as `droppable5.html`. We also need some new styles for this example. Create a new style sheet in your text editor, and add to it the following selectors and rules:

```
#drag {
   width:114px; height:114px; margin-bottom:5px; z-index:2;
   cursor:move; background:url(../img/draggable.png) no-repeat;

}
#target {
   width:250px; height:200px; border:3px solid #000;
   position:absolute; right:20px; top:20px; z-index:1;
}
#status {
   width:230px; padding:10px; border:3px solid #000;
   position:absolute; top:223px; right:20px; color:#000;
}
#message { margin:0px; font-size:80%; }
```

Save this file as `droppableEvents.css` in the `css` directory. Don't forget to update the `<link>` in the `<head>` of the page, to point to the new style sheet:

```
<link rel="stylesheet" href="css/droppableEvents.css">
```

The `<body>` of the page contains, along with the droppable, a new status bar, which in this case is a simple `<div>` element. In the script, we define our configurable options, specifying that the function `eventCallback` should be executed when each of the events are detected.

Next, we define an object literal, in which the key for each property is set to one of the event types that may be triggered. The value of each property is the message that we want to display for any given event.

We then define our callback function. Like other components, the callback functions used in the droppables component automatically pass two objects—the `event` object and an object representing the drag element.

We use the `type` property of the `event` object to retrieve the appropriate message from the `eventMessages` object. We then use standard jQuery element creation and manipulation methods to add the message to the status bar.

Here's how the status bar should look following an interaction:

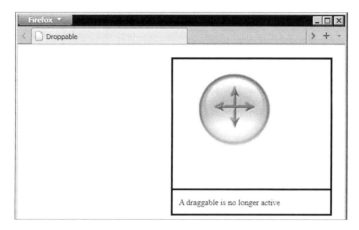

After playing around with the page, it may appear that one of our messages is not being displayed. When the drag object is dropped onto the droppable, our `drop` message is not shown.

Actually, the message is shown, but because the `deactivate` event is fired immediately after the `drop` event, the `drop` message is overwritten right away. There are a number of ways we could work around this; the simplest, of course, would be not to use the `drop` and `deactivate` options together.

Although we only make use of the event object (`e`) in this example, a second object is also passed automatically to any callback functions we use with the event options. This object contains information relevant to the droppable such as the following:

Property	Value
`ui.draggable`	The current drag object
`ui.helper`	The current drag helper
`ui.position`	The current relative position of the helper
`ui.offset`	The current absolute position of the helper

Scope

Both the draggables and droppables feature the `scope` configuration option that allows us to easily define groups of drag objects and drop targets. In this next example, we can look at how these options can be configured and the effect that configuring them has. We'll link to another new style sheet in this example, so in the `<head>` of `droppable5.html`, change the `<link>` element, so that it appears as follows:

```
<link rel="stylesheet" href="css/droppableScope.css">
```

We need a number of new elements for this example. Change the <body> of the page in droppable5.html, so that it contains the following elements:

```
<div id="target_a">A</div>
<div id="target_b">B</div>
<div id="group_a">
  <p>A</p>
  <div id="a1" class="group_a">a1</div>
  <div id="a2" class="group_a">a2</div>
  <div id="a3" class="group_a">a3</div>
</div>
<div id="group_b">
  <p>B</p>
  <div id="b1" class="group_b">b1</div>
  <div id="b2" class="group_b">b2</div>
  <div id="b3" class="group_b">b3</div>
</div>
```

To make these elements behave correctly, change the final <script> element to the following:

```
<script>
  (function($) {
    var dragOpts_a = {
      scope: "a"
    },
    dragOpts_b = {
      scope: "b"
    },
    dropOpts_a = {
      hoverClass: "over",
      scope: "a"
    },
    dropOpts_b = {
      hoverClass: "over",
      scope: "b"
    };
    $(".group_a").draggable(dragOpts_a);
    $(".group_b").draggable(dragOpts_b);
    $("#target_a").droppable(dropOpts_a);
    $("#target_b").droppable(dropOpts_b);
  })(jQuery);
</script>
```

Save this file as `droppable6.html`. Next, we need to create the new CSS file; in a new page in your text editor, add the following code:

```
#target_a, #target_b, #group_a, #group_b {
   width:150px; height:150px; padding:50px;
   margin:0 20px 20px 0; border:2px solid black; float:left;
   font-family:Georgia; font-size:100px; color:red;
   text-align:center;
}
#group_a, #group_b {
   width:518px; height:115px; padding:5px 0 5px 5px;
   margin-bottom:20px; clear:both;
}
p { float:left; margin:0 20px 0; }
.group_a, .group_b {
   width:94px; height:94px; padding:20px 0 0 20px;
   margin-right:20px; float:left; font-family:arial;
   font-size:14px; color:red; text-align:left;
   background:url(../img/draggable.png) no-repeat;
}
.over { background-color:#ccffcc; }
```

Save this as `droppableScope.css` in the `css` folder.

The page has two drop targets and two groups of three drag objects, all of which are labeled to show the group they belong to. In the script, we define two configuration objects for the two groups of draggables, and two configuration objects for the drop targets. Within each configuration object, we set the `scope` option.

The values we set for the `scope` of each drop target matches the `scope` of each drag object. Therefore, if we want to use `scope`, it must be defined for both the drag object and drop target. If we try to set the `scope` of a droppable, but don't give at least one drag object the same `scope`, an error is thrown.

Setting the `scope` gives us another technique for defining which drag objects are accepted by which drop targets, but it is provided as an alternative to the `accept` option; the two options should not be used together.

The following screenshot shows how the page should appear:

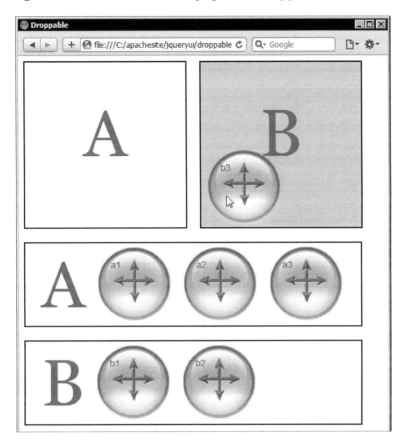

Greedy

The final option that we are going to look at in connection with the droppable component is the greedy option. This option can be useful in situations where there is a droppable nested within another droppable. If we don't use this option, both droppables will fire events during certain interactions.

The greedy option is an easy way to avoid event-bubbling problems in an efficient and cross-browser manner. Let's take a closer look at this option with an example. Change the <link> in droppable6.html, so that it links to a new style sheet:

```
<link rel="stylesheet" href="css/droppableNesting.css">
```

Then change the `<body>`, so that it contains the following elements:

```
<div id="drag"></div>
<div class="target" id="outer">
  <div class="target" id="inner"></div>
</div>
<div id="status"></div>
```

Finally, change the last `<script>` element, so that it appears as follows:

```
<script>
  (function($) {
    $(".target").css({ opacity:"0.5" });
    var dragOpts = {
      zIndex: 3
    },
    dropOpts = {
      drop: dropCallback,
      greedy: true
    };
    function dropCallback(e) {
      var message = $("<p></p>", {
        id: "message",
        text: "The firing droppable was " + e.target.id
      });
      $("#status").append(message);
    }
    $("#drag").draggable(dragOpts);
    $(".target").droppable(dropOpts);
  })(jQuery);
</script>
```

Save this example as `droppable7.html`. The CSS for this example is simple and builds on the CSS of previous examples.

```
#drag {
  width:114px; height:114px; margin-bottom:5px; cursor:move;
  background:url(../img/draggable.png) no-repeat;
}
#outer {
  width:300px; height:300px; border:3px solid #000;
  float:right;
  background-color:#99FF99;
}
#inner {
  width:100px; height:100px; border:3px solid #000;
  position:relative; top:100px; left:100px;
```

```
    background-color:#FFFF99;
  }
  #status {
    width:280px; padding:10px; border:3px solid #000;
    float:right; clear:right; color:#000;
  }
  #message { margin:0px; font-size:80%; }
```

Save this as `droppableNesting.css` in the `css` folder.

In this example, we have a smaller droppable nested in the center of a larger droppable. Their opacity is set using the standard jQuery library's `css()` method. In this example, this is necessary, because if we alter the `zIndex` of the elements, so that the drag object appears above the nested droppables, the target element is not reported correctly.

In this example, we use the `zIndex` option of the draggables component to show the drag object above the droppables, while a drag is in progess. The `dropCallback` function is used to add a simple message to the status bar, notifying us which droppable was the `target` of the drop.

Our droppables configuration object uses the `drop` option to wire-up our callback function. However, the key option is the `greedy` option that makes whichever target the draggable is dropped on, to stop the event from escaping into other targets.

If you run the page, and drop the drag object onto one of the droppables, you should see something as shown in the following screenshot:

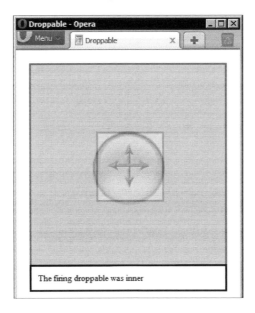

The net effect of setting the `greedy` option to `true` is that the inner droppable prevents the event from propagating into the outer droppable and firing again. If you comment out the `greedy` option and drop the draggable onto the inner droppable, the status message will be inserted twice, once by the inner droppable and once by the outer droppable.

Droppable methods

Like the draggable component, droppable has only the common API methods shared by all library components. This is another component that is primarily option-driven. The methods available to us are the same ones exposed by draggable, namely the standard methods shared by all library components.

A drag and drop game

We've now reached the point where we can have a little fun by putting what we've learned about these two components into a fully working example. In our final drag and drop example, we're going to combine both of these components to create a simple maze game.

The game will consist of a draggable marker that will need to be navigated through a simple maze to a specified droppable at the other end of the maze. We can make things a little more challenging, so that if any of the maze walls are touched by the marker, it will return to the starting position.

The following screenshot shows what we're going to build:

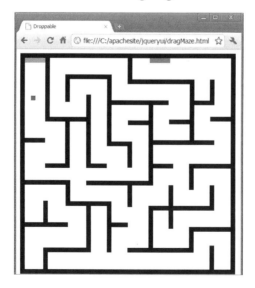

Let's start with the markup. In a new page in your text editor, add the following code:

```
<!DOCTYPE html>
<html>
  <head>
    <meta charset=utf-8">
    <link rel="stylesheet" href="css/dragMaze.css">
    <title>jQuery UI Draggable Maze Game</title>
  </head>
  <body>
    <div id="maze">
      <div id="drag"></div>
      <div id="start"></div>
      <div id="end"></div>
    </div>
    <script src="development-bundle/jquery-1.4.4.js"></script>
    <script src="development-bundle/ui/jquery.ui.core.js">
    </script>
    <script src="development-bundle/ui/jquery.ui.widget.js">
    </script>
    <script src="development-bundle/ui/jquery.ui.mouse.js">
    </script>
    <script src="development-bundle/ui/jquery.ui.draggable.js">
    </script>
    <script src="development-bundle/ui/jquery.ui.droppable.js">
    </script>
    <script></script>
  </body>
</html>
```

Save this file as `dragMaze.html`. On the page, we have our outer container that we've given an `id` of `maze`. We have `<div>` elements for the starting and ending positions, as well as for the drag marker. Our map will need walls. Rather than hand-coding the 46 required walls for the map pattern that we're going to use, I thought we could use jQuery to do this for us.

We left an empty `<script>` element at the bottom of our page. Let's fill that up next with the following code:

```
(function($) {
  var dragOpts = {
    containment: "#maze"
  },
  dropOpts = {
    tolerance: "touch",
```

```
      over: function(e, ui) {
        $("#drag").draggable("destroy").remove();
        $("<div />", {
          id: "drag",
          css: {
            left: 0,
            top: 0
          }
        }).appendTo("#maze");
        $("#drag").draggable(dragOpts);
      }
    },
    endOpts = {
      over: function(e, ui) {
        $("#drag").draggable("destroy").remove();
        alert("Woo! You did it!");
      }
    };
    for (var x = 1; x < 47; x++) {
      $("<div />", {
        id: "a" + x,
        class: "wall"
      }).appendTo("#maze");
    }
    $("#drag").draggable(dragOpts);
    $(".wall").droppable(dropOpts);
    $("#end").droppable(endOpts);
})(jQuery);
```

We also need to style up the walls of the maze, but we can't use any simple JavaScript pattern for this. Unfortunately, we have to hardcode them. In another new file in your text editor, add the following selectors and rules:

```
#maze {
  width:441px; height:441px; border:10px solid #000000;
  position:relative; background-color:#ffffff;
}
#drag {
  width:10px; height:10px; z-index:1;
  background-color:#0000FF;
}
#start {
  width:44px; height:10px; background-color:#00CC00;
  position:absolute; top:0; left:0; z-index:0;
}
```

```
#end {
  width:44px; height:10px; background-color:#FF0000;
  position:absolute; top:0; right:130px;
}
.wall { background-color:#000000; position:absolute; }
#a1 { width:10px; height:133px; left:44px; top:0; }
#a2 { width:44px; height:10px; left:0; top:167px; }
#a3 { width:44px; height:10px; left:44px; top:220px; }
#a4 { width:89px; height:10px; left:0; bottom:176px; }
#a5 { width:94px; height:10px; left:0; bottom:88px; }
#a6 { width:10px; height:41px; left:40px; bottom:0; }
#a7 { width:10px; height:48px; left:88px; top:44px; }
#a8 { width:78px; height:10px; left:54px; top:123px; }
#a9 { width:10px; height:97px; left:88px; top:133px }
#a10 { width:10px; height:45px; left:40px; bottom:98px; }
#a11 { width:88px; height:10px; left:89px; bottom:132px; }
#a12 { width:10px; height:97px; left:132px; bottom:35px; }
#a13 { width:10px; height:44px; left:89px; bottom:142px; }
#a14 { width:92px; height:10px; left:40px; bottom:35px; }
#a15 { width:89px; height:10px; left:88px; top:34px; }
#a16 { width:10px; height:145px; left:132px; top:76px; }
#a17 { width:44px; height:10px; left:132px; top:220px; }
#a18 { width:133px; height:10px; left:132px; bottom:175px; }
#a19 { width:10px; height:107px; left:176px; bottom:35px; }
#a20 { width:10px; height:150px; left:176px; top:34px; }
#a21 { width:35px; height:10px; left:186px; top:174px }
#a22 { width:35px; height:10px; left:186px; bottom:88px; }
#a23 { width:122px; height:10px; left:186px; top:88px; }
#a24 { width:10px; height:44px; left:220px; top:0px; }
#a25 { width:10px; height:55px; left:220px; top:174px; }
#a26 { width:10px; height:45px; left:220px; bottom:130px; }
#a27 { width:133px; height:10px; right:88px; top:44px; }
#a28 { width:10px; height:168px; right:166px; top:98px; }
#a29 { width:44px; height:10px; right:176px; top:130px; }
#a30 { width:10px; height:98px; right:166px; bottom:35px; }
#a31 { width:133px; height:10px; right:88px; bottom:35px; }
#a32 { width:10px; height:133px; right:78px; top:44px; }
#a33 { width:44px; height:10px; right:88px; top:128px; }
#a34 { width:131px; height:10px; right:35px; top:171px; }
#a35 { width:43px; height:10px; right:123px; top:220px; }
#a36 { width:10px; height:91px; right:123px; bottom:85px; }
#a37 { width:131px; height:10px; right:35px; bottom:123px; }
#a38 { width:10px; height:55px; right:79px; top:220px; }
```

```
#a39 { width:44px; height:10px; right:0; top:122px; }
#a40 { width:10px; height:54px; right:79px; bottom:35px; }
#a41 { width:79px; height:10px; right:0; bottom:79px; }
#a42 { width:10px; height:45px; right:35px; top:44px; }
#a43 { width:43px; height:10px; right:35px; top:88px; }
#a44 { width:79px; height:10px; right:0; top:220px; }
#a45 { width:10px; height:44px; right:35px; bottom:132px; }
#a46 { width:10px; height:50px; right:35px; bottom:0; }
```

Save this file as `dragMaze.css` in the `css` folder.

Let's review what the new code does. First, we define a simple configuration object for the drag object. The only option we need to configure is the `containment` option that constrains the draggable marker element within the maze. We can then go ahead and create the draggable behavior with the `draggable` constructor method.

Next, we define the configuration object for the walls. Each wall is treated as a droppable. We specify `touch` as the value of the `tolerance` option, and add a callback function to the `over` option. Therefore, whenever the drag object touches a wall, the function will be executed.

All we do in this function is destroy the current drag object and remove it from the page. We then create a new drag object back at the starting position and make it draggable once more. There is no `cancelDrag` method that causes the drag object to act as if it had been dropped and revert to its starting position, but we can easily replicate this behavior ourselves.

We then add another droppable configuration object that configures the ending point of the maze. All we configure for this droppable is a function to execute, when the draggable is over this droppable. In this function, we remove the drag object again and present the user with an alert congratulating them.

We then use a simple `for` loop to add the walls to our maze. We use the plain-vanilla `for` loop in conjunction with jQuery to create 46 `<div>` elements, and add `id` and `class` attributes to each one, before appending them to the `maze` container. Finally, we make the drag object draggable and the walls and the end target droppables.

We can now attempt to navigate the marker from the starting point to the finish by dragging it through the maze. If any wall is touched, the marker will return to the starting point. We could make it harder (by adding additional obstacles to navigate, and so on), but for the purpose of having fun with jQuery UI draggables and droppables, our work here is complete.

Summary

We looked at two very useful library components in this chapter—the draggable and droppable components. Draggables and droppables, as we saw, are very closely related and have been designed to be used with each other, allowing us to create advanced and highly-interactive interfaces.

We've covered a lot of material in this chapter, so let's recap on what we have learned. We saw that the draggable behavior can be added to any element on the page with zero configuration. There may be implementations where this is acceptable, but usually we'll want to use one or more of the component's extensive range of configurable options.

In the second part of this chapter, we saw that the `droppables` class allows us to easily define areas on the page that draggables can be dropped onto, and can react to things being dropped on them. We can also make use of a smaller range of configurable droppable options to implement more advanced droppable behavior.

Both components feature an effective event model for hooking into the interesting moments of any drag and drop interaction. We also saw that each component has a simple set of methods for enabling or disabling drag or drop, and also a `destroy` method for removing the functionality (but not the underlying elements) from the page.

Our final example showed how both the draggables and droppables components can be used together to create a fun and interactive game. Although the game was very basic by modern gaming standards, it nevertheless provides a sound base that we can easily build upon to add features.

In the next chapter, we'll take a look at the resizable component, which allows users to resize selected elements using a familiar drag-based interface.

The Resizable Component

We have already seen resizables in action briefly when we looked at the dialog widget, earlier in the book. In this chapter, we're going to focus on it directly. However, the dialog is a perfect example of how useful the resizable component can be in a real-world implementation.

The resizable widget adds the same functionality as that, which is automatically added to `<textarea>` elements in WebKit browsers such as Safari or Chrome, or newer versions of Firefox. In these browsers, a resize handle is added to the bottom-right corner, which allows the element to be resized. With the jQuery UI resizable component, we can add this behavior to almost any element on the page.

In this chapter, we'll be looking at the following aspects of the component:

- Implementing basic resizability
- The configurable options available for use
- Specifying which resize handles to add
- Managing the resizable's minimum and maximum sizes
- The role of resize helpers and ghosts
- A look at the built-in resize animations
- How to react to resize events
- Determining the new size of a resizable
- Using a resizable with other library widgets

The resizable is a flexible component that can be used with a wide range of different elements. Throughout the examples in this chapter, we'll mostly be using simple `<div>` elements, so that the focus remains on the component and not on the underlying HTML. We will also look at some brief examples using `<img>` and `<textarea>` elements, towards the end of the chapter.

The resizable component works well with other components and is very often used in conjunction with draggables. However, while you can easily make draggable components resizable (think `dialog`), the two classes are in no way related.

A basic resizable

Let's implement the basic resizable, so we can see just how easy making elements resizable is, when you use jQuery UI as the driving force behind your pages. In a new file in your text editor add the following code:

```
<!DOCTYPE html>
<html>
  <head>
    <meta charset="utf-8">
    <title>Resizable</title>
    <link rel="stylesheet"
      href="css/smoothness/jquery-ui-1.8.9.custom.css">
    <link rel="stylesheet" href="css/resize.css">
  </head>
  <body>
    <div id="resize"></div>
    <script src="development-bundle/jquery-1.4.4.js"></script>
    <script src="development-bundle/ui/jquery.ui.core.js">
    </script>
    <script src="development-bundle/ui/jquery.ui.widget.js">
    </script>
    <script src="development-bundle/ui/jquery.ui.mouse.js">
    </script>
    <script
      src="development-bundle/ui/jquery.ui.resizable.js">
    </script>
    <script>
      (function($){
        $("#resize").resizable();
      })(jQuery);
    </script>
  </body>
</html>
```

Save this as `resizable1.html`. The basic widget method, used with no arguments for the default implementation, uses the same simplified syntax as the rest of the library. This requires just one line of code for the example to work.

Along with the CSS framework files that we need for any resizables implementation, we also use a custom style sheet to add basic dimensions and borders to our resizable `<div>`. Use the following CSS in a new file in your text editor:

```
#resize {
    width:200px; height:200px; margin:30px 0 0 30px;
    border:1px solid #7a7a7a;
}
```

Save this file as `resize.css` in the `css` folder. We've given the resizable element's dimensions in our CSS, because without them the `<div>` will stretch the width of the screen. We've also specified a border to clearly define it, as the default implementation only adds a single resize handle to the bottom-right corner of the targeted element. The following screenshot shows how our basic page should look, after the `<div>` has been resized:

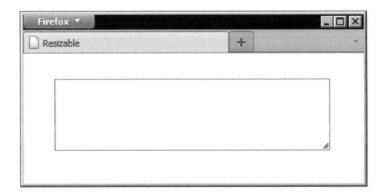

The files required for the resizable component are as follows:

- `jquery-x.x.x.js`
- `jquery. ui.core.js`
- `jquery. ui.widget.js`
- `jquery.ui.mouse.js`
- `jquery.ui.resizable.js`

The component automatically adds the three required elements for the drag handles. Although the only visible resize handle is the one in the bottom-right corner, both the bottom and right edges also allow for resizing.

Resizable options

The following table lists the configurable options that we have at our disposal when working with the resizable component:

Option	Default value	Used to...
alsoResize	false	Automatically resize specified elements in sync with the resizable.
animate	false	Animate the resizable element to its new size.
animateDuration	slow	Set the speed of the animation. Values can be integers, specifying the number of milliseconds, or one of the string values slow, normal, or fast.
animateEasing	swing	Add easing effects to the resize animation.
aspectRatio	false	Maintain the aspect ratio of the resize element. Accepts numerical custom aspect ratios in addition to Boolean values.
autoHide	false	Hide the resize handles until the resizable is hovered over with the mouse pointer.
cancel	':input,option'	Stop specified elements from being resizable.
containment	false	Constrain the resizable within the boundary of the specified container element.
delay	0	Set a delay in milliseconds from when the pointer is clicked on a resizable handle to when the resizing begins.
disabled	false	Disable the component at page load.
distance	1	Set the number of pixels the mouse pointer must move with the mouse button held down before resizing begins.
ghost	false	Show a semi-transparent helper element while the resizing is taking place.
grid	false	Snap the resize to imaginary grid lines while resizing is taking place.

Option	Default value	Used to...
handles	'e, se, s'	Define which handles to use for resizing. Accepts a string containing any of the following values: n, ne, e, se, s, sw, w, nw, or all. The string could also be an object where the properties are any of the above and the values are jQuery selectors matching the elements to use as handles.
helper	false	Add a class name to the helper element that is applied during resizing.
maxHeight	null	Set the maximum height the resizable may be changed to.
maxWidth	null	Set the maximum width the resizable may be set to.
minHeight	null	Set the minimum height the resizable may be changed to.
minWidth	null	Set the minimum width the resizable may be set to.

Configuring resize handles

Thanks to the handles configuration option, specifying which handles we would like to add to our target element is exceptionally easy. In resizable1.html, change the final <script> element, so that it appears as follows:

```
<script>
  (function($) {
    var resizeOpts = {
      handles: "all"
    };
    $("#resize").resizable(resizeOpts);
  })(jQUery);
</script>
```

Save this as resizable2.html. When you run the example in a browser, you'll see that although the component looks exactly as it did before, we can now use any edge or corner to resize the <div>.

Adding additional handle images

One thing you'll notice straight away is that although the element is resizable along any axis, there's no visual cue to make this obvious; the component will automatically add the resize stripes to the bottom-right corner, but it's up to us to add the rest.

There are several different ways to do this. Although the method doesn't add images to the other three corners, it does insert DOM elements with classnames, so we can easily target these with CSS and provide our own images. This is what we'll do next.

In a new page in your text editor, add the following style rules:

```css
#resize {
  width:200px; height:200px; margin:30px 0 0 30px;
  border:1px solid #7a7a7a;
}
.ui-resizable-sw, .ui-resizable-nw, .ui-resizable-ne {
  width:12px; height:12px;
  background:url(../img/handles.png) no-repeat 0 0;
}
.ui-resizable-sw { left:0; bottom:0; }
.ui-resizable-nw {
  left:0; top:0; background-position:0 -12px;
}
.ui-resizable-ne {
  right:0; top:0; background-position:0 -24px;
}
```

Save this file in the `css` folder as `resizeHandles.css`. We provide our own image for this example, which is a sprite file containing copies of the standard bottom-right image flipped and reversed (this can be found in the code download).

Our selectors target the classnames that are automatically added to the handle elements, by the control. Link to the new style sheet in the `<head>` of `resizable2. html` and resave it as `resizable3.html`:

```html
<link rel="stylesheet" href="css/resizeHandles.css">
```

The new style sheet should give our element the following appearance:

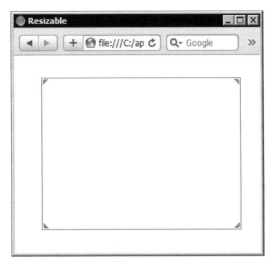

Another configuration option related to resize handles and how they are displayed is `autoHide`. Let's take a quick look at this option next. Change the configuration object in `resizable3.html` to the following:

```
var resizeOpts = {
    handles: "all",
    autoHide: true

}
```

Save this version as `resizable4.html`. We've added the `autoHide` option and set its value to `true` in this example. Configuring this option hides all of the resize handles until the mouse pointer moves onto the resizable element. This is great for a minimal intrusion of the additional DOM elements when there is pictorial content inside the resizable element.

Defining size limits

Restricting the minimum or maximum sizes that the target element can be resized to, is made exceptionally easy with four configurable options, which we will see in action in the next example. It's better to have some content in the container for this example, so add some layout text in a `<p>` element within our resizable in `resizable4.html`:

```
<p>Lorem ipsum etc, etc...</p>
```

Change the configuration object that we used in `resizable4.html` to as follows:

```
var resizeOpts = {
  maxWidth: 500,
  maxHeight: 500,
  minWidth: 100,
  minHeight: 100
};
```

Save this as `resizable5.html`. This time, the configuration object uses the dimension-boundary options to specify the minimum and maximum height and width that the resizable may be adjusted to. These options take simple integers as their values.

As we can see, when we run this example, the resizable now adheres to the sizes we have specified, whereas in previous examples, the resizable element's minimum size was the combined size of its resize handles, and it had no maximum.

So far, our resizable has been an empty `<div>` and you may be wondering how the resizable handles minimum and maximum sizes, when there is content within the target element. The restrictions are maintained, but we'll need to add `overflow:hidden` to the CSS. Otherwise, the content may overflow the resizable, if there is too much for the minimum size to handle.

Of course, we can also use `overflow:auto` as well to add a scrollbar, when there is too much content, which would sometimes be the desired behavior.

Resizing ghosts

Ghost elements are very similar to the proxy element that we used when we looked at the draggables component in the previous chapter. A ghost element can be enabled with the configuration of just one option. Let's see how this is done.

Change the configuration object we used in `resizable5.html` to the following:

```
var resizeOpts = {
  ghost: true
};
```

Save this file as `resizable6.html`. All that is needed to enable a resize ghost is to set the `ghost` option to `true`. The effect of the resizable ghost is very subtle. It is basically a clone of the existing resizable element, but is only a quarter of the opacity. This is why we've left the layout text from the previous example within the resizable element.

We're also linking to a new style sheet in this example, which is exactly the same as `resize.css` with a background color specified:

```
#resize {
  width:200px; height:200px; margin:30px 0 0 30px;
  border:1px solid #7a7a7a; overflow:hidden;
  background-color:#999;
}
```

Save this as `resizeGhosts.css` in the `css` folder. The next screenshot shows how the resizable ghost will appear while it is visible:

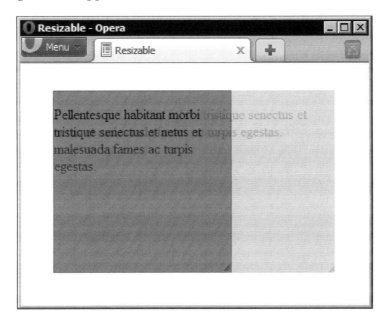

 In some versions of Internet Explorer, ghost elements may cause issues when transparent PNGs are within the resizable.

The ghost element is just a helper element that has been made semi-transparent. If this is not suitable and further control over the appearance of the helper element is required, we can use the `helper` option to specify a classname to be added to the helper element, which we can then use to style it. Change the configuration object in `resizable6.html`, so that it appears as follows:

```
var resizeOpts = {
  ghost: true,
  helper: "my-ui-helper"
};
```

Save this revision as `resizable7.html`. We've simply specified the classname that we'd like to be added as the value of the `helper` option. We can target the new classname from a CSS file. Open `resize.css` and add the following code to it:

```
.my-ui-helper { background-color:#FFFF99; }
```

Save the new style sheet as `resizeHelper.css` and don't forget to link it at the top of `resizable7.html`:

```
<link rel="stylesheet" href="css/resizeHelper.css">
```

The only thing we do in this example is give the helper a simple background color. This is how it looks when the new page is run and a resize is in action:

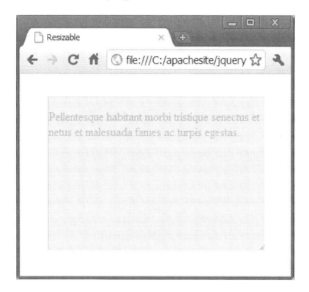

The `ghost` and `helper` options don't have to be used together; we can use either one separately, but if we use the `helper` option without the `ghost` option, we do not get the semi-transparent content within the resize helper.

Containing the resize

The resizable component makes it easy to ensure that a resized element is contained within its parent element. This is great if we have other content on the page that we don't want moving around all over the place during a resize interaction. In `resizable7.html`, change the elements on the page so that they appear as follows:

```
<div class="container">
  <img id="resize" src="img/moon.jpg" alt="Moon Landing">
</div>
```

Finally, change the configuration object to use the `containment` option:

```
var resizeOpts = {
  containment: ".container"
};
```

Save this as `resizable8.html`. On the page, we've added a container element for the resizable and have switched from using a `<div>` to an image as the resizable element.

Once again, we need some slightly different CSS for this example. In a new file in your text editor, add the following code:

```
.container {
  width:600px; height:600px; border:1px solid #7a7a7a;
  padding:1px 0 0 1px;
}
#resize { width:300px; height:300px; }
```

Save this as `resizeContainer.css` in the `css` folder and change the `<link>` in the `<head>` of the page from `resizeHelper.css` to the new style sheet:

```
<link rel="stylesheet" href="css/resizeContainer.css">
```

The `containment` option allows us to specify a container for the resizable, which will limit how large the resizable can be made, forcing it to stay within its boundaries. We specify a jQuery selector as the value of this option. When we view the page, we should see that the image cannot be resized to larger than its container.

Handling aspect ratio

In addition to maintaining the aspect ratio of the resizable element, we can also define it manually. Let's see what control this interaction gives us over the resize. Change the configuration object used in `resizable8.html` to the following:

```
var resizeOpts = {
  containment: ".container",
  aspectRatio: true
};
```

Save this file as `resizable9.html`. Setting the `aspectRatio` option to `true` ensures that our image will maintain its original aspect ratio. So in this example, the image will always be a perfect square.

For a greater degree of control, we can instead specify the actual aspect ratio that the resizable should maintain:

```
var resizeOpts = {
  containment: ".container",
  aspectRatio: 0.5
};
```

By specifying the floating-point value of 0.5, we're saying that when the image is resized, the x axis of the image should be exactly half of the y axis.

> Care should be taken when deviating from the aspect ratio of any images.

Resizable animations

The resizable API exposes three configuration options related to animations—animate, animateDuration, and animateEasing. By default, animations are switched off in resizable implementations. However, we can easily enable them to see how they enhance this component.

In this example, change the markup from the previous couple of examples, so that the resizable element goes back to a plain <div>:

```
<div id="resize"></div>
```

We should also switch back to the resizeGhost.css style sheet:

```
<link rel="stylesheet" href="css/resizeGhost.css">
```

Now, change the configuration object to use the following options:

```
var resizeOpts = {
  ghost: true,
  animate: true,
  animateDuration: "fast"
};
```

Save this as resizable10.html. The configuration object we use in this example starts with the ghost option.

> When using animations, the resizable element is not resized until after the interaction has ended, so it's useful to show the ghost as a visual cue that the element will be resized.

All we need to do to enable animation is set the `animate` option to `true`. That's it; no further configuration is required. Another option we can change is the speed of the animation, which we have done in this example, by setting the `animateDuration` option. This accepts any of the standard values that can be used with jQuery's `animate()` method.

When we run this page in a browser we should find that when we resize the element, it isn't set to its new size as soon as we let go of the mouse button, but smoothly animates to its new size.

Simultaneous resizing

We can easily make several elements on the same page individually resizable, by passing references to them to the resizable widget method. But, in addition to doing this, we can make use of the `alsoResize` property to specify additional elements that are to be resized together as a group, whenever the actual resizable element is resized. Let's see how.

First, we'll need to reference to a new style sheet once again:

```
<link rel="stylesheet" href="css/resizeSimultaneous.css">
```

Next, we'll need to change the elements in the `<body>` of the page as follows:

```
<div id="mainResize">
  <p>I am the main resizable!</p>
</div>
<div id="simultaneousResize">
  <p>I will also be resized when the main resizable is resized!</p>
</div>
```

Then change the configuration object to the following:

```
var resizeOpts = {
  alsoResize: "#simultaneousResize"
};
```

The `id` of our resizable element has also changed in this example, so be sure to update the selector accordingly:

```
$("#mainResize").resizable(resizeOpts);
```

Save this file as `resizable11.html`. We provide a selector as the value of the `alsoResize` option, in order to target the second `<div>` element. The secondary element will automatically pick up the resizable attributes of the actual resizable. So, if we limit the resizable to having just an `e` handle, the secondary element will also only resize in this direction.

The new style sheet referenced in this example should contain the following code:

```
#mainResize {
  width:100px; height:100px; margin:0 0 30px;
  border:2px solid #7a7a7a; text-align:center;
}
#simultaneousResize {
  width:150px; height:150px; border:2px solid #7a7a7a;
  text-align:center;
}
p { font-family:arial; font-size:15px; }
```

Save this file as `resizeSimultaneous.css` in the `css` folder. When we run the file, we should see that the second `<div>` element is resized at the same time as the first:

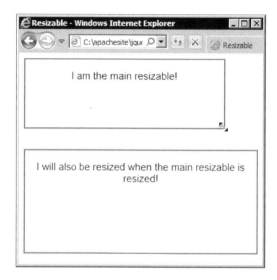

Preventing unwanted resizes

There may be times when we'd like to make an element resizable, but it also has other functionality, perhaps it listens for click events too. In this situation, it may be desirable to prevent the resize unless it is definitely required, enabling us to easily differentiate between clicks and true drags. We can use two options to achieve this.

First, in `resizable11.html`, revert to the original style sheet `resize.css`:

```
<link rel="stylesheet" href="css/resize.css">
```

We can also return to the simple empty resizable `<div>`:

```
<div id="resize"></div>
```

Then change the configuration object to the following:

```
var resizeOpts = {
  delay: 1000
};
```

Save this version as `resizable12.html`. The `delay` option accepts an integer that represents the number of milliseconds that need to pass with the mouse button held down, after clicking on a resize handle before the resize will begin.

We've used `1000` as the value in this example that is equal to one second. Try it out and you'll see that if you click on a resize handle and release the mouse button too soon, the resize won't take place.

Along with delaying the resize, we could also use the distance option instead to specify that the mouse pointer must move a certain number of pixels, with the button held down after clicking on a resize handle, before the resize occurs.

Change the configuration object in `resizable12.html`, so that it appears as follows:

```
var resizeOpts = {
  distance: 30
};
```

Save this as `resizable13.html`. Now when the page is run, instead of having to wait with the mouse button held down, the mouse pointer will need to travel `30` pixels with the mouse button held down, before the resize occurs.

Both of the these options present certain usability issues, especially when set to high as in these examples. They both make it harder to resize an element along more than one axis at a time. They should be used sparingly, with as low values as possible.

Resizable callbacks

Like other components of the library, resizable defines a selection of custom events, and allows us to easily execute functions when these events occur. This makes the most of interactions between your visitors and the elements on your pages. Resizable defines the following callback options:

Option	Triggered when...
create	The resizable is initialized
resize	The resizable is in the process of being resized
start	A resize interaction begins
stop	A resize interaction ends

Hooking into these custom methods is just as easy for resizables as it has been for the other components of the library we have looked at. Let's explore a basic example to highlight this fact.

In `resizable13.html`, change the second `<link>` to point to a new style sheet as follows:

```
<link rel="stylesheet" href="css/resizeStop.css">
```

Then change the final `<script>` element so that it appears as follows:

```
<script>
  (function($) {
    function reportNewSize(e, ui) {
      var width = Math.round(ui.size.width),
      height = Math.round(ui.size.height);
      $("<div />", {
        "class": "message",
        text: "New size: " + height + "px high, " + width + "px
          wide",
        width: width
      }).appendTo("body").fadeIn().delay(2000).fadeOut();
    }
    var resizeOpts = {
      stop: reportNewSize
    };
    $("#resize").resizable(resizeOpts);
  })(jQUery);
</script>
```

Save this as `resizable14.html`. In `resize.css`, add the following selector and rules:

```
.message {
  display:none; border:1px solid #7a7a7a; margin-top:5px;
  position:absolute; left:38px;fontSize:80%; font-weight:bold;
  text-align:center;
}
```

Save this as `resizeStop.css` in the `css` folder.

We define a function called `reportNewSize`; this function (along with all of the other event handlers) is automatically passed two objects. The first is the event object and the second is an object containing useful information about the resizable.

We can use the `size` property of the second object to find out what the `width` and `height` the resizable has been changed to. These values are stored as variables within the function. We use the JavaScript `Math.round()` function to make sure that we end up with an integer.

We then create a new `<div>` element and give it a classname for styling. We also set the text of the new element to display the `width` and `height` variables along with a brief message. We also set the `width` of the new element to match the resizable.

Once created, we append the message to the page and then fade it in with jQuery's `fadeIn()` method. We then use the `delay()` method to pause for 2 seconds before fading the message out again.

The following screenshot shows how our page looks before the `<div>` fades away:

Resizable methods

This component comes with the four basic methods found with all of the interaction components of the library, namely the `destroy`, `disable`, `enable`, and `option` methods. Unlike most of the other components, the resizable component has no custom methods unique to it. For clarification on these basic API methods, see the *API introduction* section in *Chapter 1, Introducing jQuery UI*.

Resizable tabs

In our final resizable example, let's look at combining this component with one of the widgets that we looked at earlier. This will help us see how compatible it is with the rest of the library. We'll be working with the tabs component in the following example. The following screenshot shows the page we will end up with:

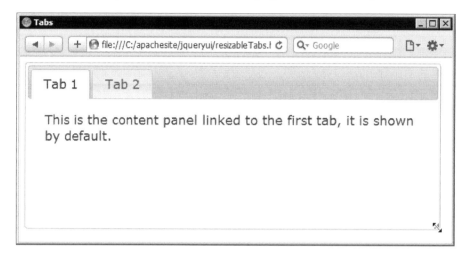

In your text editor, add the following code:

```
<!DOCTYPE html>
<html>
  <head>
    <meta charset="utf-8">
    <title>Tabs</title>
    <link rel="stylesheet"
      href="css/smoothness/jquery-ui-1.8.9.custom.css">
    <style>
      #myTabs { width:400px; height:170px; }
    </style>
  </head>
  <body>
    <div id="myTabs">
      <ul>
        <li><a href="#a">Tab 1</a></li>
        <li><a href="#b">Tab 2</a></li>
      </ul>
      <div id="a">
        This is the content panel linked to the first tab; it
          is shown by default.
```

```
        </div>
        <div id="b">
          This content is linked to the second tab and will be
            shown when its tab is clicked.</div>
        </div>
        <script src="development-bundle/jquery-1.4.4.js">
        </script>
        <script src="development-bundle/ui/jquery.ui.core.js">
      </script>
    <script src="development-bundle/ui/jquery.ui.widget.js">
    </script>
    <script src="development-bundle/ui/jquery.ui.tabs.js">
    </script>
    <script src="development-bundle/ui/jquery.ui.mouse.js">
    </script>
    <script src="development-bundle/ui/jquery.ui.resizable.js">
    </script>
    <script>
      (function($){
        var tabs = $("#myTabs").tabs(),
        resizeOpts = {
          autoHide: true,
          minHeight: 170,
          minWidth: 400
        };
        tabs.resizable(resizeOpts);
      })(jQuery);
    </script>
  </body>
</html>
```

Save this as `resizableTabs.html`. Making the tabs widget resizable is extremely easy and only requires calling the resizable method on the tab's underlying `<ul>`.

We're using a single configuration object in this example. The tabs component can be initialized with zero configuration. Apart from setting the `autoHide` option for the resizable in our configuration object, we also define `minWidth` and `minHeight` values for usability purposes.

Summary

In this chapter, we covered resizables. This is a component that allows us to easily resize any onscreen element. It dynamically adds resize handles to the specified sides of the target element and handles all of the tricky DHTML resizing for us, neatly encapsulating the behavior into a compact, easy-to-use class.

We then looked at some of the configurable options that we can use with the widget, such as how to specify which handles to add to the resizable, and how the minimum and maximum sizes of the element can be limited.

We briefly looked at how to maintain an image's aspect ratio, or how to work with custom ratios, while it is being resized. We also explored how to use ghosts, helpers, and animations to improve the usability and appearance of the resizable component.

We also looked at the event model exposed by the component's API and how we can react to elements being resized in an easy and effective way. Our final example explored resizable's compatibility with other components of the library.

The Selectables Component

12

The selectables component allows you to define a series of elements that can be chosen by dragging a selection square around them or by clicking them as if they were files on the desktop. In this way, elements on the page can be treated as objects, allowing either single elements or groups of them to be selected.

Topics that will be covered in this section include:

- Creating the default implementation
- How selectable class names reflect the state of selectables
- Filtering selectable elements
- Working with selectable's built-in callback functions
- A look at selectables' methods

A selection square has been a standard part of modern operating systems for a long time. For example, if you wanted to select some of the icons on your desktop, you could hold the mouse button down on a blank part of the desktop and drag a square around the icons you wanted to select.

The selectables interaction helper adds this same functionality to our web pages, which allows us to build more user-friendly interfaces without needing to use external environments like Flash or Silverlight.

Basic implementation

A demonstration that you can play with will tell you more about the functionality provided by this library component than merely reading about it. The first thing we should do is invoke the default implementation to get a glimpse of the basic functionality provided by this component.

In a new file in your text editor, add the following code:

```
<!DOCTYPE html>
<html>
  <head>
    <meta charset="utf-8">
    <title>Selectable</title>
    <link rel="stylesheet"
      href="css/smoothness/jquery-ui-1.8.9.custom.css">
  </head>
  <body>
    <ul id="selectables">
      <li>This list item can be selected</li>
      <li>This list item can be selected</li>
      <li>This list item can be selected</li>
      <li>This list item can be selected</li>
      <li>This list item can be selected</li>
    </ul>
    <script src="development-bundle/jquery-1.4.4.js"></script>
    <script src="development-bundle/ui/jquery.ui.core.js">
    </script>
    <script src="development-bundle/ui/jquery.ui.widget.js">
    </script>
    <script src="development-bundle/ui/jquery.ui.mouse.js">
    </script>
    <script
      src="development-bundle/ui/jquery.ui.selectable.js">
    </script>
    <script>
      (function($){
        $("#selectables").selectable();
      })(jQuery);
    </script>
  </body>
</html>
```

Save this as `selectable1.html` in the `jqueryui` folder. We simply call the `selectable` widget method on the parent `<ul>` element and then all of its child `<li>` elements are made selectable. This allows selection by clicking on them or using the selection square (like you would on your desktop).

Note that there is no styling associated with the selectables component. Default behavior includes clicking on individual elements, causing them only to be selected, and clicking outside of the selected elements to deselect them. Holding down the *Ctrl* key will enable multi-select. The following screenshot shows the selection square enclosing the list items:

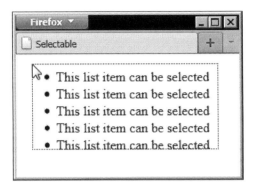

The minimum set of library files we need for a selectable implementation is as follows:

- `jquery-x.x.x.js`
- `jquery.ui.core.js`
- `jquery.ui.widget.js`
- `jquery.ui.mouse.js`
- `jquery.ui.selectable.js`

Along with building selectables from list items, we can also build them from other elements, such as a collection of `<div>` elements. Add the following link to the `<head>` of the `selectable1.html`:

```
<link rel="stylesheet" href="css/selectable.css">
```

Also replace the list elements in `selectable1.html` with the following code:

```
<div id="selectables">
   <div>This div can be selected</div>
   <div>This div can be selected</div>
   <div>This div can be selected</div>
   <div>This div can be selected</div>
   <div>This div can be selected</div>
</div>
```

Save this as `selectable2.html`. Everything is essentially the same as before. We're just basing the example on different elements. However, due to the nature of these elements, we should add a little basic styling so that we can see what we're working with.

In a new file in your text editor, add the following code:

```
#selectables div {
  width:170px; height:25px;
  padding:5px 0 0 10px; margin:10px 0 0 10px;
  border:1px solid #000;
}
```

Save this as `selectable.css` in the `css` folder. It's not much, but it helps to clarify the individual selectables in the example, as shown in the following screenshot:

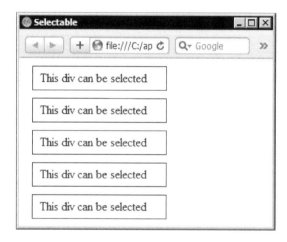

Selectee classnames

The elements that are made selectable are all initially given the class `ui-selectee`, and the parent element that contains them is given the class `ui-selectable`. While elements are selected they are given the class `ui-selected`.

While the selecting square is around selectable elements, they are given the class `ui-selecting`, and for a brief moment, when an element is deselected it is given the class `ui-unselecting`. These classnames are added purely for our benefit, so that we can highlight different states that the selectable may be in.

This extensive class system makes it very easy to add custom styling to show when elements are either in the process of being selected or have been selected. Let's add some additional styling now to reflect the *selecting* and *selected* states. Add the following new selectors and rules to `selectable.css`:

```
#selectables div.ui-selecting {
  border:1px solid #66CC00;
}
#selectables div.ui-selected {
  background:#66CC00; color:#fff;
}
```

Save this `selectableStates.css` in the `css` folder. Change the link to the style sheet reference in the `<head>` of `selectable2.html`, then save this file as `selectable3.html`:

```
<link rel="stylesheet" href="css/selectableStates.css">
```

With the addition of this very simple CSS, we can add visual cues to elements which are part of the current selection, both during and following a select interaction. The following screenshot shows some elements in the process of being selected on the left, and the same elements having been selected on the right:

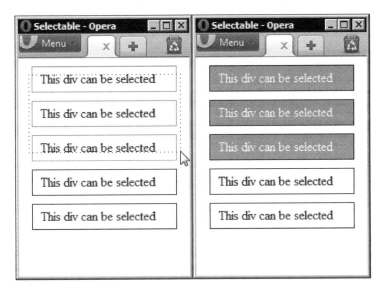

Configurable options of the selectable component

The selectable class is quite compact, with relatively few configurable options compared to some of the other components that we've looked at. The following options are available for configuration:

Option	Default value	Used to
autoRefresh	true	Automatically refresh the size and position of each selectable at the start of a select interaction.
cancel	":input,option"	Prevent the specified elements from being selected with a click. The default string contains the :input jQuery filter, which matches all <input>, <textarea>, <select>, and <button> elements along with the standard option element selector.
delay	0	Set the delay in milliseconds before the element is selected. The mouse button must be held down on the element for this length of time before the selection will begin.
disabled	false	Disable selection when the page initially loads.
distance	0	Set the distance the mouse pointer must travel, with the mouse button held down, before selection will begin.
filter	"*"	Specify child elements to make selectable.
tolerance	"touch"	Set the tolerance of the selection square. Possible values are touch or fit. If fit is specified the element must be completely within the selection square before the element will be selected.

Filtering selectables

There may be situations when we don't want to allow all of the elements within the targeted container to be made selectable. In this situation we can make use of the filter option to nominate specific elements, based on a CSS selector, that we want selecting to be enabled on. In selectable3.html change the collection of <div> elements so that it appears as follows:

```
<div id="selectables">
  <div>This div can't be selected</div>
  <div class="selectable">This div can't be selected</div>
```

```
<div class="selectable">This div can be selected</div>
<div class="selectable">This div can be selected</div>
<div class="selectable">This div can be selected</div>

</div>
```

Then change the final `<script>` element to the following:

```
<script>
  (function($) {
    var selectableOpts = {
      filter: ".selectable"
        }
    $("#selectables").selectable(selectableOpts);

  })(jQuery);
</script>
```

Save this version as `selectable4.html`. In the underlying markup, we have given a class to each element except for the first. In the JavaScript, we define a configuration object containing the `filter` option. The value of this option is the class selector of the elements that we want to be selectable; elements without this class name are filtered out of the selection:

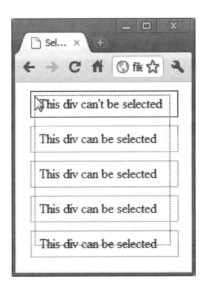

As shown in the previous screenshot, the selection square is over the unselectable element, but it's not picking up the `ui-selecting` class like the others. The component completely ignores the filtered selectable and it does not become part of the selection.

Canceling the selection

Along with indirectly making elements unselectable using the `filter` option, we can also directly make elements unselectable using the `cancel` option. This option was also exposed by the interaction helper we looked at in the last chapter, **Resizable**, although we didn't look at it in any detail. Now is the perfect opportunity to have a play with it.

Add the class name `unselectable` to the first element in the container in `selectable4.html`:

```
<div class="unselectable">This div cannot be selected</div>
```

Change the configuration object from the last example so that it uses the `cancel` option:

```
var selectableOpts = {
    cancel: ".unselectable"
}
```

Save this as `selectable5.html`. Instead of passing the class name of the selectable elements to the configuration object, we pass the class name of the unselectable element to it, but as we see when we run the example, it is only unselectable in certain situations.

The first element, with the class name `unselectable`, is still given the class `ui-selectee`. However, it is only selectable with the selection square; it cannot be selected by clicking, even with the *Ctrl* key held down.

Selectable callbacks

In addition to the standard configurable options of the selectable API, there are also a series of event callback options that can be used to specify functions that are executed at specific points during a select interaction. These options are as listed in the following table:

Option	Triggered when
selected	The select interaction ends and each element added to the selection triggers the callback.
selecting	Each selected element triggers the callback during the select interaction.
start	A select interaction begins.

Option	Triggered when
stop	This is fired once, regardless of the number of items selected, as the select interaction ends.
unselected	Any elements that are part of the selectable, but are not selected during the interaction will fire this callback.
unselecting	Unselected elements will fire this during the select interaction.

Selecting really only becomes useful when something happens to the elements once they have been selected, which is where this event model comes into play. Let's put some of these callbacks to work so that we can appreciate their use.

Change the configuration object in `selectable5.html` so that it contains the following code:

```
var selectableOpts = {
    selected: function(e, ui) {
        $(ui.selected).text("I have been selected!");
    },
    unselected: function(e, ui) {
        $(ui.unselected).text("This div was selected");
    },
    start: function(e) {
        if (!$("#tip").length) {
            $("<div />", {
                "class": "ui-corner-all ui-widget ui-widget-header",
                id: "tip",
                text: "Drag the lasso around elements, or click to
                  select",
                css: {
                    position: "absolute",
                    padding: 10,
                    left: e.pageX,
                    top: e.pageY - 30,
                    display: "none"
                }
            }).appendTo("body").fadeIn();
        }
    },
    stop: function() {
        $("#tip").fadeOut("slow", function() {
            $(this).remove();
        });
    }
};
```

Save this as `selectable6.html`. To the HTML elements, we've added `id` attributes so that we can easily target specific elements. In the `<script>`, we've added functions to the `selected`, `unselected`, `start`, and `stop` options. These will be executed at the appropriate times during an interaction.

As with other components, these functions are automatically passed two objects. The first is the original browser event object and the other is an object containing useful properties of the selected element. However, not all callbacks can successfully work with the second object—`start` and `stop`, for example. When the `ui` object is used with either of these events, the object is empty.

When a `<div>` is selected, we change its inner text to reflect the selection using the `selected` event callback. We can use the `selected` property to get the element that was selected in order to change its text content to a new message. When an element is deselected, we set the text back to its original value using the same technique. We can also alter the text of any selectable that was previously selected using the `unselected` event.

At the start of any interaction, we create a little tooltip that is appended to the `<body>` of the page, slightly offset from the mouse pointer, using the `start` event. We use a basic conditional to check that the tool tip does not already exist to prevent duplicate tips. We can make use of the framework classes `ui-corner-all`, `ui-widget`, and `ui-widget-header` to do most of the styling for us. The few styles we require that are not provided by the theme are added using the `css()` method.

We can get the pointer coordinates using the `e` (event) object, which is passed as the first argument to our callbacks, in order to position the tool tip. At the end of the selection, we remove the tool tip using the `stop` property. The following screenshot shows the results of different interactions:

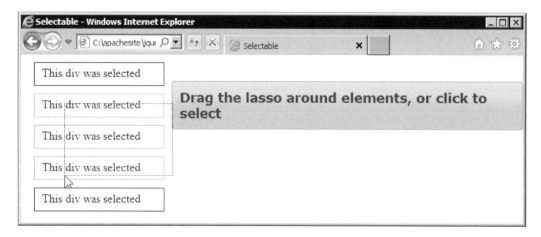

The `selecting` and `unselecting` callbacks work in exactly the same way as those we just looked at, but are fired as elements are added or removed to the selection. To see them in action change the configuration object in `selectable6.html` so that it appears as follows:

```
var selectableOpts = {
    selecting: function(e, ui) {
      $(ui.selecting).text("I am part of the selection");
    },
    unselecting: function(e, ui) {
      $(ui.unselecting).text("I was part of the selection");
      }
};
```

This time we use the `selecting` and `unselecting` properties to specify callback functions, which again change the text content of the elements at certain times during an interaction. We repeat the procedure from the last example, this time we're just using different callbacks and properties of the objects passed to them.

The second object passed to any of the selectable callbacks contains a property relating to the type of custom event. For example, the `selected` callback receives an object with a `selected` property, which can be used to gain information about the element that was added to the selection. All callbacks have a matching property that can be used in this way.

Working with vast amounts of selectables

The jQuery UI library, like jQuery itself, is already extremely efficient. It uses the ultra effective Sizzle selector engine (via jQuery) and each component has been optimized as much as possible.

However, there is only so much that the creators of the library can do. In our examples so far, we've used a maximum of five selectable elements, which isn't really many at all. What if we were to use 500 instead?

When working with great numbers of selectables there is still something we can do to make sure that the select interactions are as efficient as possible. The `autoRefresh` option is set to `true` by default, which causes the sizes and positions of all selectable elements on the page to be recalculated at the beginning of every interaction.

This can cause delays on pages with many selectable elements on it, so the autoRefresh option can be set to false when dealing with large collections of elements. We can also use the refresh method to manually refresh the selectables at appropriate times in order to improve the speed and responsiveness of the interactions. On most pages we would not need to worry about configuring this option and can leave it at its default setting.

Let's take a look at how this option can help our pages in certain situations. In the <head> of selectable7.html change the <link> for the custom style sheet to the following:

```
<link rel="stylesheet" href="css/selectableMany.css ">
```

Then change the selectables container element so that it appears as follows (with the comment shown below being changed so that the file actually contains 200 selectable elements):

```
<div id="selectables" class="ui-helper-clearfix">
  <div class="selectable">Selectable</div>
  <!—- 199 more selectables! -->
</div>
```

Then change the configuration object as follows:

```
var selectableOpts = {
  autoRefresh: false
}
```

Save this page as selectable8.html. Our page should now contain 200 individual selectables within the selectables container. We've also added a class name to the outer container so that the container is cleared properly when we float our selectables (which we will do in a moment).

 If the container is not cleared correctly the selection square will not work.

We also need a new style sheet in this example that consists of the following code:

```
#selectables div {  width:70px; height:25px; padding:5px 0 0 10px;
                    border:1px solid #000;
                      margin:10px 0 0 10px; float:left;
}
.ui-selected { background-color:#00FF66; }
```

Save this in the css folder as selectableMany.css. It's purely for layout purposes, so we don't need to discuss it further.

We can use Firebug to profile a selection of all 200 selectables with and without the `autoRefresh` option enabled (remember, it's enabled by default, so our example will disable it). The results will probably vary between tests, but you should find that the profile (in both milliseconds and the number of calls) is consistently lower with `autoRefresh` set to `disabled`.

Selectable methods

The methods that we can use to control the selectables component from our code are similar to the methods found in other interaction helpers and follow the same pattern of usage. The only unique method exposed by the selectables component is listed as follows:

Method	Usage
Refresh	Manually refreshes the positions and sizes of all selectables. Should be used when `autoRefresh` is set to `false`.

In addition to this unique method, the selectables component (like every other component) makes use of the common API methods `destroy`, `disable`, `enable`, `option`, and `widget`.

Refreshing selectables

Setting the `autoRefresh` property to `false` can yield performance gains when there are many selectables on the page, especially in IE. However, there will still be times when you will need to refresh the size and positions of the selectables, such as when this component is combined with the draggables component.

Let's take a look at the `refresh` method as it leads on perfectly from the last example. Add the following new `<button>` element directly after the selectables container:

```
<button id="refresh">Refresh</button>
```

We'll also need to link to the draggable source file for this example:

```
<script src="development-bundle/ui/jquery.ui.draggable.js">
</script>
```

Then change the final `<script>` element so that it appears as follows:

```
<script>
  (function($) {
    var selectableOpts = {
      autoRefresh: false
```

```
        };
        $("#selectables").selectable(selectableOpts);
        $("#selectables div").draggable();

        $("#refresh").click(function() {
          $("#selectables").selectable("refresh");
        });
    })(jQuery);
  </script>
```

Save this as `selectable9.html`. We've added a new `<button>` to the page and we now link to the draggable source file as well as selectable's. Each of the 200 elements is made both draggable and selectable.

Our click handler that is attached to the `<button>` will simply call the `refresh` method manually on the selectables container. When we run the page in a browser we should first make a selection of a group, but not all, of the selectable. We should then deselect the elements and move some of them around. We can move other elements that weren't selected into the selection group as well. Really shuffle them up!

When we try to select the same group again, we find that the wrong elements are being selected:

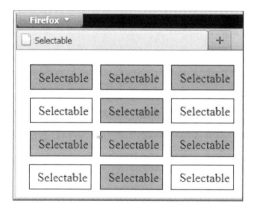

The component hasn't refreshed the positions of the selectables, so it still thinks that all of the selectables are in the same place as they were when the first selection was made. If we click on the refresh button and make a third selection, the correct elements will now be selected.

A selectable image viewer

In our final selectable example, we're going to make a basic image viewer. Images can be chosen for viewing by selecting the appropriate thumbnail. Although this sounds like a relatively easy achievement, in addition to the actual mechanics of displaying the selected image, we'll also need to consider how to handle multiple selections. The following screenshot shows an example of what we'll end up with:

Let's get started with the code. In a fresh page in your text editor, add the following page:

```
<!DOCTYPE html>
<html>
  <head>
    <meta charset="utf-8">
    <title>Selectable</title>
```

```html
    <link rel="stylesheet"
      href="css/smoothness/jquery-ui-1.8.9.custom.css">
    <link rel="stylesheet" href="css/selectableViewer.css">
  </head>
  <body>
    <div id="imageSelector"
      class="ui-widget ui-corner-all ui-helper-clearfix">
      <div id="status"
        class="ui-widget-header ui-corner-all">Crab</div>
      <div id="viewer">
        <img src="img/crab.jpg">
      </div>
      <div id="thumbs">
        <img class="ui-selected" id="crab" src="img/crab.jpg">
        <img class="right" id="orion" src="img/orion.jpg">
        <img id="omega" src="img/omega.jpg">
        <img class="right" id="egg" src="img/egg.jpg">
        <img id="triangulum" src="img/triangulum.jpg">
        <img class="right" id="rosette" src="img/rosette.jpg">
        <img id="ring" src="img/ring.jpg">
        <img class="right" id="boomerang"
          src="img/boomerang.jpg">
      </div>
    </div>
    <script src="development-bundle/jquery-1.4.4.js"></script>
    <script src="development-bundle/ui/jquery.ui.core.js">
    </script>
    <script src="development-bundle/ui/jquery.ui.widget.js">
    </script>
    <script src="development-bundle/ui/jquery.ui.mouse.js">
    </script>
    <script
      src="development-bundle/ui/jquery.ui.selectable.js">
    </script>
    <script src="development-bundle/ui/jquery.ui.tabs.js">
    </script>
  </body>
</html>
```

Save this as `imageSelector.html`. On the page we have a parent `<div>` with an `id` of `imageSelector` into which all of our other elements go.

Within the parent, we have a `<div>` that will act as a status bar to display the names of individually selected images, and a `<div>` that will act as the viewing panel and will display the full-sized version of the image. Finally, we have our thumbnail images, which will be made selectable.

Styling the image selector

Our example is also heavily reliant on CSS to provide its overall appearance. In a new file in your text editor, create the following new style sheet:

```
#imageSelector {
  width:676px; height:497px; border:1px solid #adadad;
  margin:0 auto; position:relative; background-color:#dfdede; }
#status {
  width:380px; height:21px; padding:10px; position:absolute;
  left:17px; top:17px; font-size:19px; text-align:center;
  background-color:#adadad; border:1px solid #adadad;
  text-transform:capitalize;
}
#viewer {
  width:400px; height:400px; border:1px solid #fff;
  position:absolute; left:17px; top:78px;
}
#thumbs {
  width:222px; height:460px; position:absolute; right:17px;
  top:17px;
}
#thumbs img {
  width:100px; height:100px; float:left; margin:0 18px 18px 0;
  cursor:pointer; border:1px solid #fff;
}
#thumbs img.right { margin-right:0; }
#thumbs img.ui-selected { border:1px solid #99ff99; }
#tabs {
  padding:0; border:none; position:absolute; left:17px;
  background:none;
}
#tabs .ui-tabs-panel { padding:0; }
#tabs .ui-tabs-nav {
  padding:0; border:none; position:relative; top:54px;
  background:none;
}
#tabs .ui-tabs-nav li { margin:0; }
#tabs .ui-tabs-nav li a {
  padding:5px 4px; font-size:11px; text-transform:capitalize; }
#tabs .ui-tabs-nav li.ui-tabs-selected a,
#tabs .ui-tabs-nav li.ui-state-disabled a,
#tabs .ui-tabs-nav li.ui-state-processing a {
  font-weight:bold;
}
```

Save this in the `css` folder as `selectableViewer.css`. Most of the styles are arbitrary and are required purely for layout or visual appearance. We're using some of the framework classes in our mark-up in order to add the rounded corners, so the amount of CSS we need to write is minimal. The last few selectors are required in order to override some of the tab widget's default styling.

Adding the behaving

Next we need to add the script that makes the image selector work, so directly after the final `<script>` element add the following code:

```
<script>
  (function($) {

    var selectOpts = {
      stop: function(e, ui) {
        $("#imageSelector")
        .children().not("#thumbs").remove();

        $("<div />", {
          id: "viewer"
        }).insertBefore("#thumbs");

        if ($(".ui-selected", "#thumbs").length == 1) {
          singleSelect();
        } else {
          multiSelect();
        }
      }
    };

    function singleSelect() {
      var id = $(".ui-selected", "#thumbs").attr("id");

      $("<div />", {
        id: "status",
        text: id,
        "class": "ui-widget-header ui-corner-all"
      }).insertBefore("#viewer");

      $("<img />", {
        src: "img/" + id + ".jpg",
        id: id
      }).appendTo("#viewer");
    }
```

```
        function multiSelect() {
          $("<div />", {
            id: "tabs"
          }).insertBefore("#viewer");

          var tabList = $("<ul />", {
            id: "tabList"
          }).appendTo("#tabs");

          $(".ui-selected", "#thumbs").each(function() {
            var id = $(this).attr("id"),
                tabItem = $("<li />").appendTo(tabList),
                tabLink = $("<a />", {
                text: id,
                href: "#tabpanel_" + id
              }).appendTo(tabItem),
                panel = $("<div />", {
                id: "tabpanel_" + id
              }).appendTo("#viewer");

            $("<img />", {
              src: "img/" + id + ".jpg",
              id: id
            }).appendTo(panel);
          });

          $("#viewer").css("left", 0).appendTo("#tabs");
          $("#tabs").tabs();
        }

        $("#thumbs").selectable(selectOpts);
      })(jQuery);
    </script>
```

The first thing we do is define the configuration object for the selectables. We use the `stop` `callback` function to do some prep work such as removing the contents of the image selector container (except for the thumbnails) and creating an empty `viewer` container. We then use an `if` conditional to call either the `singleSelect()` or `multiSelect()` functions.

We define these two functions next. One of these functions will be invoked every time a selection is made. If a single thumbnail image is selected, the first function is called, and if more than one of the elements are selected the second function will be called.

In the `singleSelect()` function we first cache the `id` of the selected element; we'll be referring to this several times so it's more efficient to store it in a variable.

Next we create a new status bar and set its `innerText` to the `id` value that was cached a moment ago, remember this will be the `id` attribute of whichever thumbnail is selected. We give the new element some of the framework classes to style the element and then insert it into the image selector container.

The last thing we do in this function is create the full-sized version of the thumbnail. To do this we create a new image, set its `src` attribute to match the large version of the thumbnail that was selected (both the large and thumbnail versions of each image have the same filename). The full-size image is then inserted into the `viewer` container.

Next we define the `multiSelect()` function. This time we start by creating a new `<div>` element, give it an `id` of `tabs` and insert it before the `viewer` container. Following this we create a new `<ul>` element as this is a required component of the tabs widget (that we looked at in *Chapter 3*). This element is appended to the `tabs` container we created a moment ago.

We then use jQuery's `each()` method to iterate over each of the thumbnails that were selected. For each item we create a series of variables, which will hold the different elements that make up the tab headings. We cache the `id` attribute of each image and create a new `<li>` and a new `<a>` element. The link will form the clickable tab heading and is given the `id` of the thumbnail as its text content.

We then create the new tab panel that will match the tab heading that we just created. Notice that we create a unique `id` for the content panel based on the thumbnail's `id` attribute and some hardcoded text. Note that the `id` will precisely match the `href` attribute that we set on the `<a>` element. Each new image is created in the same way as in the `singleSelect()` function.

After the `each()` method, we set a CSS property on the `viewer` container to tidy up its appearance and then append it to the `tabs` container. Finally the `tabs()` method is called on the `tabs` container, transforming it into the tabs widget. At the end of the script the thumbnails are made selectable.

When we run the example in a browser, we should see something similar to what is shown in the previous screenshot. When a single thumbnail is selected the full-size version of the image will be displayed. When multiple images have been selected, tabs are created at the top of the viewer, which allow all of the selected images to be shown.

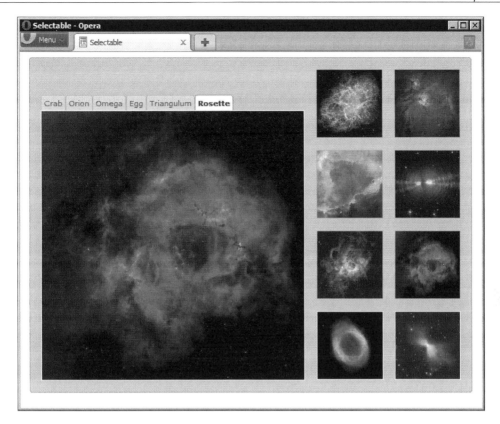

Summary

The selectables component provides a powerful set of behaviors for selecting elements on the page, much like how we would select them in a file explorer, such as explorer on Windows or finder on the Mac.

We first looked at the default implementation and then moved on to look at the configurable options, along the numerous callback properties, which can be used to perform different actions at different points in an interaction.

Next we looked at how the performance of a page can be improved when there are a large number of selectables on the page, and how the single unique method exposed by the component, refresh, is used.

Lastly we looked at a fun example that brought together what we had learned throughout the chapter and combined the selectables component with the tabs component to create an image viewer capable of handling single or multiple selections.

13
The Sortables Component

The final interaction helper that we're going to look at is the sortables component. This component allows us to define one or more list of elements (not necessarily actual <ul> or <ol> elements), where the individual items in the list(s) can be re-ordered by dragging.

We'll be looking at the following aspects of the component in this chapter:

- The default sortable implementation
- Basic configurable properties
- Working with placeholders
- Sortable helpers
- Sortable items
- Connected sortables
- Sortables' wide range of built-in event handlers
- A look at sortables' methods
- Submitting the sorted result to a server
- Adding drag elements to a sortable

The sortables component is like a specialized implementation of drag-and-drop, with a very specific role. It has an extensive API, which caters for a wide range of behaviors.

The default implementation

A basic sortable list can be enabled with no additional configuration. Let's do this first, so that you can get an idea of the behavior enabled by this component. In a new file in your text editor, add the following code:

```html
<!DOCTYPE html>
<html>
  <head>
    <meta charset="utf-8">
    <title>Sortable</title>
    <link rel="stylesheet"
      href="css/smoothness/jquery-ui-1.8.9.custom.css">
  </head>
  <body>
    <ul id="sortables">
      <li>Sortable 1</li>
      <li>Sortable 2</li>
      <li>Sortable 3</li>
      <li>Sortable 4</li>
      <li>Sortable 5</li>
    </ul>
    <script src="development-bundle/jquery-1.4.4.js"></script>
    <script src="development-bundle/ui/jquery.ui.core.js">
    </script>
    <script src="development-bundle/ui/jquery.ui.widget.js">
    </script>
    <script src="development-bundle/ui/jquery.ui.mouse.js">
    </script>
    <script src="development-bundle/ui/jquery.ui.sortable.js">
    </script>
    <script>
      (function($){
        $("#sortables").sortable();
      })(jQuery);
    </script>
  </body>
</html>
```

Save this as `sortable1.html`. On the page, we have a simple unordered list with five list items. Code-wise, the default implementation is the same as it has been for each of the other components. We simply call the `sortable` widget method on the parent `<ul>` element of the list items that we want to make sortable.

Thanks to the sortables component, we should find that the individual list items can be dragged to different positions in the list, as shown in the following screenshot:

A lot of behaviors are added to the page to accommodate this functionality. As we drag one of the list items up or down in the list, the other items automatically move out of the way, creating a slot for the item that is currently being sorted to be dropped on.

Additionally, when a sortable item is dropped, it will slide quickly, but smoothly into its new position in the list. The library files that were needed for the basic implementation are as follows:

- jquery-x.x.x.js
- jquery.ui.core.js
- jquery.ui.widget.js
- jquery.ui.mouse
- jquery.ui.sortable.js

As I mentioned earlier, the sortables component is a flexible addition to the library that can be applied to many different types of elements. For example, instead of using a list, we could use a series of `<div>` elements as the sortable list items, in place of the `<ul>` element in the previous example:

```
<div id="sortables" class="ui-widget">
   <div class="ui-widget-header ui-corner-all">Sortable 1</div>
   <div class="ui-widget-header ui-corner-all">Sortable 2</div>
   <div class="ui-widget-header ui-corner-all">Sortable 3</div>
   <div class="ui-widget-header ui-corner-all">Sortable 4</div>
   <div class="ui-widget-header ui-corner-all">Sortable 1</div>
</div>
```

This can be saved as `sortable2.html`. As you can see, the behavior exhibited by this version is exactly the same as it was before. All that's changed is the underlying markup. We've added some of the CSS framework classes in order to add some basic styling to our elements, and we can also use a custom style sheet to add a few extra styles.

Create a new file and add the following styles:

```
#sortables { width:300px; }
#sortables div { padding:2px 0 2px 4px; margin-bottom:8px; }
```

Save this in the `css` folder as `sortable.css`. Link to the CSS file in the `<head>` of `sortable2.html`:

```
<link rel="stylesheet" href="css/sortable.css">
```

With our new style sheet, the page should now appear as follows:

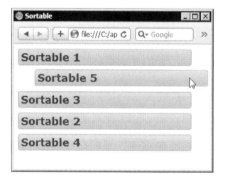

Configuring sortable options

The sortables component has a huge range of configurable options, much more than any of the other interaction components (but not as many as some of the widgets). The following table shows the range of options at our disposal:

Option	Default value	Used to...
appendTo	"parent"	Set the element that helpers are appended to, during a sort.
axis	false	Constrain sortables to one axis of movement. Possible values are the strings x or y.
cancel	":input, button"	Specify elements that cannot be sorted, if they are the elements being sorted.

Option	Default value	Used to...
connectWith	false	Enable one-way sorting from the current list to the specified list.
containment	false	Constrain sortables to their container while they are being sorted. Values can be the strings parent, window, or document, or can be a jQuery selector or element node.
cursor	"auto"	Define the CSS cursor to apply while dragging a sortable element.
cursorAt	false	Specify the coordinates that the mouse pointer should be at, while a sort is taking place. Accepts an object with the keys top, right, bottom, or left with integers as the values.
delay	0	Set the time delay in milliseconds before the sort begins, once a sortable item has been clicked (with the mouse button held down).
disabled	false	Disable the widget on page load.
distance	1	Set how far in pixels the mouse pointer should move, while the left button is held down before the sort begins.
dropOnEmpty	true	Allow linked items from linked sortables to be dropped onto empty slots.
forceHelperSize	false	Force the helper to have a size when set to true.
forcePlaceholderSize	false	Force the placeholder to have a size when set to true. The placeholder is the empty space that a sortable can be dropped on to.
grid	false	Set sortables to snap to a grid while being dragged. Accepts an array with two items—the x and y distances between gridlines.
handle	false	Specify an element to be used as the drag handle on sortable items. Can be a selector or an element node.
helper	"original"	Specify a helper element that will be used as a proxy, while the element is being sorted. Can accept a function that returns an element.

Option	Default value	Used to...
items	">*"	Specify the items that should be made sortable. The default makes all children sortable.
opacity	false	Specify the CSS opacity of the element being sorted. Value should be an integer from 0.01 to 1, with 1 being fully opaque.
placeholder	false	Specify a CSS class to be added to empty slots.
revert	false	Enable animation when moving sortables into their new slots, once they have been dropped.
scroll	true	Enable page scrolling when a sortable is moved to the edge of the viewport.
scrollSensitivity	20	Set how close a sortable must get, in pixels, to the edge of the viewport, before scrolling should begin.
scrolSpeed	20	Set the distance in pixels that the viewport should scroll, when a sortable is dragged within the sensitivity range.
tolerance	"intersect"	Control how much of the element being sorted must overlap other elements, before the placeholder is moved. Another possible value is the string pointer.
zIndex	1000	Set the CSS zIndex of the sortable or helper, while it is being dragged.

Let's work some of these properties into our previous example to get a feel for the effect they have on the behavior of the component. First wrap the #sortables container in a new <div>:

```
<div id="container">
  <div id="sortables" class="ui-widget">
    <div class="ui-widget-header ui-corner-all">Sortable 1
    </div>
    <div class="ui-widget-header ui-corner-all">Sortable 2
    </div>
    <div class="ui-widget-header ui-corner-all">Sortable 3
    </div>
    <div class="ui-widget-header ui-corner-all">Sortable 4
    </div>
```

```
      <div class="ui-widget-header ui-corner-all">Sortable 5
      </div>
    </div>
  </div>
```

Then change the final `<script>` element in `sortable2.html`, so that it appears as follows:

```
<script>
  (function($) {
    var sortOpts = {
      axis: "y",
      containment: "#container",
      cursor: "ns-resize",
      distance: 30
    };
    $("#sortables").sortable(sortOpts);
  })(jQuery);
</script>
```

Save this as `sortable3.html`. We also need to add a little padding to our new container element. Update `sortable.css`, so that it contains the following new code:

```
#container { padding:10px 0 20px; }
```

Resave this file as `sortableContainer.css` and update the `<link>` in the `<head>` of `sortable3.html`, so that it points to the new style sheet.

We use four options in our configuration object; the `axis` option is set to `y`, to constrain the motion of the sortable currently being dragged to just up-and-down. The `containment` option specifies the element that the sortables should be contained within. The sortables will now not be able to move outside of the bounds of the container element.

Sortable spacing

Care should be taken when using the `containment` option. This is specifically why we added some padding to the container element in our style sheet. Without this padding, the first sortable element is flushed against the top of the container and the last element is flushed against the bottom. In order to be able to push a sortable element out of the way, there must be some space above or below it.

We also specify the cursor option that automatically adds the CSS ns-resize cursor. Like with the draggable component that we looked at in *Chapter 10, Drag and Drop,*the cursor is not actually displayed until the sort begins.

Finally, we configure the distance option with a value of 30, which specifies that the mouse pointer should move 30 pixels before the sort begins. The distance option works in the same way with sortables as it did with draggables, and is great for preventing unwanted sorts, but in practice, we'd probably use a much lower threshold than 30 pixels.

Let's look at some more options. Change the underlying <div> elements in sortable3.html, so that they appear as follows:

```
<div id="sortables" class="ui-widget">
  <div class="ui-widget-header ui-corner-all">Sortable 1
    <span class="ui-icon ui-icon-triangle-2-n-s"></span>
  </div>
  <div class="ui-widget-header ui-corner-all">Sortable 2
    <span class="ui-icon ui-icon-triangle-2-n-s"></span>
  </div>
  <div class="ui-widget-header ui-corner-all">Sortable 3
    <span class="ui-icon ui-icon-triangle-2-n-s"></span>
  </div>
  <div class="ui-widget-header ui-corner-all">Sortable 4
    <span class="ui-icon ui-icon-triangle-2-n-s"></span>
  </div>
  <div class="ui-widget-header ui-corner-all">Sortable 5
    <span class="ui-icon ui-icon-triangle-2-n-s"></span>
  </div>
</div>
```

We can get rid of the #container element for this example. We also need a modified style sheet for this example. Change sortable.css, so that it includes the following new styles:

```
#sortables span { margin:2px 2px 0 0; float:right; }
```

Save the new style sheet as sortableHandles.css in the css folder and update the <link> element to point to the new style sheet.

Finally, change the configuration object as follows:

```
var sortOpts = {
  revert: "slow",
  handle: "span",
  delay: 1000,
  opacity: 0.5
};
```

Save this as `sortable4.html`. We've made a slight change to the page. Within each sortable element is a new `<span>` element that will be used as the sort handle. We give this element some CSS framework classes in order to reduce the CSS we need to add manually.

The `revert` option has a default value of `true`, but can also take one of the speed integer or string values (`slow`, `normal`, or `fast`) that we've seen in other animation options in other components.

The `delay` option accepts a value in milliseconds that the component should wait, before allowing the sort to begin. If the mouse pointer is moved away from the handle while the left-button is held down, the sort will still occur after the specified time. If the mouse-button is released, however, the sort will be canceled.

The value of the `opacity` option is used to specify the CSS opacity of the element that is being sorted, while the sort takes place. The value should be a floating-point number between `0` and `1`, with `1` corresponding to full opacity and `0` specifying no opacity.

Another option we've used is the `handle` option, which allows us to define a region within the sortable, which must be used to initiate the sort. Dragging on other parts of the sortable will not cause the sort to begin.

You can see how the handle will appear in the following screenshot:

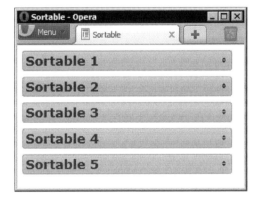

 Make my handles bigger

For usability reasons, we should probably use a bigger handle than the one used in the previous example.

Placeholders

A placeholder defines the empty space or slot that is left, while one of the sortables is in the process of being moved to its new position. The placeholder isn't rigidly positioned. It will dynamically move to whichever sortable has been displaced, by the movement of the sortable that is being sorted.

There are two options that are specifically concerned with placeholders—the very aptly named `placeholder` option and the `forcePlaceholderSize` option. Let's take a look at these two options in action. Remove the `<span>` elements from the sortable `<div>` elements in `sortable4.html` and then change the configuration object, so that it appears as follows:

```
var sortOpts = {
  placeholder: "empty ui-corner-all",
  forcePlaceholderSize: true
};
```

Save this as `sortable5.html`. Next, we should add the new selector and rules to a CSS file. Change `sortable.css`, so that it contains the following styles:

```
.empty { border:1px solid #029000; background-color:#cdfdcd; }
```

Save this as `sortablePlaceholder.css` in the `css` folder.

The `placeholder` option allows us to define a CSS class that should be added to the placeholder element. This is a useful property that we can use often in our implementations. Remember this is a classname, not a class selector, so no period is used at the start of the string. It can accept multiple classnames.

The `forcePlaceholderSize` option ensures that the placeholder is the same size as the actual sortables. If we left this option at its default value of `false`, in this example, the placeholder would just be a thin line made up of the padding that we applied to the sortable `<div>` elements.

When we run the new HTML file in a browser, we should be able to see the specified styles applied to the placeholder, while the sort is taking place:

Sortable helpers

We looked at helper/proxy elements back when we looked at the draggables component earlier in the book. Helpers can also be defined for sortables that function in a similar way to those of the draggable component, although there are some subtle differences in this implementation.

With sortables, the original sortable is hidden when the sort interaction begins, and a clone of the original element is dragged instead. So with sortables, helpers are an inherent feature.

Like with draggables, the `helper` option of sortables may take a function as its value. The function, when used, will automatically receive the `event` object and an object containing useful properties from the sortable element as arguments.

The function must return the element to use as a helper. Although it's very similar to the draggable helper example, let's take a quick look at it when used in conjunction with sortables. In `sortable5.html`, change the last `<script>` block, so that it appears as follows:

```
<script>
  (function($) {
    var helperMaker = function(e, ui) {
      return $("<div />", {
        text: $(ui).text(),
        "class": "ui-corner-all",
        css: {
          opacity: 0.5,
          border: "4px dashed #cccccc",
          textAlign: "center"
        }
      });
    },
    sortOpts = {
      helper: helperMaker
    };
    $("#sortables").sortable(sortOpts);
  })(jQwery);
</script>
```

Save this file as `sortable6.html`. We define a `helperMaker` function that creates and returns the element to be used as the helper, while the sort is in progress. We set some basic CSS properties on the new element, so that we don't need to provide additional rules in the style sheet.

The following screenshot shows how the helper will appear while a sort is taking place:

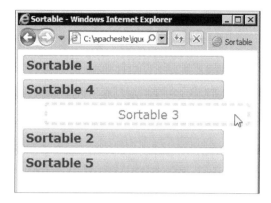

Sortable items

By default, all children of the element that the `sortable` method is called on, are turned into sortables. While this is a useful feature of the component, there may be times when we don't necessarily want all child elements to become sortable.

The `items` option controls which child elements of the specified element should be made sortable. It makes all child elements sortable using the string `>*` as its default value, but we can alter this to specify only the elements we want. Change the sortable `<div>` elements in `sortable6.html`, so that the last element has a new classname:

```
<div class="ui-widget-header ui-corner-all unsortable">
  Sortable 5
</div>
```

Then, change the configuration object to make use of the `items` option:

```
var sortOpts = {
  items: ">:not(.unsortable)"
};
```

Save this as `sortable7.html`. In the `<script>`, we've specified the selector `">:not(.unsortable)"` as the value of the `items` option, so the element with the classname `unsortable` will not be made sortable, while the rest of the `<div>` elements will.

When we run the page in a browser, we should find that the last item in the collection cannot be sorted, and other sortable items cannot be moved into the space that the last item occupies.

Connected lists

So far, the examples that we have looked at have all centered on a single list of sortable items. What happens when we want to have two lists of sortable items, and more importantly, can we move items from one list to another?

Having two sortable lists is of course extremely easy and involves simply defining two containers and their child elements, and then passing a reference to each container to the `sortable()` method.

Allowing separate lists of sortables to exchange and share sortables is also extremely easy. This is thanks to the `connectWith` option that allows us to define an array of sortable containers, who can share their sortable contents.

Let's look at this in action. Change the underlying markup on the page, so that it appears as follows:

```
<div id="sortablesA" class="ui-widget">
  <div class="ui-widget-header ui-corner-all">Sortable 1A</div>
  <div class="ui-widget-header ui-corner-all">Sortable 2A</div>
  <div class="ui-widget-header ui-corner-all">Sortable 3A</div>
  <div class="ui-widget-header ui-corner-all">Sortable 4A</div>
  <div class="ui-widget-header ui-corner-all">Sortable 5A</div>
</div>
<div id="sortablesB" class="ui-widget">
  <div class="ui-widget-header ui-corner-all">Sortable 1B</div>
  <div class="ui-widget-header ui-corner-all">Sortable 2B</div>
  <div class="ui-widget-header ui-corner-all">Sortable 3B</div>
  <div class="ui-widget-header ui-corner-all">Sortable 4B</div>
  <div class="ui-widget-header ui-corner-all">Sortable 5B</div>
</div>
```

Save this as `sortable8.html`. Everything on the page is pretty similar to what we have worked with before. We also need a new style sheet for this example. In a new page, add the following styles:

```
#sortablesA, #sortablesB {
  width:300px; margin-right:50px; float:left;
}
.ui-widget div { padding:2px 0 2px 4px; margin-bottom:8px; }
```

Save this as `sortableConnected.css` in the `css` folder. Don't forget to point to the new style sheet in the `<head>` of the new page. Finally, change the last `<script>` element, so that it appears as follows:

```
<script>
  (function($){
    var sortOpts = {
      connectWith: ["#sortablesA", "#sortablesB"]
    };
    $("#sortablesA, #sortablesB").sortable(sortOpts);
  })(jQuery);
</script>
```

We still define a single configuration object, which can be shared between both sets of sortable elements. The `connectWith` option is able to accept multiple selectors if they are passed in as an array, and it's this option that allows us to share individual sortables between the two sortable containers.

This configuration option only provides a one-way transmission of sortables, so if we were to only use the configuration object with `sortablesA` and specify just the selector `#sortablesB`, we would only be able to move items from `sortablesA` to `sortablesB`, not the other way.

Specifying both sortables' `id` attributes in the option and selecting both of the containers when calling the `sortable()` method, allows us to move items between both elements, and allows us to cut down on coding.

When we run the page in a browser, we find that not only can the individual items be sorted in their respective elements, but that items can also be moved between elements, as shown in the following screenshot:

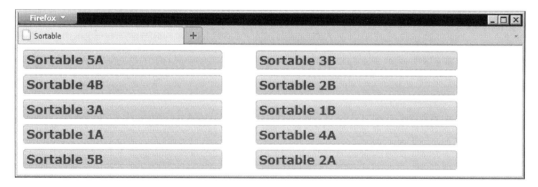

Reacting to sortable events

In addition to the already large list of configurable options defined in the sortables class, there are also a whole lot more in the form of event callbacks, which can be passed functions to execute at different points during a sortable interaction. These are listed in the following table:

Event	Fired when...
activate	Sorting starts on a connected list.
beforeStop	The sort has stopped, but the original slot is still available.
change	The DOM position of a sortable has changed and the sort is still in progress.
create	The widget is initialized.
deactivate	Sorting stops on a connected list.
out	A sortable is moved out of a connected list.
over	A sortable is over a connected list. This is great for providing visual feedback while a sort is taking place.
receive	A sortable is received from a connected list.
remove	A sortable is moved from a connected list.
sort	A sort is taking place.
start	A sort starts.
stop	A sort ends.
update	The sort has ended and the DOM position has changed.

Each of the components that we've looked at in the preceding chapters has defined it's own suite of custom events, and the sortables component is no exception.

Many of these events will fire during any single sort interaction. The following list shows the order in which they will fire:

1. start
2. sort
3. change
4. beforeStop
5. stop
6. update

As soon as one of the sortables is **picked up,** the start event is triggered. Following this, on every single mouse move, the sort event will fire, making this event very intensive.

As soon as another item is displaced by the current sortable, the `change` event is fired. Once the sortable is **dropped**, the `beforeStop` and `stop` events fire, and if the sortable is now at a different position, the `update` event is fired last of all.

For the next few examples, we'll work some of these event handling options into the previous example, starting with the `start` and `stop` events. Change the configuration object in `sortable8.html`, so that it appears as follows:

```
var sortOpts = {
  connectWith: ["#sortablesA", "#sortablesB"],
  start: function(e, ui) {
    $("<p />", {
      id: "message",
      text: ui.helper.text() + " is active",
      css: {
        clear:"both"
      }
    }).appendTo("body");
  },
  stop: function() {
    $("#message").remove();
  }
};
```

Save this as `sortable9.html`. Our event usage in this example is minimal. When the sort starts, we simply create a new paragraph element and add some text to it, including the text content of the element that is being sorted. The text message is then duly appended to the `<body>` of the page. When the sort stops, we remove the text.

Using the second object passed to the callback function is very easy, as you can see. The object itself refers to the parent sortables container, and the `helper` property refers to the actual item being sorted (or its helper). As this is a jQuery object, we can call jQuery methods, such as `text`, on it.

When we run the page, the message should appear briefly until the sort ends, at which point it's removed.

Let's look at one more of these simple callbacks, before we move on to look at the additional callbacks used with connected sortables. Change the final `<script>` element in `sortable9.html` to the following:

```
<script>
  (function($){
    var getPlaces = function(e, ui) {
      var extraMessage = (e.type === "sortreceive") ? " in a new
        list" : "";
      $("#message").remove();
      $("<p />", {
        id: "message",
        text: [
          "Item now at position ",
          (ui.item.index() + 1).toString(),
          extraMessage
        ].join(" "),
        css: {
          clear: "both"
        }
      }).appendTo("body");
    },
    sortOpts = {
      connectWith: ["#sortablesA", "#sortablesB"],
      beforeStop: getPlaces,
      receive: getPlaces
    };
    $("#sortablesA, #sortablesB").sortable(sortOpts);
  })(jQuery);
</script>
```

Save this as `sortable10.html`. In this example, we work with the `receive` and `beforeStop` callbacks to provide a message, indicating the position within the list that any sortable is moved to, as well as which list it is in. We also make use of the `ui.item` property from the object, which is automatically passed to any callback functions used by the events.

We first define a variable called `extraMessage`, which is initially set to an empty string. We then define a function called `getPlaces`. This function will be used as a callback function for sortable events and will, therefore, automatically receive `e` and `ui` objects.

Within the function, we first check whether the event object's `type` property has a value of `sortreceive`; if it does, we know that a sortable has moved lists and can, therefore, set the extra part of the message.

We then remove any pre-existing messages, before creating a new `<p>` element and setting a message, indicating its new position in the list. We can obtain the new position of the element that was sorted using the `item` property of the second object passed to our callback in conjunction with jQuery's `index()` method, which we convert to a string and concatenate into a message.

In our configuration object, we connect the two lists using the `connectWith` option as before, and make use of both the `receive` and `beforeStop` options, which both point to our `getPlaces` function.

The `receive` event is fired whenever a sortable container receives a new sortable element from a connected list. The `beforeStop` event is fired just before the sort interaction ends. In terms of event order, in this example the `beforeStop` event is fired first, followed by the `receive` event.

The `receive` event will only be fired if a sortable element moves to a new sortable container. The following screenshot shows how the page should look following a sort interaction:

Connected callbacks

Six of the available callbacks can be used in conjunction with connected sortables. These events fire at different times during an interaction, alongside the events that we have already looked at.

Like the standard unconnected events, not all of the connected events will fire in any single interaction. Some events, such as `over`, `off`, `remove`, and `receive` will fire only if a sort item moves to a new list.

Other events, such as the activate and deactivate, will fire in all executions, whether any sort items change lists or not. Additionally, some connected events, such as activate and deactivate, will fire for each connected list on the page.

Provided at least one item is moved between lists, events will fire in the following order:

1. start
2. activate
3. sort
4. change
5. beforeStop
6. stop
7. remove
8. update
9. receive
10. deactivate

Let's now see some of these connected events in action. Change the final <script> element in sortable10.html, so that it appears as follows:

```
<script>
  (function($){
    var sortOpts = {
      connectWith: ["#sortablesA", "#sortablesB"],
      activate: function() {
        $("<p />", {
          text: $(this).attr("id") + " has been activated",
          css: {
            clear:"both"
          }
        }).appendTo("body");
      },
      deactivate: function() {
        $("<p />", {
          text: $(this).attr("id") + " has been deactivated",
          css: {
            clear:"both"
          }
        }).appendTo("body");
      },
      receive: function(e, ui) {
        $("<p />", {
```

```
          text: ui.item.text() + " was moved from " +
            ui.sender.attr("id") + " into " + $(this).attr("id"),
          css: {
            clear:"both"
          }
        }).appendTo("body");
      }
    };
    $("#sortablesA, #sortablesB").sortable(sortOpts);
  })(jQuery);
</script>
```

Save this as `sortable11.html`. The `activate` and `deactivate` events are fired for each connected list at the start of any sort interaction. Within our callback functions, `$(this)` refers to each sortable container. We can easily determine which sortable list the item originated in using the `sender` property of the second object, passed to our function.

When we run the page in a browser, we see that as soon as a sort begins, both of the sortables are activated, and when the sort ends, both of them are deactivated. If an item is moved between lists, the message generated by the `receive` callback is shown:

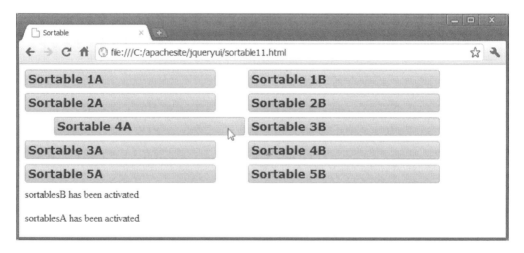

Sortable methods

The sortables component exposes the usual set of methods for making the component do things, and like the selectables component that we looked at before, it also defines a couple of unique methods not seen in any of the other components. The following table lists sortables' unique methods:

Method	Used to...
cancel	Cancel the sort and cause elements to return to their original positions.
refresh	Reload the set of sortables.
refreshPositions	Trigger a cache refresh of the set of sortables.
serialize	Construct a query string that can be used to send a new sort order to the server, for further processing or storage.
toArray	Serialize the sortables into an array of strings.

Serializing

The serialize and toArray methods are great for storing the new order of the sortables. Let's see this in action. Change the underlying markup on the <body> of the page in sortable11.html to as follows:

```
<div id="sortablesA" class="ui-widget">
  <div id="sortablesA_1"
    class="ui-widget-header ui-corner-all">Sortable 1A</div>
  <div id="sortablesA_2"
    class="ui-widget-header ui-corner-all">Sortable 2A</div>
  <div id="sortablesA_3"
    class="ui-widget-header ui-corner-all">Sortable 3A</div>
  <div id="sortablesA_4"
    class="ui-widget-header ui-corner-all">Sortable 4A</div>
  <div id="sortablesA_5"
    class="ui-widget-header ui-corner-all">Sortable 5A</div>
</div>
```

Then change the final <script> element, so that it appears as follows:

```
<script>
  (function($) {
    var sortOpts = {
      stop: function(e, ui) {
        var order = $("#sortablesA").sortable("serialize");
        $("#message").remove();
        $("<p />", {
          id: "message",
          text: order,
          css: {
            clear:"both"
          }
```

```
        }).appendTo("body");
      }
    };
    $("#sortablesA").sortable(sortOpts);
  })(jQuery);
</script>
```

Save this as `sortable12.html`. We've dropped the second set of sortables for this example and have added `id` attributes to each of the sortable items in the format of the name of the parent sortable and a number, separated by an underscore.

We use the `stop` event to execute an anonymous function, after each sort interaction. Within this function, we store the result of the `serialize` method in a variable, and then display this variable in a new `<p>` element on the page:

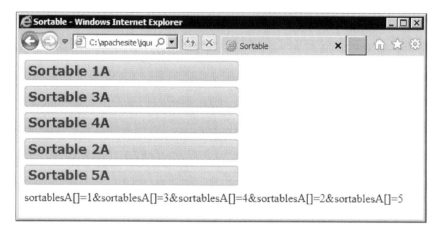

As you can see, the format of the serialized string is quite straight-forward. The sortable items appear in the order that the items appear on the page, and are separated by an ampersand. Each serialized item is made up of two parts—a hash of the `id` attribute of each sortable item followed by an integer representing the item's new order.

In the previous example, all we do is display the serialized string on the page, but the string is in the perfect format for use with jQuery's `ajax` method to pass to a server for further processing.

The `serialize` method is also able to accept a configuration object to tailor how the serialization occurs. The options we can configure are listed in the following table:

Option	Default value	Used to...
attribute	id	Specify the attribute to use when parsing each item in the list of sortables and generating the hash.
connected	false	Include all connected lists in the serialization.
expression	`"(.+)[-=_](.+)"`	Specify the `regexp` to use to parse the sortable list.
key	The first part of the id attribute of each sortable item	Specify the string to be used as the first part of each item in the serialized output.

The `toArray` method works in a similar way to serialize, except that with `toArray`, the output is not a string, but an array of strings.

Widget compatibility

In the previous chapter, we saw that both the resizable and the selectable components worked well with the tabs widget (and we already know how well the dialog and resizables components go together). The sortable component is also highly compatible with other widgets. Let's look at a basic example. In a new page in your text editor, add the following code:

```
<!DOCTYPE html>
<html>
  <head>
    <meta charset="utf-8">
    <title>Sortable Tabs</title>
    <link rel="stylesheet"
      href="css/smoothness/jquery-ui-1.8.9.custom.css">
  </head>
  <body>
    <div id="tabs">
      <ul>
        <li><a href="#0"><span>Sort Tab 1</span></a></li>
        <li><a href="#1"><span>Sort Tab 2</span></a></li>
        <li><a href="#2"><span>Sort Tab 3</span></a></li>
      </ul>
      <div id="0">The first tab panel</div>
      <div id="1">The second tab panel</div>
      <div id="2">The third tab panel</div>
    </div>
```

```
<script src="development-bundle/jquery-1.4.4.js"></script>
<script src="development-bundle/ui/jquery.ui.core.js">
</script>
<script src="development-bundle/ui/jquery.ui.widget.js">
</script>
<script src="development-bundle/ui/jquery.ui.mouse.js">
</script>
<script src="development-bundle/ui/jquery.ui.sortable.js">
</script>
<script src="development-bundle/ui/jquery.ui.tabs.js">
</script>
<script>
  (function($){
    var sortOpts = {
      axis: "x",
      items: "li"
    };
    $("#tabs").tabs().sortable(sortOpts);
  })(jQuery);
</script>
</body>
</html>
```

Save this page as `sortable13.html`. There is nothing in the code that we haven't seen before, so we won't go into any great detail about it. Note that only the `tabs()` and `sortable()` methods are called on the same element—the outer containing `<div>` element.

When we run the page in a browser, we should find that the components work in exactly the way that we want them to. The tabs can be sorted horizontally to any order, but as the tabs are linked to their panel by `href`, they will still show the correct panel, when selected.

Sorting the tabs works on the `mousedown` event and selecting the tabs works on the `mouseup` event, so there are no event collisions and no situations arising where you want to select a tab, but end up sorting it. The next screenshot shows how the tabs may appear after sorting:

Adding draggables

When we looked at draggables and droppables, earlier in the book, we saw that there was a configuration option for draggables called `connectToSortable`. Let's take a look at that option now that we've been introduced to the fundamentals of the sortables component. In this example, we'll create a sortable task list that can have new tasks dragged into it. The resulting page will appear as follows:

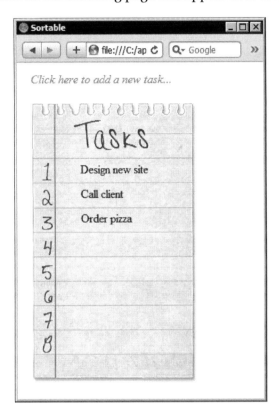

In a new file in your text editor, add the following code:

```
<!DOCTYPE html>
<html>
  <head>
    <meta charset="utf-8">
      <title>Sortable</title>
      <link rel="stylesheet"
        href="css/smoothness/jquery-ui-1.8.9.custom.css">
      <link rel="stylesheet" href="css/sortableTasks.css">
  </head>
  <body>
```

```html
    <ul id="drag">
      <li>Click here to add a new task...</li>
    </ul>
    <a id="add" href="#"></a>
    <div id="taskList">
      <ul id="tasks">
        <li>Design new site</li>
        <li>Call client</li>
        <li>Order pizza</li>
      </ul>
    </div>
    <script src="development-bundle/jquery-1.4.4.js"></script>
    <script src="development-bundle/ui/jquery.ui.core.js">
    </script>
    <script src="development-bundle/ui/jquery.ui.widget.js">
    </script>
    <script src="development-bundle/ui/jquery.ui.mouse.js">
    </script>
    <script src="development-bundle/ui/jquery.ui.sortable.js">
    </script>
    <script src="development-bundle/ui/jquery.ui.draggable.js">
    </script>
  </body>
</html>
```

Save this as `sortable14.html`. On the page, we have a couple of `<ul>` elements; the first contains a single item which provides an instruction to the visitor and the second is the task list. The second list is wrapped in a container `<div>`, mostly for styling purposes.

We also use a new style sheet for this example. Add the following code to a new page in your text editor:

```css
#drag { padding:0 0 0 11px; margin:0; float:left; }
#drag li { font-style:italic; color:#999; }
#drag li input { width:175px; }
#taskList {
  width:250px; height:400px; clear:both;
  background:url(../img/paper.jpg) no-repeat;
}
#tasks {
  width:170px; padding:89px 0 0; margin:0; float:right;
}
#tasks li, #drag li {
```

```
      height:28px; padding-top:5px; list-style-type:none;
}
#add {
  display:none; width:24px; height:24px; position:absolute;
  left:218px; top:13px;
  background:url(../img/add.png) no-repeat;
}
#add.down { background:url(../img/down.png) no-repeat; }
```

Save this as `sortableTasks.css` in the `css` folder. Mostly this is just decorative, superficial stuff for the purposes of the example.

Finally we can add the script that wires it all up. Add the following `<script>` element, after the library resources:

```
<script>
  (function($){
    var dragItem = $("#drag li"),
    addButton = $("#add"),
    sortOpts = {
      axis: "y",
      stop: function() {
        addButton.css("display", "none");
        dragItem.text("Click here to add new task...")
          .draggable("option", "disabled", true)
          .removeClass("ui-state-disabled");
      }
    },
    dragOpts = {
      connectToSortable: "#tasks",
      helper: "clone",
      disabled: true
    };
    $("#tasks").sortable(sortOpts);
    dragItem.draggable(dragOpts).live("click", function() {
      if ($("#tasks").children().length > 7) {
        alert("too many tasks already!");
      } else {
        var input = $("<input />", {
          id: "newTask"
        });
        $(this).text("").append(input);
        input.focus();
        addButton.removeClass("down").css("display", "block");
      }
    });
```

```
      addButton.live("click", function(e) {
        e.preventDefault();
        if ($("#drag input").val() !== "") {
          dragItem.text($("#newTask").val())
            .draggable("option", "disabled", false);
          $("#drag input").remove();
          addButton.addClass("down")
            .attr("title", "drag new task into the list");
        }
      });
    })(jQuery);
  </script>
```

We first cache a couple of selectors that we'll be using frequently throughout the script, then define the configuration object for the sortables. We restrict sorting to the vertical axis and specify a callback function for the `stop` event.

Within this function, we hide the `add` button and reset any text that has been added to the draggable, then use the `option` method of the draggable to disable dragging on the element, so that the text label cannot be dragged into the task list.

Additionally, when we set the `disabled` option of the draggable, it adds a CSS framework class that reduces the opacity of the draggable. This is not necessary for our example, so we also remove this classname.

Following this, we define the draggable configuration object and set the `connectToSortable` option to an `id` selector that matches the parent sortables container, and the `helper` option to clone. The dragging is initially disabled. We then initialize the sortable and draggable components.

We add a click handler to the draggable element using jQuery's `live()` method. When the draggable `<li>` is clicked, it checks that there aren't too many tasks in the list already, and if not, it will create a new `<input>` field and append it to the `<li>` in the first `<ul>`. The hidden `add` button is also displayed. The visitor can then enter a new task and make the new task draggable, by clicking the button. The text box and icon will appear as shown in the following screenshot:

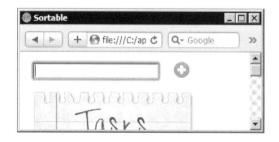

We also add a click handler for the `add` button that we create, again using jQuery's `live()` method. This function checks that the `<input>` contains some text, and provided it does, it then gets the text and then removes the text field. The text is then added to the draggable `<li>` element, and the `<li>` is made draggable by setting the `disabled` option to `false`. Finally, the `<input>` is removed, and the message and button are set back to their original state.

Summary

We've finished our tour of the interaction components of the library, by looking at the sortables component. Like the other modules that we looked at before, it has a wide range of properties and methods that allow us to configure and control its behavior and appearance in both simple and more complex implementations.

We started off the chapter with a look at a simple, default implementation with no configuration to see the most basic level of functionality added by the component. We looked at some of the different elements that can be made sortable and added some basic styling to the page.

Following this, we looked at the range of configurable options that are exposed by the sortable API. The list is extensive and provides a wide range of functionality that can be enabled or disabled with ease.

We moved on to look at the extensive event model used by this component that gives us the ability to react to different events, as they occur in any sort operation, initiated by the visitor.

Connected lists offer the ability to be able to exchange sortable items between lists or collections of sortables. We saw the additional options and events that are used specifically with connected sortable lists.

In the last part of the chapter, we looked at the methods available for use with the sortables component, and focused on the highly useful `serialize` method, and also had a quick look at its compatibility with other members of the jQuery UI library in the form of the sortable tabs example. We've now looked at all of the current interaction components found in the library. In the next and final chapter, we'll look at all of the different animation effects that jQuery UI brings to the table.

14
UI Effects

We've so far looked at a range of incredibly useful widgets and interaction helpers. All are easy to use, but at the same time are powerful and highly configurable. Some have had their subtle nuances, which have required consideration and thought during their implementation.

The effects provided by the library, on the other hand, are for the most part extremely compact, with very few options to learn and no methods at all. We can use these effects quickly and easily, with minimum configuration.

The effects that we'll be looking at in this chapter are as follows:

- Blind
- Bounce
- Clip
- Drop
- Explode
- Fold
- Highlight
- Pulsate
- Scale
- Shake
- Slide
- Transfer

The core effects file

Like the individual components themselves, the effects require the services of a separate core file. It provides essential functionality to the effects, such as creating wrapper elements and controlling the animations. Most, but not all, of the effects have their own source files, which build on the core foundation to add functionality specific to the effect.

All we need to do to use an effect is include the core file (`jquery.effects.core.js`) in the page, before the effect's source file. Unlike the `jquery.ui.core.js` file, however, the `jquery.effects.core.js` file has been designed to be used, in part, completely standalone.

When using the core effect file on its own, we can take advantage of color animations. This includes changing the background color of an element to another color (and not just a snap change, but a smooth morphing of one color into another), class transitions, and advanced easing animations.

Using color animations

Let's look at creating color animations. First, create the following new page:

```html
<!DOCTYPE html>
<html>
  <head>
    <meta charset="utf-8">
    <title>Color Animations</title>
    <link rel="stylesheet" href="css/effectColor.css">
  </head>
  <body>
    <form action="#">
      <div><label>Name: </label><input type="text"></div>
      <div><label>Age: </label><input type="text"></div>
      <div><label>Email: </label><input type="text"></div>
      <button type="submit">Submit</button>
    </form>
    <script src="development-bundle/jquery-1.4.4.js"></script>
    <script src="development-bundle/ui/jquery.effects.core.js">
    </script>
    <script>
      (function($){
        $("form").submit(function() {
          $("input").each(function() {
            ($(this).val().length == 0) ? $(this).animate({
```

```
                    backgroundColor:"#ff9999",
                    borderTopColor: "#ff0000",
                    borderRightColor: "#ff0000",
                    borderBottomColor: "#ff0000",
                    borderLeftColor: "#ff0000"
                }) : $(this).animate({
                    backgroundColor:"#ccffcc",
                    borderTopColor: "#00ff00",
                    borderRightColor: "#00ff00",
                    borderBottomColor: "#00ff00",
                    borderLeftColor: "#00ff00"
                });
            });
        });
    })(jQuery);
    </script>
  </body>
</html>
```

Save the page as `effectColor.html`. As you can see, all we need are jQuery and the `jquery.effects.core.js` file to create attractive color transitions. On the page, we have a simple `<form>` element enclosing three container elements and three sets of `<label>` and `<input>` elements. The `animate` method is part of jQuery rather than jQuery UI specifically, but the `jquery.effects.core.js` file extends jQuery's `animate` method, by allowing it to specifically work with colors and classes.

When the **Submit** button is clicked, we simply use the `animate` method to apply a series of new CSS properties to the target elements, based on whether the text inputs have been filled out or not. If they have been completed, we color them green, and if not, we color them red. We also use a basic style sheet in this example. In another new page in your text editor, add the following basic selectors and rules:

```
div { margin-bottom:5px; }
label { display:block; width:100px; float:left; }
input { border:1px solid #000000; }
```

Save this as `effectColor.css` in the `css` folder. When we view this page in our browser, we should see that any fields that are left blank, smoothly turn red when the **Submit** button is clicked, while fields that are not empty, smoothly turn green. It's most attractive, however, when a field changes from red to green.

The following screenshot shows the page once the **Submit** button has been clicked:

The style attributes that color animations can be used on are as follows:

- `backgroundColor`
- `borderTopColor`
- `borderRightColor`
- `borderBottomColor`
- `borderLeftColor`
- `color`
- `outlineColor`

Colors may be specified using either RGB, hexadecimal (in the format #xxx[xxx]), or even standard color names. Although there can be cross-browser issues when using color names, they are best avoided in most cases.

Using class transitions

In addition to animating individual color attributes, `jquery.effects.core.js` also gives us the powerful ability to animate between entire classes. This allows us to switch styles smoothly and seamlessly without sudden, jarring changes. Let's look at this aspect of the file's use in the following example.

Change the `<link>` in the `<head>` of `effectColor.html` to point to a new style sheet:

```
<link rel="stylesheet" href="css/effectClass.css">
```

Then change the final `<script>` element so that it appears as follows:

```
<script>
  (function($) {
    $("form").submit(function(e) {
      e.preventDefault();
```

```
    $("input").each(function() {
      if ($(this).hasClass("error")) {
        ($(this).val().length == 0) ? null :
          $(this).switchClass("error", "pass", 2000);
      } else if ($(this).hasClass("pass")) {
        ($(this).val().length != 0) ? null :
          $(this).switchClass("pass", "error", 2000);
      } else {
        ($(this).val().length == 0) ? $(this)
          .addClass("error", 2000) : $(this)
          .addClass("pass", 2000);
      }
    });
  });
}) (jQuery);
</script>
```

Save this as `effectClass.html`. The `jquery.effects.core.js` file extends the jQuery class API, by allowing us to specify a duration over which the new classname should be applied, instead of just switching it instantly. We can also specify an easing effect.

The `switchClass` method of the `jquery.effects.core.js` file is used when the fields already have one of the classnames and need to change to a different classname. The `switchClass` method requires several arguments; we specify the classname to remove, followed by the class name to add. We also specify a duration as the third argument.

Essentially, the page functions as it did before, although using this type of class transition allows us to use non-color-based style rules as well, so we can adjust widths, heights, or many other style properties if we want to. Note that background images cannot be transitioned in this way.

As in the previous example, we have a style sheet attached. This is essentially the same as in the previous example, except with some styles for our two new classes. Add the following selectors and rules to the bottom of `effectColor.css`:

```
.error { border:1px solid #ff0000; background-color:#ff9999; }
.pass { border:1px solid #00ff00; background-color:#ccffcc; }
```

Save the updated file as `effectClass.css` in the `css` folder.

Advanced easing

The `animate` method found in standard jQuery has some basic easing capabilities built-in, but for more advanced easing, you have to include an additional easing plugin (ported to jQuery by GSGD).

 See the easing plugin's project page for further information: `http://gsgd.co.uk/sandbox/jquery/easing/`.

The `jquery.effect.core.js` file has all of these advanced easing options built in, so there is no need to include additional plugins. We won't be looking at them in any real detail in this section; however, we will be using them in some of the examples later on in the chapter.

Highlighting specified elements

The highlight effect temporarily applies a light yellow coloring to any element that it's called on (the effect is also known as **Yellow Fade Technique** (**YFT**)). Let's put a simple example together, so we can see the effect in action:

```
<link rel="stylesheet" href="css/effectHighlight.css">
```

The `<script>` element that refers to the effect's source file, so that it uses the `jquery.effects.highlight.js` file:

```
<script src="development-bundle/ui/jquery.effects.highlight.js">
</script>
```

Then remove the `<form>` from the `<body>` of the page and replace it with the following markup:

```
<h1>Choose the correct download below:</h1>
<a id="win" href="#"><img src="img/iconWin.png"></a>
<a id="mac" href="#"><img src="img/iconMac.png"></a>
<a id="linux" href="#"><img src="img/iconLinux.png"></a>
<button id="hint">Hint</button>
```

Lastly, change the final `<script>` element so that ends up as follows:

```
<script>
  (function($) {
    $("#hint").click(function() {
      var os = navigator.userAgent;
      if (os.search(/windows/i) !== -1) {
```

```
      var el = $("#win");
    } else if (os.search(/mac/i) !== -1) {
      var el = $("#mac");
    } else if (os.search(/linux/i) !== -1) {
      var el = $("#linux");
    }
    $(el).effect("highlight");
  });
}) (jQuery);
</script>
```

Save this page as `effectHighlight.html`. The code that invokes the highlight effect takes the same familiar form as other library components. The `effect` method is called and the actual effect is specified as a string argument to the method.

We simply sniff the `userAgent` string and see if a search for either windows, mac, or linux returns a positive integer. If a positive integer is found, the `userAgent` string contains the search word; if `-1` is returned, the search term was not found.

We also need to create the new style sheet, not for the effect to work, but just to tidy things up a little. In a new page in your text editor, add the following selectors and rules:

```
a { padding:10px; float:left; }
a img { display:block; border:none; }
button {
  display:block; position:relative; top:10px; clear:both;
}
```

Save this file as `effectHighlight.css` in the `css` folder.

View the example and click the **Hint** button. The icon for whichever operating system you are using should be highlighted briefly:

While our example may seem a little contrived, it is easy to see the potential for this effect as an assistance tool on the front-end. Whenever there is a sequence of actions that needs to be completed in a specific order, the `highlight` effect can instantly give the visitor a visual cue as to the step that needs to be completed next.

Additional effect arguments

Each of the `effect` methods, as well as the argument that dictates which effect is actually applied, can take up three additional arguments that control how the effect works. All of these arguments are optional, and consist of the following (in the listed order):

1. An object containing additional configuration options.
2. An integer representing in milliseconds, the duration of the effect, or a string specifying one of `slow`, `normal`, or `fast`.
3. A callback function that is executed when the effect ends.

The `highlight` effect has only one configurable option that can be used in the object passed as the second argument, and that is the highlight color.

Let's add some of these additional arguments into our highlight example to clarify their usage. Change the call to the `effect` method in the final `<script>` element in `effectHighlight.html`, so that it appears as follows:

```
$(el).effect("highlight", {}, function() {
  $("<p />", {
    text: "That was the highlight"
  }).appendTo("body").delay(2000).fadeOut();
});
```

Save this as `effectHighlightCallback.html`. Perhaps the most striking feature of our new code is the empty object passed as the second argument. In this example, we don't use any additional configurable options, but we still need to pass in the empty object, in order to access the third and fourth arguments.

The callback function, passed as the third argument, is perhaps the least useful callback in the history of JavaScript, but it does serve to illustrate how easy it is to arrange additional post-animation code execution following an effect.

Bouncing

Another simple effect we can use with little configuration is the bounce effect. To see this effect in action change the contents of the <body> in effectHighlight.html to the following:

```
<div id="ball">
  <img src="img/ball.png">
</div>
```

We also need to use the source file for the bounce effect; change the reference to the jquery.effects.highlight.js file, so that it points to the bounce source file:

```
<script src="development-bundle/ui/jquery.effects.bounce.js">
</script>
```

Save this as effectBounce.html. We need to add a tiny bit of styling to really see the effect in full, but it's probably not worth creating a whole new style sheet so simply replace the <link> element in the <head> of the page with the following:

```
<style>
  #ball { position:relative; top:150px; }
</style>
```

Finally, change the final <script> element so that it appears as follows:

```
<script>
  (function($){
    $("#ball").click(function() {
      $(this).effect("bounce", { distance: 140 });
    });
  })(jQuery);
</script>
```

Using the bounce effect, in this example, shows how easy it is to add this simple but attractive effect. We configure the distance option to set how far the element travels. Other options that can be configured are listed in the following table:

Option	Default value	Used to...
direction	"up"	Set the direction of the bounce.
distance	20	Set the distance in pixels of the first bounce.
times	5	Set the number of times the element should bounce.

You'll notice when you run the example that the bounce effect has an ease-out easing feature built into it, so the distance of the bounce will automatically decrease as the animation proceeds.

One thing to note is that with most of the different effects, including the bounce effect (but not the highlight effect we looked at earlier), the effect is not actually applied to the specified element. Instead a wrapper element is created and the element targeted by the effect is appended to the inside of the wrapper. The actual effect is then applied to the wrapper.

This is an important detail to be aware of, because if you need to manipulate the element that has the effect applied to it in mid-animation, then the wrapper will need to be targeted instead of the original element. Once the effect's animation has completed, the wrapper is removed from the page.

Shaking an element

The shake effect is very similar to the bounce effect, but with the crucial difference of not having any built-in easing. So, the targeted element will shake the same distance for the specified number of times, instead of lessening each time (although it will come to a smooth stop at the end of the animation).

Let's change the previous example so that it uses the shake effect instead of the bounce effect. Change `effectBounce.html` so that it uses the shake source file instead of the bounce source file:

```
<script src="development-bundle/ui/jquery.effects.shake.js">
</script>
```

Then change the click-handler in the final `<script>` element at the bottom of the `<body>`, so that it appears as follows:

```
$("#ball").click(function() {
  $(this).effect("shake", { direction: "up" }, 100);
});
```

Save this as `effectShake.html`. This time we've made use of the `direction` configuration option and the duration argument. The configuration option controls the direction of the shake. We set this to override the default setting for this option, which is `left`. The duration we use, speeds up the animation.

This effect shares the same options as the bounce effect, although the defaults are set slightly differently. The options are listed in the following table:

Option	Default value	Used to...
direction	"left"	Set the direction of the shake.
distance	20	Set the distance of the shake in pixels.
times	3	Set the number of times the element should shake.

Transferring an element's outline

The transfer effect is different from others, in that it doesn't directly affect the targeted element. Instead, it transfers the outline of a specified element to another specified element. To see this effect in action, change the `<body>` of `effectShake.html` so that it contains the following elements:

```
<div id="container">
  <div id="productContainer">
    <img alt="GTX 280" src="img/gcard.jpg"></img>
    <p>BFG GTX 280 OC 1GB GDDR3 Dual DVI HDTV Out PCI-E Graphics Card
    </p>
    <p id="price">Cost: $350</p>
    <div id="purchase"><button id="buy">Buy</button></div>
  </div>
  <div id="basketContainer">
    <div id="basket"></div>
      <p>Basket total: <span id="total">0</span></p>
  </div>
</div>
```

Save this as `effectTransfer.html`. We've created a basic product listing; when the **Buy** button is clicked, the transfer effect will give the impression of the product being moved into the basket. To make this happen, change the final `<script>` element, so that it contains the following code:

```
<script>
  (function($){
    $("#buy").click(function() {
      $("#productContainer img").effect("transfer", {
        to:"#basket"
      }, 750, function() {
        var currentTotal = $("#total").text(),
        numeric = parseInt(currentTotal, 10);
        $("#total").text(numeric + 1);
```

```
        });
      });
    })(jQuery);
  </script>
```

Of course, a proper shopping cart application would be exponentially more complex than this, but we do get to see the transfer effect in all its glory. Don't forget to update the effect's source file:

```
<script src="development-bundle/ui/jquery.effects.transfer.js">
</script>
```

We also need some CSS for this example, so create the following new style sheet:

```
#container { width:607px; margin:0 auto; }
#productContainer img {
  width:92px; height:60px; border:2px solid #000000;
  position:relative; float:left;
}
#productContainer p {
  width:340px; height:50px; padding:5px;
  border:2px solid #000; border-left:none; margin:0;
  font-family:Verdana; font-size:11px; font-weight:bold;
  float:left;
}
p#price {
  height:35px; width:70px; padding-top:20px; float:left;
}
#purchase {
  height:44px; width:75px; padding-top:16px;
  border:2px solid #000; border-left:none; float:left;
  text-align:center;
}
#basketContainer {
  width:90px; margin-top:100px; float:right;
}
#basket {
  width:65px; height:31px; position:relative; left:13px;
  background:url(../img/basket.gif);
}
.ui-effects-transfer { border:2px solid #66ff66; }
```

Save this as `effectTransfer.css` in the `css` folder. The key rule in our new style sheet is the one that targets the element which has a class of `ui-effects-transfer`. This element is created by the effect and together with our styling produces the green outline that is transferred from the product to the basket.

Run the file in your browser. I think you'll agree that it's a nice effect which would add value to any page that it was used on. Here's how it should look while the transfer is occurring:

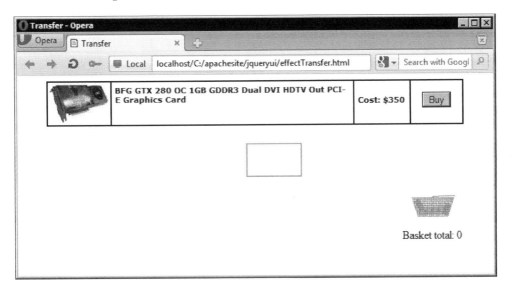

The transfer effect has just two configurable options, one of which is required and that we have already seen. For reference, both are listed in the following table:

Option	Default value	Used to...
className	"ui-effects-transfer"	Apply a custom classname to the effect helper element.
to	"none"	Set the element the effect will be transferred to. This property is mandatory.

The four effects that we've looked at so far all have one thing in common—they can only be used with the effect method. The remaining effects can be used not only with the effect method, but also with jQuery's toggle and the show/hide methods. Let's take a look.

Element scaling

The scale effect is highly configurable and is used to shrink an element. It is very effective when used to hide elements. In this example we'll use the hide() method to trigger the effect, instead of using the effect method.

We'll use a few of the CSS framework classes in this example, as well as a few custom styles; so add two new `<link>` elements to the `<head>` of `effectTransfer.html`:

```
<link rel="stylesheet"
  href="css/smoothness/jquery-ui-1.8.9.custom.css">
<link rel="stylesheet" href="css/effectScale.css">
```

Then, replace the underlying markup in the `<body>` with the following:

```
<div class="ui-widget ui-widget-content ui-corner-all">
  <div class="ui-widget-header ui-corner-all">
    A dialog box
    <a id="close" class="ui-icon ui-icon-closethick" href="#">
      Close
    </a>
  </div>
  <div class="content">
    Close the dialog to see the scale effect
  </div>
</div>
```

Don't forget to change the `<script>` element for the effect, to the scale effect's source file:

```
<script src="development-bundle/ui/jquery.effects.scale.js">
</script>
```

Finally, change the last `<script>` element, so that it appears as follows:

```
<script>
  (function($){
    $("#close").click(function(e) {
      e.preventDefault();
      $(this).closest(".ui-widget").hide("scale", {}, 900);
    });
  })(jQuery);
</script>
```

Save the new page as `effectScale.html`. The custom style sheet we use is as follows:

```
.ui-widget { padding:3px; width:300px; }
.ui-widget-header, .content { padding:5px 10px; }
.ui-widget-header a { margin-top:2px; float:right; }
```

Save this file as `effectScale.css` in the `css` folder. These styles are used to give the example a vaguely dialog-like appearance.

In the script, we simply add a click handler for the close icon and call the `effect()` method on the outer container of the dialog box. An empty object is passed as the second argument to the method, and a relatively long duration is passed as the third argument, as this effect proceeds quite rapidly. The following screenshot shows the effect in action:

Using the `hide()` method instead of the `effect` method is advantageous to us in this example, because we want the dialog box to remain hidden after the effect has completed. When the `effect()` method is used instead, bits of the widget remain visible at the end of the animation.

 The `percent` configuration option must be configured when using the `effect` method in conjunction with the scale effect.

There are several configuration options which can be used with scale; these are as listed in the following table:

Option	Default value	Used to...
direction	"both"	Set the direction to scale the element in. May be a string specifying either both, vertical, or horizontal.
from	{}	Set the starting height and width of the element to be scaled.
origin	["middle","center"]	Set the vanishing point, used with show/hide animations.
percent	0	Set the end size of the scaled element.

Element explosion

The explosion effect is truly awesome. The targeted element is literally exploded into a specified number of pieces, before disappearing completely. It's an easy effect to use and has few configuration properties, but the visual impact of this effect is huge, giving you a lot of effect in return, for very little code. Let's see a basic example. Create the following new page:

```
<!DOCTYPE html>
<html>
  <head>
    <meta charset="utf-8">
    <title>Explode</title>
  </head>
  <body>
    <p>Click the grenade to pull the pin!</p>
    <img id="theBomb" src="img/nade.jpg">
    <script src="development-bundle/jquery-1.4.4.js"></script>
    <script src="development-bundle/ui/jquery.effects.core.js">
    </script>
    <script src="development-bundle/ui/jquery.effects.explode.js">
    </script>
    <script>
      (function($){
        $("#theBomb").click(function() {
          $(this).hide("explode");
        });
      })(jQuery);
    </script>
  </body>
</html>
```

Save this as `effectExplode.html`. As you can see, the code is extremely simple and can be used completely out of the box with no additional configuration. This effect has only one configurable property, which is the `pieces` property, and it determines how many pieces the element is exploded into. The default is 9. The effect works equally as well with the `effect()` method as it does with the `hide()` method.

Once the specified element has been exploded, it will be hidden from view by having its `style` attribute set to `display:none`. This is the default behavior. However, it will still remain in the DOM of the page. The following screenshot shows the explosion in progress:

Physicists sometimes speculate as to why the arrow of time seems to only point forwards. They invariably ask themselves philosophical questions like *why do we not see grenades spontaneously forming from a large cloud of debris?* (Actually the object is usually an egg, but I don't think an egg-based example would have had quite the same impact!)

jQuery UI cannot help our understanding of entropy, but it can show us what a grenade spontaneously reassembling might look like. We'll need to hide the `<img>` in order to show it. The easiest way to do this is with an inline `style` attribute:

```
<img id="theBomb" src="img/nade.jpg" style="display:none">
```

Then, change the final `<script>` element so that it appears as follows:

```
<script>
  (function($){
    $("#theBomb").show("explode");
  })(jQuery);
</script>
```

Save this variant as `effectExplodeShow.html`. This time we use the `show()` method instead of the `hide()` method to trigger the animation, which occurs once the page has loaded.

The animation is the same, except that it is shown in reverse and this time, the grenade is not hidden from view once the animation ends. Like the other effects, explode can also make use of specific durations and callback functions.

The puff effect

Similar to the explode effect, but slightly more subtle is the puff effect, which causes an element to grow slightly before fading away. Like explode, there are few configuration options to concern ourselves with.

Consider a page that has AJAX operations occurring on it. It's useful to provide a loading image that shows the visitor that something is happening. Instead of just hiding an image like this when the operation has completed, we can puff it out of existence instead.

Remove the `<p>` and change the `<img>` from the previous example, so that it points to a new image:

```
<img id="loader" src="img/ajax-loader.gif">
```

Then change the effect's source file to the scale effect:

```
<script src="development-bundle/ui/jquery.effects.scale.js">
</script>
```

Finally, change the last `<script>` element, so that it appears as follows:

```
<script>
  (function($){
    $("#loader").click(function() {
      $(this).hide("puff");
    });
  })(jQuery);
</script>
```

Save this as `effectPuff.html`. We're actually not detecting whether a given process has finished loading in this example. It would require too much work just to see the effect we're looking at. Instead, we tie the execution of the effect into a simple click-handler.

You'll notice that we used the `jquery.effect.scale.js` source file for this effect. The puff effect is the only effect that does not have its own source file, and instead it's a part of the very closely related scale effect's source file.

Like the explode effect that we looked at in the last section, this effect has just one configuration option that can be passed in an object as the second argument of the `effect` method. This is the `percent` option and controls the size the image is scaled up to. The default value is `150` percent. Like the explode effect, the target element is hidden from view once the animation ends. This happens whether `effect()` or `hide()` is used.

The effect stretches the targeted element (and its children, if it has any), while at the same time reducing its opacity. It works well on proper images, background colors, and borders, but you should note that it does not work so well with background images specified by CSS. Nevertheless, it's a great effect. The following screenshot shows it in action:

The pulsate effect

The pulsate effect is another effect that works with the opacity of a specified element. This effect reduces the opacity, temporarily, a specified number of times, making the element appear to pulsate.

In the following basic example, we'll create a simple countdown time that counts down from 15. When the display reaches 10 seconds, it will begin to flash red. In effectPuff.html, change the link in the <head> of the page to point to a new style sheet:

```
<link rel="stylesheet" href="css/effectPulsate.css">
```

Then remove the loading <img> from the page and add the following element in its place:

```
<div id="countdown">15</div>
```

Next, change the source file of the effect so that the jquery.effects.pulsate.js file is used:

```
<script src="development-bundle/ui/jquery.effects.pulsate.js">
</script>
```

Finally, change the last <script> element so that it appears as follows:

```
<script>
  (function($) {
    var age = 15,
    countdown = $("#countdown"),
    adjustAge = function() {
```

```
        countdown.text(age--);
        if (age === 0) {
          clearInterval(timer);
        } else if (age < 10) {
          countdown.css({
            backgroundColor: "#ff0000",
            color: "#fff"
          }).effect("pulsate", { times: 1 });
        }
      },
      timer = setInterval(function() { adjustAge() }, 1000);
    })(jQuery);
  </script>
```

Save this as `effectPulsate.html`. The page itself contains just a simple `<div>` element with the text 15 inside it. The code first sets a counter variable and then caches a selector for the `<div>`. We then define the `adjustAge()` function.

This function first decreases the text content of the countdown element and at the same time, reduces the value of the counter variable by one. It then checks whether the counter variable has reached 0 yet; if yes, it clears the interval we are about to set.

If the counter variable is greater than 0 but less than 11, the function applies a background color of red to the element and white to the element's text content, and then runs the pulsate effect.

We use the `times` configuration option to specify how many times the element should pulsate. As we'll be executing the method once every second, we can set this to just pulsate once each time. This is the only configurable option.

After our `adjustAge` function, we start the interval using JavaScript's `setInterval` function. This function will repetitively execute the specified function after the specified interval, which in this example is `1000` milliseconds, or 1 second. We avoid using the `window` object by using an anonymous function to call our named function.

The new style sheet is very simple and consists of the following code:

```
#countdown {
  width:100px; border:1px solid #000; margin:10px auto 0;
  font-size:60px; text-align:center;
}
```

Save this in the `css` folder as `effectPulsate.css`.

Dropping elements onto the page

The drop effect is simple. Elements appear to drop off (or onto) the page, which is simulated by adjusting the element's `position` and `opacity`.

This effect exposes the following configurable options:

Option	Default value	Used to...
direction	"left"	Set the direction of the drop.
distance	The outer width or height of the element (depending on the direction) divided by 2	Set the distance the element drops.
easing	*none*	Set the easing function used during the animation.
mode	"hide"	Set whether the element is hidden or shown.

There are many situations in which the drop effect would be useful, but the one that instantly springs to mind is when creating custom tooltips. We can easily create a tooltip that appears when a button is clicked, but instead of just showing the tooltip, we can drop it onto the page. We'll use the button widget and the `position` utility in this example, as well as the effect.

Add a link to the CSS framework file and change the style sheet link in the `<head>` of `effectPulsate.html`:

```
<link rel="stylesheet"
  href="css/smoothness/jquery-ui-1.8.9.custom.css">
<link rel="stylesheet" href="css/effectDrop.css">
```

Remove the countdown `<div>` from the page, and add the following element instead:

```
<a id="button" href="#" title="This button does nothing">
  Click me!
</a>
```

Now we need to change the effect's source file and add the source files for the position and button widgets:

```
<script src="development-bundle/ui/jquery.effects.drop.js">
</script>
<script src="development-bundle/ui/jquery.ui.core.js">
</script>
```

```
<script src="development-bundle/ui/jquery.ui.widget.js">
</script>
<script src="development-bundle/ui/jquery.ui.position.js">
</script>
<script src="development-bundle/ui/jquery.ui.button.js">
</script>
```

Lastly, change the final `<script>` element, so that it appears as follows:

```
<script>
  (function($){
    $("#button").button().click(function() {
      var button = this,
      positionOpts = {
        of: button,
        my: "right center",
        at: "left center",
        offset: "-30 0"
      },
      tip = $("<span />", {
        id: "tip",
        text: button.title
      }),
      tri = $("<span />", {
        id: "tri"
      }).appendTo(tip);
      tip.appendTo("body").position(positionOpts)
        .show("drop", { direction: "up" }, function() {
        $(this).delay(1000).fadeOut();
      });
    });
  })(jQuery);
</script>
```

Save this file as `effectDrop.html`. When the button is clicked, we first store a reference to the DOM node of the button. We then add a configuration object for the `position` utility, in order to position our tooltip to the right of the button.

We then create a new `<span>` element to use as the tooltip, which has its text content set to the title text of the button. We also create another element used to create a triangular CSS shape to give the tooltip a pointer. This element is appended to the tooltip.

Once created, the tooltip is appended to the `<body>` of the page and is then shown using the drop effect. The `direction` configuration option is used to make the tooltip appear to drop down; we have to specify the opposite direction here, because our tooltip is absolutely positioned.

There is also some minimal CSS required for this example, in addition to the styles provided by the CSS framework, to style the tooltip. Create the following style sheet:

```
#tip {
  display:none; padding:10px 20px 10px 10px;
  position:absolute; background-color:#cecece;
}
#tri {
  border-top:20px solid transparent;
  border-right:30px solid #cecece;
  border-bottom:20px solid transparent; position:absolute;
  left:-30px; top:0;
}
```

Save this in the `css` folder as `effectDrop.css`. The styling here is purely for aesthetics.

When you run the file in your browser, you should see your tooltip, as in the following screenshot:

Sliding elements open or closed

The remaining effects of the jQuery UI library all work by showing and hiding elements in different ways, rather than using opacity like most of the effects we have already looked at.

The slide effect is no exception and shows (or hides) an element by sliding it into (or out of) view. It is similar to the drop effect that we just looked at. The main difference is that it does not use opacity.

The slide effect contains the following configuration options:

Option	Default value	Used to...
direction	"left"	Set the direction of the slide.
distance	The outer width or height of the element (depending on the direction)	Set the distance the element slides.
easing	*none*	Set the easing function used during the animation.
mode	"show"	Set whether the element is hidden or shown.

These are the same configuration options used by the drop effect that we looked at in the previous example, except that some of the default values are different.

For our next example, we can create exactly this kind of functionality. In effectDrop.html, change the `<link>` element in the `<head>` of the page from effectDrop.css to effectSlide.css:

```
<link rel="stylesheet" href="css/effectSlide.css">
```

Then remove the `<a>` from the `<body>` of the page and add the following HTML in its place:

```
<aside id="basket" class="ui-widget">
  <h1 class="ui-widget-header ui-corner-all">
    Basket
    <a id="toggle" title="Show basket contents"
      class="ui-icon ui-icon-circle-triangle-s" href="#">
      Open
    </a>
  </h1>
  <div class="ui-widget-content ui-corner-bottom">
    <ul>
      <li>
        <img src="img/placeholder.gif">
        <h2>Product name</h2>
        <h3>Brief descriptive subtitle</h3>
        <span>£xx.xx</span>
      </li>
      <li>
        <img src="img/placeholder.gif">
        <h2>Product name</h2>
        <h3>Brief descriptive subtitle</h3>
        <span>£xx.xx</span>
```

```
      </li>
      <li>
        <img src="img/placeholder.gif">
        <h2>Product name</h2>
        <h3>Brief descriptive subtitle</h3>
        <span>£xx.xx</span>
      </li>
    </ul>
  </div>
</aside>
```

The outer element in this collection is an `<aside>`, which is the perfect element for a mini-basket widget that sits in the right-column of a site. Within this element, we have a `<h1>` that serves as the heading for the basket. The heading contains a link, which will be used to show or hide the contents of the basket. The contents of the basket will consist of an unordered list of products within a container `<div>`.

Don't forget to change the `<script>` element for the effect's source file to use `jquery.effects.slide.js`, and remove the `<script>` files for `jquery.ui.core.js`, `jquery.ui.widget.js`, `jquery.ui.position.js`, and `jquery.ui.button.js`:

```
<script src="development-bundle/ui/jquery.effects.slide.js">
</script>
```

The final `<script>` element will need to be changed to the following code:

```
<script>
  (function($){
    $("#toggle").live("click", function(e) {
      var slider = $("#basket").find("div"),
      header = slider.prev();
      if (!slider.is(":visible")) {
        header.addClass("ui-corner-top")
          .removeClass("ui-corner-all");
      }
      slider.toggle("slide", {
        direction: "up"
      }, "slow", function() {
        if (slider.is(":visible")) {
          header.css("borderBottomWidth", 0).find("a")
            .addClass("ui-icon-circle-triangle-n")
            .removeClass("ui-icon-circle-triangle-s");
        } else {
          header.css("borderBottomWidth", 1)
            .addClass("ui-corner-all")
```

```
              .removeClass("ui-corner-top").find("a")
              .addClass("ui-icon-circle-triangle-s")
              .removeClass("ui-icon-circle-triangle-n");
          }
        });
      });
    })(jQuery);
  </script>
```

Save this as `effectSlide.html`. All of the functionality resides within a click-handler, which we attach to the icon in the basket header. When this element is clicked, we first initialize the variables `slider` and `header`, as these are the elements that we will be manipulating.

We then check whether the `slider` (which is the basket contents container) is hidden; if it is hidden, we know that it is about to be opened and so remove the rounded corners from the bottom of the header. This is so that the `slider` element sits flush up to the bottom of the `header`, even while it is sliding open.

We then use jQuery's `toggle()` method to call the effect, which we specify using the first argument of the method. We then set the configuration option, `direction`, in an object passed as the second argument. The duration of the animation is lengthened using the string `slow` as the third argument, and an anonymous callback function is used as the fourth argument. This function will be executed at the end of the slide animation.

Within this function, we check the state of the `slider` to see if it is hidden or open. If it is open at the end of the animation, we remove the border from the bottom of the `header` and then change the icon in the `header`, so that it points up to indicate that the basket can be closed by clicking the icon again.

If the `slider` is now closed, we add the bottom border and rounded corners to the `header` once again, and change the icon back to an arrow pointing down.

We also use a little CSS in this example. Create the following style sheet:

```
#basket { width:380px; float:right; }
#basket h1 { padding:5px 10px; margin:0; }
#basket h1 a { float:right; margin-top:8px; }
#basket div { display:none; }
#basket ul { margin:0; padding:0; list-style-type:none; }
#basket li { padding:10px; border-bottom:1px solid #aaa; }
#basket li:last-child { border-bottom:none; }
#basket li:after {
  content:""; display:block; width:100%; height:0;
```

```
        visibility:hidden; clear:both;
    }
    #basket img { margin:2px 10px 0; float:left; }
    #basket h2 { margin:0 0 10px; font-size:14px; }
    #basket h3 { margin:0; font-size:12px; }
    #basket span { margin-top:6px; float:right; }
```

Save this as `effectSlide.css` in the `css` folder. We don't need much CSS in this example, because we are using the CSS framework classes.

The effect in progress should appear as in the following screenshot:

In this example, we could easily just use jQuery's native `slideToggle()` method; the main benefit of using jQuery UI's slide effect is that we can also slide left or right.

Using easing

I said earlier that the `jquery.effects.core.js` file had the built-in ability to seamlessly use easing with the effects. Let's see how easy this is to achieve. Change the last `<script>` element in `effectSlide.html`, so that it appears as follows:

```
<script>
  (function($){
    $("#toggle").live("click", function(e) {
      var slider = $("#basket").find("div"),
```

```
        header = slider.prev(),
        easing = (slider.is(":visible")) ?
        "easeOutQuart" :
        "easeOutBounce";
        if (!slider.is(":visible")) {
          header.addClass("ui-corner-top")
            .removeClass("ui-corner-all");
        }
        slider.toggle("slide", {
          direction: "up",
          easing: easing
        }, "slow", function() {
          if (slider.is(":visible")) {
            header.css("borderBottomWidth", 0).find("a")
              .addClass("ui-icon-circle-triangle-n")
              .removeClass("ui-icon-circle-triangle-s");
          } else {
            header.css("borderBottomWidth", 1)
              .addClass("ui-corner-all")
              .removeClass("ui-corner-top").find("a")
              .addClass("ui-icon-circle-triangle-s")
              .removeClass("ui-icon-circle-triangle-n");
          }
        });
      });
    })(jQuery);
  </script>
```

Save this as `effectsSlideEasing.html`. See how easy that was? All we need to do is add the `easing` option within the effect's configuration object and define one or more of the easing methods as the option value.

In this example, we specify a different easing method for each toggle state, by setting a variable which uses the JavaScript ternary condition to set an easing function, depending on whether the slider is visible or not.

When the basket slides down, it bounces slightly at the end of the animation with `easeOutBounce`. When it slides back up, it will gradually slow down over the course of the animation using `easeOutQuart`.

The full range of easing methods we can make use of with the any of the effects are shown on an excellent page on the jQueryUI site and can be seen at: `http://jqueryui.com/demos/effect/easing.html`.

The window-blind effect

The blind effect is practically the same as the slide effect. Visually, the element appears to do the same thing, and the two effects' code files are also extremely similar. The main difference between the two effects that we need to worry about is that with this effect we can only specify the axis of the effect, not the actual direction.

The blind effect has the following configuration options:

Option	Default value	Used to...
direction	"vertical"	Set the axis of motion.
easing	*none*	Set the easing function used during the animation.
mode	"hide"	Set whether the element is hidden or shown.

The `direction` option that this effect uses for configuration only accepts the values `horizontal` or `vertical`. We'll build on the last example to see the blind effect in action. Change the `<script>` resource for the blind effect in `effectSlide.html`, so that it refers to the `jquery.effects.blind.js` file:

```
<script src="development-bundle/ui/jquery.effects.blind.js">
</script>
```

Now change the `toggle()` method, so that it uses the blind effect, and change the value of the `direction` configuration option:

```
slider.toggle("blind", {
    direction: "vertical"
}, "slow", function() {
    if (slider.is(":visible")) {
        header.css("borderBottomWidth", 0).find("a")
            .addClass("ui-icon-circle-triangle-n")
            .removeClass("ui-icon-circle-triangle-s");
    } else {
        header.css("borderBottomWidth", 1)
            .addClass("ui-corner-all")
            .removeClass("ui-corner-top").find("a")
            .addClass("ui-icon-circle-triangle-s")
            .removeClass("ui-icon-circle-triangle-n");
    }
});
```

Save this as `effectBlind.html`. Literally, all we've changed is the string specifying the effect, in this case to `blind`, and the value of the `direction` property from `up` to `vertical`. Notice the subtle difference when we view the file between sliding the element and blinding it up.

When the login form slides up, the bottom of the element remains visible at all times, as if the whole basket is moving up into or out of the header. With the blind effect, however, the element is shown or hidden starting with the bottom first, just like a window blind opening or closing.

Clipping elements

The clip effect is very similar to the slide effect. The main difference is that instead of moving one edge of the targeted element towards the other, to give the effect of the element sliding out of view, the clip effect moves both edges of the targeted element in towards the center.

The clip effect has the same configuration options as the blind effect and these options have the same default values.

At the end of *Chapter 5, The Dialog*, we created an example that showed a full-size image in a dialog when a thumbnail image was clicked. When the close button on the dialog was pressed, the dialog was simply removed from the page instantly. We could easily use the clip effect to close our dialog instead.

In `diaog14.html`, add the source files for the clip effect after the existing library files:

```
<script src="development-bundle/ui/jquery.effects.core.js">
</script>
<script src="development-bundle/ui/jquery.effects.clip.js">
</script>
```

Then, change the dialog configuration object so that it appears as follows:

```
var dialogOpts = {
  modal: true,
  width: 388,
  height: 470,
  autoOpen: false,
  open: function() {
    $("#ajaxDialog").empty();
      $("<img>").attr("src", filename).appendTo("#ajaxDialog");
    $("#ajaxDialog").dialog("option", "title", titleText);
  },
  close: function() {
    $(this).parent().hide("clip");
  }
};
```

Save this as `effectClip.html`. In this simple addition to the existing file, we use the clip effect in conjunction with the `close` event callback to hide the dialog from view. The default configuration value of `vertical` for the `direction` option and the default speed of normal are both fine, so we just call the `hide` method, specifying clip with no additional arguments.

The following screenshot shows the dialog being clipped:

Folding elements

Folding is a neat effect that gives the appearance that the element it's applied to is being folded up like a piece of paper. It achieves this by moving the bottom edge of the specified element up to `15` pixels from the top, then moving the right edge completely over towards the left edge.

The distance from the top that the element is shrunk to in the first part of this effect is exposed as a configurable property by the effect's API. So, this is something that we can adjust to suit the needs of our implementation. This property is an integer.

We can see this effect in action by modifying the dialog example once again. In `effectClip.html`, change the effect source file for clip to fold:

```
<script src="development-bundle/ui/jquery.effects.fold.js">
</script>
```

Then change the `close` event callback to the following:

```
close: function() {
  $(this).parent().hide("fold", { size: 200 }, 1000);
}
```

Save this as `effectFold.html`. This time we make use of the `size` configuration option to make the effect stop in the first fold, `200` pixels before the top of the dialog. We also slow the animation down a little, by setting the duration to `1000` milliseconds. It's a really nice effect; the following screenshot shows the second part of the animation:

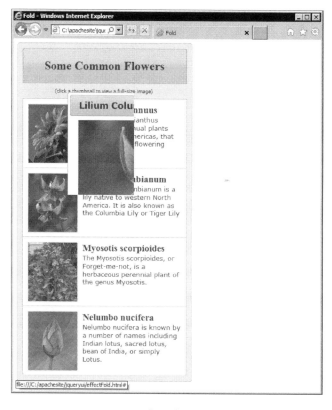

Summary

In this chapter, we've covered the complete range of UI effects available in the jQuery UI library. We've seen how easy it is to use the `jquery.effects.core.js` base component to construct attractive color animations and smooth class transitions.

We also saw that the following effects can be used in conjunction with the simple effect API:

- Bounce
- Highlight
- Shake
- Transfer

An important point is that most of the individual effects can be used not only with the effect API but can also make use of `show`/`hide` and `toggle` logic, making them incredibly flexible and robust. The following effects can be used with this advanced API:

- Blind
- Clip
- Drop
- Explode
- Fold
- Puff
- Pulsate
- Scale
- Slide

We also saw that the jQuery UI effects' core files also include all of the easing functions used in the `jquery.easing.js` plugin that must be used with jQuery when we are not using jQuery UI.

This now brings us to not only the end of this chapter, but also the end of the book. There is a saying that I'm sure almost all of you will have heard before. It's the *give a man a fish...*, saying. I hope that during the course of this book, I've taught you how to fish, instead of just giving you a fish.

Index

H

handle option 245, 249, 250, 327, 331
handles option 285
header activation, accordion widget 107
header property 95
height option 117, 123
helper elements, draggable components
        250-252
helperMaker function 333
helperMaker() function 252
helper option 245, 285, 327, 333
helper property 256
hide() method 365, 367
hide option 117, 122
highlight effect 358-360
hoverClass option 261-264
href attribute 211

I

icons 34, 35
icons option 212, 213
icons property 95
iframeFix option 246
image positioning 30
images 30
index file 12
interaction cues 30, 35-37
interactions 33, 34
interaction states 30
isOpen method 127, 128
items option 328, 334

J

jquery.effect.core.js file 358
jquery.effects.core.js file 354, 357
jquery.effects.highlight.js file 361
jQuery UI
    about 7, 8
    accordion widget 89
    browser support 17
    datepicker widget 159
    draggables component 242
    droppable component 259, 260

progressbar widget 193
    resizable component 281
    selectables component 301, 302
    sortables component 324-326
    ThemeRoller 13, 15
    UI tabs widget 61
jQuery UI 1.7
    about 25
    CSS framework 25
jquery.ui.accordion.css file 26
jquery.ui.all.css file 26, 27
jquery.ui.base.css file 26, 27
jquery.ui.core.css file 26, 27
jquery. ui.core.js file 244, 260, 283, 303, 325,
        354
jquery.ui.datepicker.css file 26
jquery.ui.dialog.css file 26
jquery. ui.draggable.js 261
jquery.ui.draggable.js file 244
jquery. ui.droppable.js 261
jQuery UI library
    book examples 18
    component categories 16, 17
    development environment, setting up 11
    downloading 8-10
    higher-level widgets 17
    licensing 18, 19
    low-level interaction helpers 16
    structure 12
jquery .ui.mouse.js file 303
jquery.ui.mouse.js file 244, 261, 283, 325
jquery.ui.progressbar.css file 26
jquery.ui.resizable.css file 26
jquery.ui.resizable.js file 283
jquery .ui.selectable.js file 303
jquery.ui.slider.css file 26
jquery.ui.sortable.js file 325
jQuery UI tabs
    about 62
    adding 77
    clicks, simulating 78
    custom theme, applying 66, 67
    disabling 76
    enabling 76
    removing 77

iso8601Week 184
noWeekends 184
parseDate 184
regional 184
setDefaults 184

V

value method 149, 150
values method 149, 150
vertical slider
  creating 143

W

WebKit browsers 281
widget
  creating 49, 50
  using 57

widget factory 48
widget method 20, 127, 219
widget style sheet 57
width option 118, 123

Y

Yellow Fade Technique. *See* YFT
YFT 358

Z

zIndex option 118, 123, 124, 246, 328

Thank you for buying
jQuery UI 1.8
The User Interface Library for jQuery

About Packt Publishing

Packt, pronounced 'packed', published its first book "*Mastering phpMyAdmin for Effective MySQL Management*" in April 2004 and subsequently continued to specialize in publishing highly focused books on specific technologies and solutions.

Our books and publications share the experiences of your fellow IT professionals in adapting and customizing today's systems, applications, and frameworks. Our solution based books give you the knowledge and power to customize the software and technologies you're using to get the job done. Packt books are more specific and less general than the IT books you have seen in the past. Our unique business model allows us to bring you more focused information, giving you more of what you need to know, and less of what you don't.

Packt is a modern, yet unique publishing company, which focuses on producing quality, cutting-edge books for communities of developers, administrators, and newbies alike. For more information, please visit our website: www.packtpub.com.

About Packt Open Source

In 2010, Packt launched two new brands, Packt Open Source and Packt Enterprise, in order to continue its focus on specialization. This book is part of the Packt Open Source brand, home to books published on software built around Open Source licences, and offering information to anybody from advanced developers to budding web designers. The Open Source brand also runs Packt's Open Source Royalty Scheme, by which Packt gives a royalty to each Open Source project about whose software a book is sold.

Writing for Packt

We welcome all inquiries from people who are interested in authoring. Book proposals should be sent to author@packtpub.com. If your book idea is still at an early stage and you would like to discuss it first before writing a formal book proposal, contact us; one of our commissioning editors will get in touch with you.

We're not just looking for published authors; if you have strong technical skills but no writing experience, our experienced editors can help you develop a writing career, or simply get some additional reward for your expertise.

jQuery UI 1.7: The User Interface Library for jQuery

ISBN: 978-1-847199-72-0   Paperback: 392 pages

Build highly interactive web applications with ready-to-use widgets from the jQuery User Interface library

1. Organize your interfaces with reusable widgets: accordions, date pickers, dialogs, sliders, tabs, and more

2. Enhance the interactivity of your pages by making elements drag-and-droppable, sortable, selectable, and resizable

3. Packed with examples and clear explanations of how to easily design elegant and powerful front-end interfaces for your web applications

jQuery 1.4 Animation Techniques: Beginners Guide

ISBN: 978-1-84951-330-2   Paperback: 344 pages

Quickly master all of jQuery's animation methods and build a toolkit of ready-to-use animations using jQuery 1.4

1. Create both simple and complex animations using clear, step-by-step instructions, accompanied with screenshots

2. Walk through each of jQuery's built-in animation methods and see in detail how each one can be used

3. Over 50 detailed examples of different types of web page animations

4. Attractive pictures and screenshots that show animations in progress and how the examples should finally appear

Please check **www.PacktPub.com** for information on our titles

11611844R0024

Made in the USA
Lexington, KY
19 October 2011